Good Practices and Capacity Building for Sustainable Development Goals

Good Practices and Capacity Building for Sustainable Development Goals

Editors

Dr. Upinder Dhar
Dr. Santosh Dhar
Dr. Namrata Jain

ALLIED PUBLISHERS PVT. LTD.

New Delhi • Mumbai • Kolkata • Chennai • Bangalore • Hyderabad

ALLIED PUBLISHERS PRIVATE LIMITED

1/13-14 Asaf Ali Road, **New Delhi**–110002
Ph.: 011-23239001 • E-mail: delhi.books@alliedpublishers.com

17 Chittaranjan Avenue, **Kolkata**–700072
Ph.: 033-22129618 • E-mail: cal.books@alliedpublishers.com

15 J.N. Heredia Marg, Ballard Estate, **Mumbai**–400001
Ph.: 022-42126969 • E-mail: mumbai.books@alliedpublishers.com

No. 25/10, Commander-in-Chief Road, Ethiraj Lane (Next to Post Office)
Egmore, **Chennai**–600008
Ph.: 044-28223938 • E-mail: chennai.books@alliedpublishers.com

P.B. No. 9932, No. 15, 3rd Floor (Next to Vijaya Bank), 5th Cross, Gandhinagar, Karnataka,
Bangalore–560009, Ph.: 080-41530285 / 22386239
• E-mail: bngl.journals@alliedpublishers.com / apsabng@airtelmail.in

Sri Jayalakshmi Nilayam, No. 3-4-510, 3rd Floor (Above More Super Market)
Barkatpura, **Hyderabad**–500027
Ph.: 040-27551811, 040-27551812 • E-mail: hyd.books@alliedpublishers.com

Website: www.alliedpublishers.com

ISBN: 978-93-89934-29-8

Published by Sunil Sachdev and printed by Ravi Sachdev at Allied Publishers Pvt. Ltd.,
1/13-14 Asaf Ali Road, New Delhi–110002

Prologue

Habits as Antecedents of the Quality of Life

Quality of life should always be a priority for everyone. If you are having less money, you want to have more. If you have good income, it may not appear enough to you. If you have a busy social life, it might bore you over the period of time. If you dream, you want it to happen in reality. There are number of such ifs and buts in our lives. We constantly aspire to have a higher standard of living than what we have. Living standard refers to a person's ability to acquire more and better materialistic goods. One may acquire the goods of better quality and in greater quantity, because income influences the purchasing power of a person directly. The more one earns, the more is the urge to consume. On the other hand, the quality of life is a person's contribution to the world that promotes social well-being. It includes everything that results in happiness, peace and satisfaction at both, the personal and collective levels. This could be a vacation at any price, or a simple pleasant chat.

Many cities in India and Bangladesh have grown very fast in the globalized world. The living standard of the inhabitants of certain cities has increased exponentially each year, because their economic development is brisk and impressive. On the other hand, there is Thimphu, the capital of Bhutan, a small country far from the hustle and bustle of globalization, financial markets and other economic worries. While many cities of India are ever more industrial and contaminated—but with high living standard—the people of Bhutan live with nature, among rivers, and are working mostly in agriculture as their main occupation with a per capita income of $1,300 only.

Now arises the question that whom do you think has the better quality of life? An inhabitant of Bhutan lives in peace, working in nature, without much stress. He does not strive for more than what he has. In fact years ago, one king of Bhutan perceived the concept of the Gross National Happiness. On the other hand, countries like Brazil, India or China, which are constantly and rapidly growing, and even developed European countries like Spain, Germany and France, experience stress. So, all the nations on the international plane, both developed and developing, have standards of living that are high or growing. But, at what cost? What is better: to accumulate money and riches or quality time and happiness?

Waking up each day to the same repetitive cycle that seems never-ending may result in the quality of life declining over time, resulting in the loss of energy, vitality, and enthusiasm for the future. Experiences may bring frustration from time to time. Life may bring traumatic experiences even in the case of the most intelligent or influential individuals. The tough times may appear to get stretched without understanding where our lives are headed and why. Usually, the people may "give up." However, life does not mean defeat, and it most certainly, does not mean frustration. One can improve the quality of life by making small adjustments in the routine by changing the behavior and way of thinking.

Many of us grow through long periods of frustration, anxiety, fear, and worry. It is easy to overcome some of our tendencies to prevent ourselves from slipping into the state of depression. Sometimes life does not turn out the way we want it to be, but many times the quality of our lives has more to do with the habits that we have developed and we routinely demonstrate them on daily basis. We can improve the quality of our lives by changing our habits. It has been proven that those who think that the quality of life is equivalent to the standard of living are wrong. The standard of living, which essentially equates to one's income, does have a marginal impact on the quality of life, but they are not synonymous. Quality of life has constituents like health, happiness, vitality, leisure, and income.

This approach helps to present a better picture of the overall quality. Many people simply equate their quality of life with the amount of money they earn. And, while money is a good barometer, it is not the full equation. Money does make the world go round. People with access to money and precious resources are able to improve the standard of their lives. But it has also been observed that many such people are not necessarily happier. Increase in income only equates to a temporary improvement in happiness. Eventually, happiness levels baseline again. May be a person received promotion that he/she was expecting for a long time. For a short period, one may be happy. Happiness does not last forever. While money gives access to material goods, the saying "the best things in life are free" stands true for antecedents of quality.

Hedonic Adaptation refers to the natural tendency of human beings to revert back to the set point of happiness after major changes – either positive or negative – in their lives. The Hedonic set point, then, is a baseline or standard level of happiness that we all have, which we tend to revert to, even after things like a traumatic event or winning a lottery. The lottery winners and paraplegics all returned to the baseline or standard level of happiness some time after the event. It is believed that all of us have a baseline or standard level of Hedonic set point, which is determined through hereditary and experiential learning. Although the baseline levels of happiness might be different for everyone, the concept is very important for understanding the causes of happiness while improving the quality of life.

Increasing materialistic goods as well as income are obvious to people than say increasing happiness, health or vitality. One may either have money or not. It is easy to quantify. Health, happiness, vitality, and leisure are important aspects of the quality of life. To improve these aspects of the quality of life, the promotion and adherence to a certain set of positive habits is necessary. Good habits improve the quality of life. If one wants to improve the quality of life, he/she can achieve that by inculcating good habits.

There are number of people who have contributed in making this book possible. We would specially like to express our gratitude to all the authors. We would also like to thank all the conveners, reviewers and members of the organizing committee of *Sanmantrana - 2021* for their unconditional support. Last but not the least, we acknowledge the help and cooperation received from all the faculty and staff members of Shri Vaishnav Vidyapeeth Vishwavidyalaya, Indore.

Date: 09.01.2021

Dr. Upinder Dhar
Dr. Santosh Dhar

About the Editors

DR. UPINDER DHAR

Dr. Upinder Dhar is Vice Chancellor of Shri Vaishnav Vidyapeeth Vishwavidyalaya (Indore). Earlier, he was Group Additional Vice Chancellor and Pro-Vice Chancellor (Academics), Amity University (Noida); Founder Vice Chancellor of JK Lakshmipat University (Jaipur); Director - Institute of Management, Dean - Faculty of Management, and Dean - Faculty of Doctoral Studies and Research, Nirma University (Ahmedabad); Director - Prestige Institute of Management and Research (Indore); Professor of Management at NITIE (Mumbai); Reader at IMS-DAVV (Indore); and Lecturer at M.D. University (Rohtak). He has conducted more than 650 management and faculty development programs for the executives of major business houses and faculty members of academic institutions respectively. He has also been Guest Faculty at IIM Calcutta, IIM Indore, IIM Trichy and IIT Roorkee. Besides undertaking consultancy assignments, he has authored/co-authored/edited more than 700 publications. Thirty-Six (36) scholars have been awarded Ph.D. degree under his supervision by various universities.

A Fellow of ISTD and a strong proponent of Case Method, Dr. Dhar was conferred **Ravi J Matthai National Fellow Award** by the *Association of Indian Management Schools (AIMS) in 2018.* He has been on the Panel of Reviewers of number of international journals, such as International Journal of Training and Development, Human Resources International, Journal of Global Business and Technology, and South Asian Journal of Management. He has also been on the Panel of Experts maintained by the NAAC (Bangalore), NBA (Bangalore); ICSSR (New Delhi); and SAQS (Hyderabad). He was President of Anthropological and Behavioural Sciences Section of the Indian Science Congress Association in 2007–08, Indian Society for Training and Development in 2008–09 and Association of Indian Management Schools in 2014–15. He has also been Member of the Council of Management of AIMA, Member of ATMA, All India Board of Management Studies of AICTE, Rajasthan State Productivity Council, Governing Board of DELNET, and Member of the Executive Board of AMDISA.

Dr. Dhar was awarded Commonwealth Fellowship twice to present his papers at the South Asian Management Forums held at Royal Institute of Management, Bhutan and Lahore University of Management Science, Lahore. He was invited by the American Society for Engineering Management as resource person for Case Method during its international annual Conference held at Minnesota in 2013. He had the opportunity to visit Ivy league institutions like Harvard Business School, MIT Sloan School of Management, and Yale University School of Management. He has also visited 18 countries for professional and academic interest. He has been on the high powered Expert Committees constituted by MHRD, UGC, AICTE and Hon'ble Governor of Uttar Pradesh. Currently, he is a Member of the *Standing Committee on Specification of Degrees u/s 22* of the *UGC Act, 1956*. He has also been resource person in the Leadership for Academicians Program (LEAP) sponsored by MHRD and organized by IIT Roorkee in 2018 and BHU Varanasi in 2019.

DR. SANTOSH DHAR

Dr. Santosh Dhar is Dean - Faculty of Doctoral Studies and Research at Shri Vaishnav Vidyapeeth Vishwavidyalaya, Indore. She has been engaged in teaching, research, corporate training and consultancy for the last forty years. She has widely published her work and has more than 356 publications to her credit. Her earlier assignments have been Professor, Shri Vaishnav Institute of Management, Indore; Professor, Amity Business School, Amity University, Greater Noida campus; Professor, Institute of Management and Dean - Research, JK Lakshmipat University, Jaipur; Senior Professor, OB/HR, Jaipuria Institute of Management, Jaipur; Professor and Chairperson - OB/HR Area, Institute of Management, Nirma University, Ahmedabad and Guest Faculty at IIM Kolkata and MICA Ahmedabad. Many research scholars have been awarded Ph.D degree under her supervision. She has designed and conducted management development programs for the executives of several business houses, such as Grasim Industries, JK Tyre, Bridgestone, Hindustan Motors, ONGC and GAIL to name a few. She has been on the Panel of Reviewers of Oxford University Press and Tata McGraw-Hill. She was Managing Editor of Prestige Journal of Management and Research and Prestige Research Abstracts. She has been Chairperson of Indian Society for Training and Development (Indore and Jaipur Chapters) and was on the Editorial Board of Indian Journal of Training and Development. She has presented papers in several national and international conferences/seminars and had the opportunity to visit Kathmandu (Nepal), Male (Maldives), Bangkok (Thailand), Beijing, Shangai, Guanzhou, Shenzen, Hong Kong (China), Seoul (South Korea) Dubai (UAE), Tumu (Myanmar), Poland and United States in connection with various professional and academic assignments.

Dr. Dhar had coordinated the implementation of a project on the *Empowerment of Women through Enterprise* in North India (2000–2002), which was funded by Canadian International Development Agency (CIDA). She has completed the research projects on *Problems of Women Trainers in India* and *Quality of Work Life as a Determinant of Mental Health in Pharmaceutical Industry*. She has also been principal investigator for Asian Development Bank funded and Rajasthan Government sponsored RUIDP Consultancy project on *Capacity Building of ULBs* of Different Towns of Rajasthan. She has twice been chairperson of Indian Society for Training and Development Jaipur and Indore Chapter & Chairperson of the Best Paper Award of the Indian Society for Training and Development, New Delhi. Dr. Dhar was conferred *National Fellowship* for her contributions to HR by the Indian Society for Training and Development in 2006–07. She is life member of Indian Society for Training and Development (ISTD), National Human Resource Development Network (NHRDN), and Indian Society for Technical Education (ISTE).

DR. NAMRATA JAIN

Dr. Namrata Jain is PhD in e-waste management, faculty, Shri Vaishnav School of Management and Member Secretary, Centre of Excellence in Sustainable Development, Shri Vaishnav Vidyapeeth Vishwavidyalaya, Indore. She has been engaged in teaching and research work for around 14 years in the area of IT, General Management and Environmental Management. She is a lifetime member of The Indian Society for Training and Development. She has participated in a number of workshops, faculty development programme, national and international conferences and has several research publications to her credit. She has visited many e-waste management agencies in the states of Maharashtra, Karnataka, Rajasthan, Madhya Pradesh, Chhattisgarh, Delhi and discussed issues pertaining to e-waste. Based on these interactions she has authored many cases. Her research work on e-waste management and handling rules was recognized in an International conference organized by Amity University, Noida in association with the University of Northampton, UK.

Dr. Jain has been the resource person for National Level Workshops on E-waste Management organized/sponsored by: Science and Engineering Research Board—A Status Body Under Department of Science and Technology, Government of India; National Institute of Urban Affairs, New Delhi; Ministry of Housing and Urban Affairs, Government of India; State Pollution Control Boards; International Institute of Waste Management—A Scientific and Industrial Research Organization of Department of Science and Industrial Research, Ministry of Science and Technology, Government of India; Engineering Staff College of India, Hyderabad; Tata Consultancy Services Limited; UGC—Human Resource Development Centre, Devi Ahilya Vishwavidyalaya, Indore and Virtual Info Systems Private Limited, Mumbai. She is a recipient of Rajya Puraskar, known as the Governor's Award, the highest award Scouts and Guides can earn at the State-level.

Contents

An Assessment of Conventional and Computational Methods for Handwriting Examination

Hansi Bansal[1] and Swati Dubey Mishra[2]

[1]Govt. Institute of Forensic Science, Nagpur, Maharashtra

[2]Shri Vaishnav Institute of Forensic Science,
Shri Vaishnav Vidyapeeth Vishwavidyalaya, Indore, Madhya Pradesh

E-mail: [1]hansi.fsc@gmail.com; [2]swati.dubeymishra@gmail.com

ABSTRACT: Different forms of writing and documents may be encountered during the course of investigation. It is important on the part of the investigating officer to understand the various types of questioned documents, the problems related to document examination and the correct method of examination. Crimes involving robbery, fraud, property related crimes, anonymous letters, threatening letters, etc. may involve various types of documents such as bills, driving licenses, wills, sale deeds, contracts, passports, educational documents, and many more. Different methods have been adopted for the examination of these questioned documents which have their owns pros and cons.

Analysis of handwriting is an important part of the questioned document examination. Identification of disguised writing is problematic for forensic document examiners and attracts higher misleading and inconclusive rates on authorship opinions than the genuine writing. Different researchers have adopted various techniques for the examination of handwriting. Author Identification and comparison of handwriting have been done by various researchers using computer assisted tools and algorithms. Different tools which have multi functionality features as well as automated methods for handwriting examination and author identification are adopted by various forensic document examiners. This paper assesses and identifies the different advantages of conventional, manual and computational methods for handwriting examination and analyses the need for further research in this area of document examination.

Keywords: CEDAR-FOX, Computer Assisted Tools, FISH, Handwritten Documents, Questioned Document.

INTRODUCTION

Questioned Documents have an evidentiary value thus, they need to be authentic to be made admissible in court. Due to their significance, criminals manipulate the documents with the intent to cause fraud (Khumalo *et al.*, 2018). As a result, forensic examination of questioned document is quite necessary for the purpose of authentication. Whether identification of a person is possible by handwriting or not is of major importance to law enforcement system as well as to provide justice. Numerous challenges have been faced by the document examiners for providing testimony in court (Saini *et al.*, 2015a; Saini *et al.*, 2015b). These challenges occur regarding the scientific validation of handwriting as an evidence. At various occasions, the acceptability of the evidence relies upon the credibility of the document examiner as compared to the evidence itself (Khumalo *et al.*, 2018; Saini *et al.*, 2015a).

Questioned Document examination serves the purpose to provide information about a document for justice (Lindblom *et al.*, 2006). Identification of the writer of the questioned document, recognition of forged or simulated signatures are the major concerns in document examination. In the process of identification of a person on the basis of handwriting, it is must that all the characteristics of the questioned samples as well as of the known writings must be taken into consideration. For a scientific basis of the document examination, handwriting has to be studied under different situations, keeping in mind the factors that may have impact on the handwriting of a person. In order to study the handwriting of an individual, it is important to study both intra and inter variations in handwriting of an individual (Khumalo *et al.*, 2018).

MANUAL AND INSTRUMENTAL EXAMINATION OF DOCUMENTS

Examination of Questioned Document deals with the analysis and comparison of documents, printing, writing instruments with the purpose to identify or eliminate suspects as the source. Questioned document may consist of identification cards, wills, titles, seals, deeds, stamps, bank cheque, handwritten correspondence, machine generated documents (photocopies, fax machines, printers) currency and electronic documents.

The characteristics of handwriting are compared by the document examiner by analyzing handwritten documents to determine the uniqueness of the document. Important handwriting features such as style of handwriting, slope, spacing, initial strokes etc. are examined. Various documents have been examined by spectroscopic analysis, ultraviolet and infrared to determine any alterations in a questioned document. Different destructive and non-destructive methods have been employed by the document examiner for the analysis of questioned document. Imaging and chromatographic (destructive techniques) have been used for the examination of questioned document. Destructive methods have been adopted for the quantitative analysis (Saini *et al.*, 2015a).

Manual comparison of handwriting is based on the likelihood that no two persons write in an exactly same manner, keeping in mind the variabilities of the writing of the same person (Srihari *et al.*, 2002). Various methods are used to determine the authenticity of documents by handwriting examination. Forensic examination involves the comparison of handwriting and handwritten signatures (Calcerrada *et al.*, 2015). The purpose of handwriting examination is to determine whether two samples of handwriting have a common authorship (Srihari *et al.*, 2002). The examination relies upon the visual examination of handwriting and comparison of similarities and differences in the characteristics of handwriting.

Handwriting is a neuro muscular function. Various models have been established to study and analyze the handwriting. These models have been categorized into two major types i.e., top-down models and bottom-up models. "Top-down models deal with approaches that are based on high level information processing varying from semantics to basic motor control problems. Bottom-up models deal with the synthesis and analysis of low-level neuro muscular process which are involved in the production of allographs, words, single stroke etc. Bottom level models are sub classified into two types. They are oscillatory and discrete models. Oscillatory models deal with oscillation as a basic movement and the complex movements are generated by regulating amplitude and frequency. In discrete models, single stroke is obtained by the coactivation of two neuromuscular systems, agonist and antagonist that control the velocity of the pen-tip" (Plamondon *et al.*, 1989; Plamondon *et al.*, 2000).

COMPUTER ASSISTED METHODS OF HANDWRITING EXAMINATION

Various computer assisted tools have been developed by researchers and document examiners for the effective analysis of handwriting. Forensic Information Handwriting System (FISH) is one effective system for handwriting examination developed by German Law Enforcement. FISH enables the retrieval of closest match from a large database of handwriting samples (Srihari *et al.*, 2003, Franke *et al.*, 2000, K^ppen *et al.*, 2001).

WANDA

WANDA is a framework for the examination of handwriting and signature veryfication. It utilizes an open software which allows the integration of computer-based methods and promote newer computer assisted examination and techniques. According to Franke *et al.*, (2003), five stages have been used for the actual use of forensic handwriting systems for the processing of the samples. These are:

Step 1: (a) Case Entry
(b) Scanning
(c) Pre-processing.

Step 2: (a) Annotation
(b) Measurement
(c) Feature Extraction.

Step 3: (a) Normalization
(b) Comparison.

Step 4: (a) Normalization
(b) Pre-selection
(c) Identification matching
(d) Hit list inspection.

Step 5: (a) Report Generation.

These stages include both interactive and batch processing mode (Franke *et al.*, 2004).

CEDAR

CEDAR-FOX system is an information processing model of handwriting examination and has an autonomous operation. It serves the function of writer verification, signature matching and writer identification. This facilitates the search of a digital repository of handwritten documents using different modes like spotting of a word, recognition of words or text-based search (Srihari *et al.*, 2002).

This writer verification system works on two modules.

Writer Independent **Writer Dependent**

In writer independent module, no training on a specific writer is needed. For writer dependent module, the system is trained on a set of documents from a given writer.

According to Srihari *et al.*, (2008), different steps involved in the application of CEDAR FOX as an interactive tool for forensic document examination are as follows:

1. The image is scanned.
2. Unwanted images or noise is eliminated.
3. Preparing the document for preprocessing.
4. Processing of the document.
5. Transcript mapping.

6. Computation of macro and micro features.
7. Similar features are computed for bigrams.
8. Determination of distances amid the writing elements.
9. Calculation of binary string correlation distance.
10. Computation of ratio of probabilities and comparison of LLRs.
11. Mapping of LLR to an opinion scale.

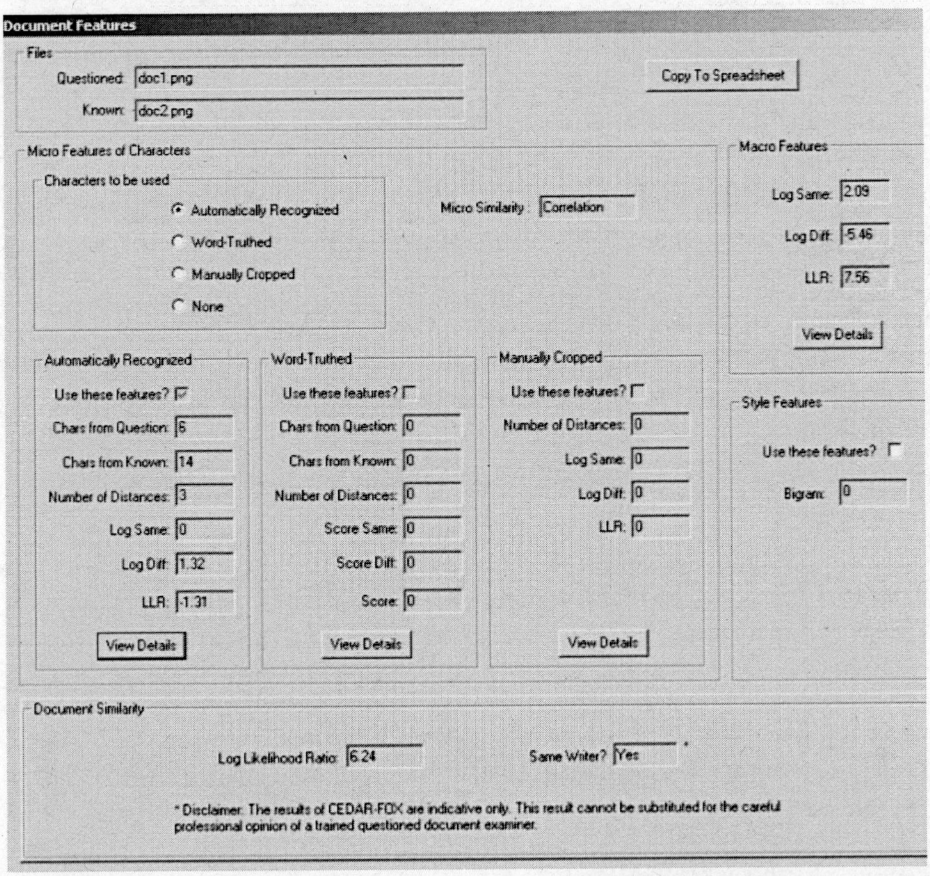

Fig. 1: Screenshot of CEDAR-FOX Writer Verification of Two Documents (Srihari *et al.*, 2008)

Signature verification system have also been in use for providing a scientific basis for the examination of handwritten documents and signatures (Calcerrada *et al.*, 2015). Computational signature analysis adopted by various soft biometric technologies include preprocessing of signature, feature extraction and evaluation (Franke *et al.*, 2003). Bayesian approaches have also been in use for the purpose of signature verification (Plamodon *et al.*, 2000; Srihari *et al.*, 2003).

CONCLUSION

Questions have always been raised about the consistency of handwriting as a reliable evidence in court of law. Manual or conventional methods of handwriting examination may prove to be unreliable in circumstances where they fail to identify the minute peculiarities in the handwriting like pressure identification and recognition of characters (Khumalo *et al.*, 2018; Saini *et al.*, 2015). This examination of handwriting may be subjected to human errors due to the non-availability of the quantification of data, standardized methods and absence of statistical tests (Saini *et al.*, 2015; Plamondon *et al.*, 2000).

On the other hand, computational methods may prove to be useful in reproducing the results. These methods could not help to resolve the legal concerns raised over the admissibility of handwriting as an evidence but prove to be a useful tool for the questioned document examiners. But computer assisted tools fail in producing conventional features of handwriting through algorithms (Plamondon *et al.*, 2000).

Further research is required in the area of questioned documents to prove the scientific reliability of the evidence. For further advancement in the area of document examination, practice and growth of non-destructive methods for examination is the need of the hour.

REFERENCES

[1] Calcerrada, M. and Garcia-Ruiz, C. (2015). Analysis of questioned documents: A review. *Analytica Chimica Act*, 853, 142–166.

[2] Franke, K. and K^ppen, M. (2000). Fuzzy image processing by using dubois and prade fuzzy norms in *Proc. 15th International Conference on Pattern Recognition (ICPR).*

[3] Franke, K. and Schomaker, L. (2003). Pen orientation characteristics of on-line handwritten signatures. *Proc. 11th Conference of the International Graphonomics Society (IGS)*, 224–227.

[4] Franke, K., Guyon, I. Schomaker, L. and Vuurpijl, L. (2004). The WANDA markup language for digital document annotation, *Proceedings of the 9th Intl Workshop on Frontiers in Handwriting Recognition (IWFHR-9)*, 563–68.

[5] Franke, K., Schomaker, L., Veenhuis, C., Taubenheim, C., Guyon, I., Vuurpijl, Van Erp, M. and Zwarts, G. (2003). WANDA: A generic framework applied in forensic handwriting analysis and writer identification, Design and Application of Hybrid Intelligent Systems, *Proc. 3rd International Conference on Hybrid Intelligent Systems (HIS03)*, 927–38.

[6] K^ppen, M. Franke, K. and Unold, O. (2001). A survey on fuzzy morphology. *5th International Conference on Pattern Recognition and Image Analysis: New Information Technologies (PRIA)*, 424–427.

[7] Khumalo, N.B. and Bhebhe, S.S. (2018). Analysis of selected methods used in forensic paper-based document examination. *Chemistry and Materials Research*, 10(7), 20–28.

[8] Plamandon, R. and Marsee, F.J. (1989). An Evaluation of motor models of handwriting. *IEEE Trans. Systems, Man and Cybernetics*, 19(5), 1060–1072.

[9] Plamondon, R. and Srihari, S. (2000). On-line and off-line handwriting recognition: A comprehensive survey. *IEEE Transactions on Pattern Analysis and Machine Intelligence*, 22(1), 63–84.

[10] Saini, K. and Kaur, S. (2015a). Forensic examination of computer- manipulated documents using image processing techniques. *Egyptian Journal of Forensic Sciences*, 6, 317–322.

[11] Saini, M. and Kapoor, A.K. (2015b). Conventional and computational features in document examination. *Journal of Forensic Science Criminology*, 3(3), 301. doi: 10.15744/2348-9804.3.301.

[12] Srihari, S. and Leedham, G. (2003). A survey of computer methods in forensic handwritten document examination. *Proceedings of the Eleventh International Graphonomics Society Conference,* Scottsdale AZ, 278–281.

[13] Srihari, S., Huang, C. and Srinivasan, H. (2008). On the discriminability of the handwriting of twins. *Journal of Forensic Sciences,* 53(2), 430–446.

[14] Srihari, S.N., Cha, S.H., Arora, H and Lee, S. (2002). Individuality of handwriting. *Journal of Forensic Science*, 47, 856–72.

[15] Srihari, S.N., Zhang, B., Tomai, C., Lee, S., Shi, Z. and Shin, Y.C. (2003). A system for handwriting matching and recognition. *Proceedings of the Symposium on Document Image Understanding Technology (SDIUT 03),* Greenbelt, MD, 67–75.

Application of Nature Inspired Algorithm in Non-Linear Flood Routing Model: A Review

Almas Qureshi[1]**, Ananda Babu K.**[2] **and Vijayant Pandey**[3]
Shri Vaishnav Institute of Technology and Science,
Shri Vaishnav Vidyapeeth Vishwavidyalaya, Indore, Madhya Pradesh
E-mail: [1]786almasq@gmail.com; [2]bujjianand@gmail.com; [3]vijayantcivil@gmail.com

ABSTRACT: Floods have huge devastating effects on surrounding environment such as breaking levees, inundation of houses, major damage on transportation system, damaging crops besides erosion of fertile land. Flood prediction and control are major concerns for designers and water resource planners to avoid flood disasters. Flood routing is the technique which is mostly used in areas such as flood forecasting, flood warning system, flood protection and many fields. One of the commonly used hydrological model technique for flood forecasting is Muskingum model. This model is used due to its simplicity as the parameters can be estimated from past inflow/ outflow data. However, application of non-linear Muskingum model suffers from hydrological parameters estimation as they cannot be obtained from past inflow and outflow hydrograph. Thus, in order to cope up with this complexity and to determine parameters of non-linear Muskingum model for accurate flood routing, several metaheuristic approaches have been used.

Among nature inspired metaheuristic methods especially those based on swarm intelligence are gaining attention in research since they are very effective for optimization where objective function is making gradient-based method unsuitable for complex problem. This paper is based on review of application of nature inspired technique—Bat Algorithm (BA), based on swarm intelligence approach to determine parameters of nonlinear Muskingum model for channel routing on some flood events. This paper is an attempt to analyze performance of BA in flood routing in various research studies where various flood events are used as benchmark and their results for parameter values by BA are compared by the researcher with another optimization algorithm.

Keywords: Bat Algorithm, Flood Routing, Hydrological Model, Metaheuristic Approach, Muskingum Model.

INTRODUCTION

Floods cause huge devastation on surrounding environment such as damaging crops, inundation of houses, major damage to transportation system and erosion of fertile land. Thus, flood prediction and flood control are major concern for designers and water resource planners for overcoming their effects (Ehteram *et al.*, 2018). Flood routing is an important technique applied for design of structural and non-structural flood control measures. Flood routing works on principle of predicting changes observed in shape, velocity and magnitude of flood wave as a function of time at different points of river (Farzin *et al.*, 2018). This technique has wide application in several fields such as water engineering, flood forecasting, watershed simulation, geographical planning and several other areas (Sànchez *et al.*, 2019). Muskingum model is the commonly used flood routing method proposed by Mc.Carthy in 1938. The model is simple as the parameters can be determined from past inflow and outflow data. Thus, the first step in applying Muskingum model is to effectively determine its parameters (Sànchez *et al.*, 2019).

Several optimization algorithms have been applied for the parameters estimation in past studies but they suffer from limitation of slow convergence and get trapped in local optimum (Ehteram *et al.*, 2018). In recent years, nature inspired algorithm have gained more interest due to their better performance and adaption in solving complex optimization problem which can't be solved by traditional mathematical programming methods (Azad *et al.*, 2020). This paper is based on review of nature inspired swarm intelligence approach—Bat Algorithm in non-linear flood routing model. This algorithm aims to overcome the problem of trapping in local optimum, slow convergence and algorithm is based on high ability of bat to receive sounds.

METHODOLOGY

Procedure for Non-linear flood routing model is given below:

Linear Muskingum model uses following continuity and storage equation: (Ehteram *et al.*, 2018; Gill, 1978; Tung, 1985).

$$\frac{\Delta S_t}{\Delta t} = I_t - O_t \qquad \dots (1)$$

$$S_t = K\left[XI_t + (1-X)O_t\right] \qquad \dots (2)$$

Where,

St: channel storage at time t, It: rate of inflow,

Ot: outflow rate at time t,

K: storage-time constant for river reach (T), whose value nearly close to travel time flow from river reach,

X: dimensionless factor of weighting whose value vary between 0.0–0.3 for stream channel.

However, it has been seen in past studies that linear Muskingum model doesn't have better computation for few rivers; hence, nonlinear Muskingum models have been preferred over linear Muskingum model (Ehteram *et al.*, 2018; Tung, 1985).

$$\Delta S_t = K_t[XI_t + (1-X)O_t]^m \qquad \dots (3)$$

$$S_t = K\left[XI_t^m + (1-X)O_m^t\right] \qquad \dots (4)$$

Some studies used 4 parameter Muskingum model considering $S_t = K\left[XI_t^{\alpha} + (1-X)O_t^{\alpha}\right]^m$, while some studies considered lateral flow taking by rearranging (3) and substituting the obtained value in (1), time rate of change of storage volume is written as:

$$\frac{\Delta S_t}{\Delta t} = -\left[\frac{1}{1-X}\right]\left[\frac{S}{K}\right]^{\frac{1}{m}} + \left[\frac{1}{1-X}\right].\bar{I}_{t+1} \qquad \dots (5)$$

Accumulated storage can be expressed as:

$$S_{t+1} = S_t + \Delta S_t \qquad \dots (6)$$

Bat Algorithm

Bat algorithm is a nature inspired-swarm intelligence algorithm approached by Yang (2010) to solve optimization problem (Sànchez *et al.*, 2019). BA is based on powerful ability of living bat to detect sounds from their surroundings (Ehteram *et al.*, 2018). Bats show a mysterious behaviour and they do not depend on their eyesight for food acquisition and have great ability to orient themselves to their surrounding environment. Bats can distinguish their environment by analyzing returning echoes in auditory system which helps them to find prey. The high ability of auditory system of bats has generated interest in the research communities in recent years for solution of optimization problem (Farzin *et al.*, 2018).

Bat algorithm follows three principles: (Bozorg-Haddad *et al.*, 2014; Ehteram *et al.*, 2018).

A. All bats use echolocation for detection of prey and obstacles based on perceived sounds and frequency.
B. All bats fly with velocity (v_1) at position (y_1) and loudness, frequency, wavelength values are A_0, f_1, λ respectively.
C. The loudness varies from large positive values (A_0) to small positive values (A_{min}).

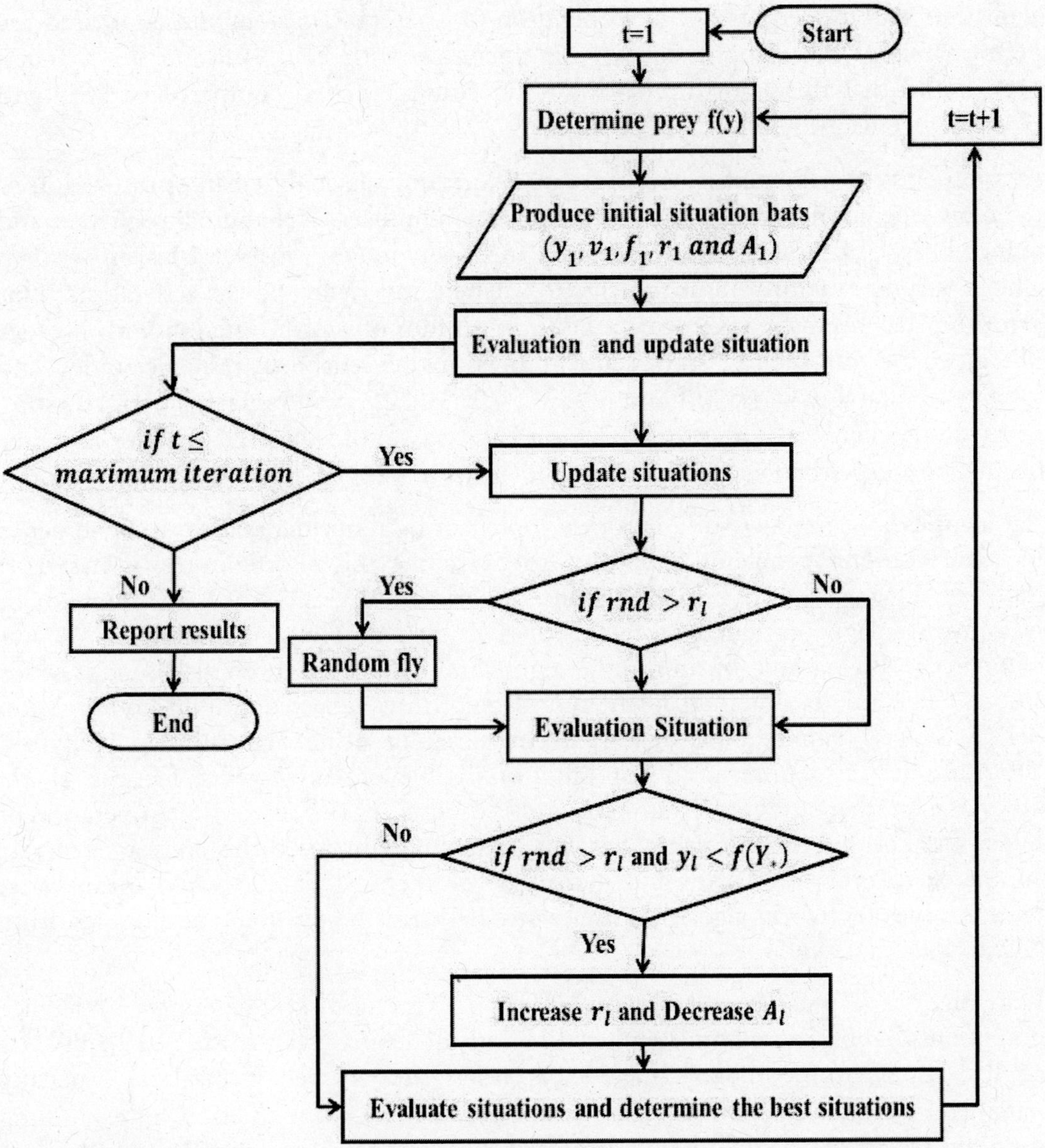

Fig. 1: Bat Algorithm Procedure

REVIEW OF LITERATURE

Due to high ability of bat in perceiving sound and faster convergence, Bat Algorithm have been used in many optimization problems such as rainfall forecasting, runoff prediction, optimal operation of reservoir system, monthly mean stream flow prediction, optimization of multi-reservoir system, and many other fields. Bat algorithm was applied for optimal operation of 4 reservoir system and compared the performance of BA in optimal reservoir operation with LP, NLP and PSO. It has been found that this algorithm shows faster convergence as compared to PSO and GA (Azad *et al.*, 2020).

In another study, the performance of bat algorithm was analyzed in optimization of reservoir operation considering three evaluation indices—reliability, resilience and vulnerability. Two case studies were examined—Aydoughmoush and Karoun-4 dam whose purpose was to minimize irrigation deficit and hydro power generation. This algorithm has been shown to converge to minimum objective function with 3-order rule curve for both the case studies and attained higher reliability, resilience index, and lowest vulnerability index (Ehteram *et al.*, 2018). BA was evaluated for forecasting urban water demand. The proposed algorithm was found to achieve better accuracy in prediction of urban water consumption (Pel *et al.*, 2018).

Bat algorithm sometimes suffers from trapping in local optima and slow convergence in some complex problems and thus, to overcome this shortcoming, it has been modified by applying hybrid algorithm. Hybrid of BA and PSO was applied for minimizing irrigation deficit on multi-reservoir system. The performance of BA was compared with various optimization algorithm which has been used in previous studies. The results obtained from hybrid algorithm achieved minimum irrigation deficit during examined period when compared to other algorithm. The hybrid algorithm has also minimized computational time of convergence (Yaseen *et al.*, 2019). In another study, hybrid of BA and PSO was applied for optimal operation of reservoir. The hybrid algorithm has been shown to increase the convergence rate compared to other algorithm and increased volumetric reliability. Also mean water release values by hybrid algorithm met water demands better than another algorithm (Zarei *et al.*, 2019).

Bat Algorithm was coupled with XGBoost method to determine reference evapotranspiration in arid and semi-arid regions of China (Han *et al.*, 2019). BA was applied to determine the parameters of SVM (support vector machine)—penalty parameter C, kernel parameter η for monthly stream flow prediction by examining monthly stream flow. The results indicated that proposed model was more accurate than ANN and cross validation based SVM. Bat algorithm was suggested to combine with local optimization algorithm to overcome the problem of time consuming and low accuracy in break point of dry years (Xing *et al.*, 2016). Improved Bat algorithm was analyzed by coupling Bat Algorithm with Differential Evolution for hydro power operation of multi-reservoir system. The results obtained have shown that IBA gave better results as compared to traditional linear programming (Ahmadianfar *et al.*, 2016).

Bat Algorithm has been applied in flood routing for better optimal parameter values of Muskingum model. This Algorithm has been found to give higher performance in determining parameters of Muskingum model. BA was applied on non-linear Muskingum model taking Wilson flood which is used as a benchmark for different method in previous research work. The results of BA were compared with numerical results of GA and PSO for parameter values; K, X, m and LSQ error. Computation of 15 independent executions of BA were analyzed and average value was considered. BA gave better optimal parameter values in comparison to PSO and GA. This method also improved LSQ error of GA and PSO with improvement rate of 48.78% and 46.89%. The observed inflow and outflow hydrograph and observed outflow for PSO and BA were plotted and analyzed. BA gave excellent matching between observed outflow and outflow predicted. The convergence diagram of BA for max., min., and average values from 15 independent executions showed that BA converges in all cases and there is no large variation between different executions, thus depicting BA is robust for different executions (Sànchez *et al.*, 2019).

4-parameter Muskingum model was analyzed using hybrid PSO and BA to find optimal values of 4 parameter Muskingum model. In this study, 4 flood events were analysed—Wilson flood, Karahan flood, Viessman flood and Lewis flood which are used as a benchmark in flood routing study. The non-linear Muskingum model and storage equation: $S_t = K\left[XI_t^{\alpha} + (1-X)O_t^{\alpha}\right]^m$ was taken. For Wilson flood case study, SSQ was taken as objective function and variations of objective function are compared with parameters. The results computed shows that computational time of HA were 25% and 20% lower than that of BA and PSO. The SSQ based on HA was 4.234 and decreased the SSQ by 23.7% and 20.74% compared to BA and PSO. HA based on 4-parameter Muskingum model gave better results with SSQ values 65%, 72% and 47% lower than that of 3-parameter Muskingum model studied using BA, PSO and HA.

In addition, SAD value decreased by 25% and 24% compared to PSO and BA and also reduced the error EQ. For Karahan flood event, sensitivity analysis was taken as objective function and found that SSQ of HA decreased by 5.85%, 2.8% compared to PSO and BA. Also, SAD values for HA based on 4-parameter Muskingum model decreased by 0.32% and 7.54% compared to PSO and BA. EO of values decreased to 7.3% and 64% lower than PSO and BA. For Lewis and Viessman flood events, SSQ, MARE and SAD of HA was found lowest. The results showed that HA overcome the weaker solution of each algorithm i.e., BA and PSO with decreased computational time and better results for 4 parameters—K, X, m and α (Ehteram *et al.*, 2018).

IBA was applied on 3-parameter Muskingum model to predict flood routing. In this study, lateral flow was considered with inflow flow rate, $O_{lateral} = \beta I_t$ and storage equation, $S_t = K\left[X(1+\beta)I_t + (1-X)O_t\right]^m$. Three case studies—Wilson flood, Karahan flood and Myanmar river were taken and 7 different performance indices were examined and performance was compared with another algorithm. Results showed IBA reduced SSD ranging between 20% and 84% compared to another algorithm. The predicted peak discharge was also accurately close to observed values. In Karahan flood, minimum level of error indices was achieved by IBA for single reach in comparison with another algorithm. IBA gave better performance with three intervals in flood routing compared to single and two reaches. For Myanmar river, simulated hydrograph obtained by IBA with three reaches was found to be more accurate. IBA based on three intervals gave computational time of 2, 4, 6 second which was lesser than BA, GA and PSO. Further, IBA gave EP of 33, 96, 97% lesser than BA, GA and PSO (Farzin *et al.*, 2018).

In other study, BA applied on 2 flood events—Wilson flood and Lighvan flood for determining parameters of non-linear Muskingum model for flood routing and compared result with evolutionary algorithm—GA, PSO and Harmony Algorithm.. The value of objective function obtained for Wilson flood was equal to 35, 14, 22 and 76 m^3/sec. The values of SSD (sum of square deviation), SAD (sum of absolute values) and difference between observed and routed peak flow for Lighvan flood was found equal to 7, 24, 6, 23 and 0 m^3/sec (Hojat *et al.*, 2018).

CONCLUSION

Flood Routing is very important subject of research in water engineering and related fields. One of the widely used hydrological model—Muskingum Model has important influence in practical application for routing of flood in rivers and natural channel. Thus, first step in application of this model is its parameter estimation. In recent years, many metaheuristic algorithms have been applied to overcome these limitations. One of nature inspired swarm intelligence approach—Bat Algorithm has gained more interest in predicting flood routing. The literature review shows that study performed on various flood events in research taking BA gave very good optimal values and also reduced error when compared to other evolutionary algorithms which were used as a benchmark for comparing the performance of BA in predicting flood routing characteristics. However, in some complex problem, it suffers problem of tapping in local optima and thus to overcome the problem, Bat algorithm has been used in hybrid with other algorithm and has given high performance.

REFERENCES

[1] Ahmadianfar, I., Adib, A., Salarijazi, M. (2016). Optimizing multi-reservoir Operation: Hybrid of Bat Algorithm and Differential Evolution. *Journal of Water Resources Planning and Management, 142*(2), 05015010.

[3] Azad, A.S., Vintaned, J.A.G. (2020). Optimization of the hydro power energy generation using Meta-Heuristic approaches: A Review. *Energy Reports,* 6, 2230–2248.

[4] Bozorg-Haddad, O., Kairimirad, I., Seifollahi-Aghmiuni, S. and Loaiciga, H. (2014). Development and application of the bat algorithm for optimizing the operation of reservoir systems. *Journal of Water Resources Planning and Management, 141*(8), 04014097.

[5] Easa, S.M., Barati, R., Shahheydari, H., Nodashan, E.J. and Barati, T. (2014). Discussion: New and improved four-parameter non-linear Muskingum model. Proceedings Institute of Civil Engineering. *Water Management,* 167,612–615.

[6] Ehteram, M., Othman, F.B., Yaseen, Z.M., Afan, H.A., Allawi, M.F., Malek, M.B. A., Ahmed, A.N., Shahid, S., Singh, V.P. and El-shafie, A. (2018). Improving the Muskingum Flood Routing Method using a Hybrid of Particle Swarm Optimization and Bat Algorithm, *Water, 10(6)*, 807.

[7] Ethteram, M., Mousavi, S.F., Karami, H. and Farzin, S. (2018). Bat algorithm for dam-reservoir operation. *Environmental Earth Sciences, 77*(13), 510.

[8] Farzin, S., Singh, V.P., Karami, H., Farahani, N., Ehteram, M., Kisi, O., Allawi, M.F., Mohd, N.S. and El-shafie, A. (2018). Flood Routing in River Reaches using a Three-Parameter Muskingum model coupled with an Improved Bat Algorithm. *Water, 10,* 1130.

[9] Gill, M.A. (1978). Flood Routing by Muskingum method. *Journal of Hydrology, 36,* 353–363.

[10] Han, Y., Wu, J., Zhai, B., Pan, Y., Huang, G., Wu, L. and Zeng, W. (2019) Coupling a bat algorithm with XGBoost to estimate reference evapotranspiration in Arid and semiarid regions of China. *Advances in Meteorology.*

[11] Hojat, K., Ehteram, M.., Farhad, M.S., Farzin, S. and Sarkamaryan, S. (2018). Evaluation of the performance of bat algorithm in optimization of non-linear muskingum model parameters for flood routing. *Iranian Journal of Eco hydrology, 4*(4), 1025–1032.

[12] McCarthy, G.T. (1938). The Unit Hydrograph and Flood Routing. Proc., Conference of the North Atlantic Division, U.S. Army Corps of Engineers, New London, CT.

[13] Pel, X., Sun, Y. and Yeqing, R. (2018). Demand estimation of water resources via Bat Algorithm. *International Journal of wireless and Mobile Computing,* 18(1).

[14] Sànchez, R., Suàrez, P., Gàlvez, A. and Iglesias, A. (2019). Parameter estimation of a nonlinear hydrological model for channel flood routing with the bat algorithm. *International Conference on swarm Intelligence: Advances in Swarm Intelligence,* 341–351.

[15] Tung, Y. (1985). River Flood Routing by Nonlinear Muskingum Method. *Journal of Hydraulics Engineering, 111,* 1447–1460.

[16] Xing, B., Gan, R., Liu, G., Liu, Z., Zhang, J. and Ren, Y. (2016). Monthly stream flow prediction based on bat algorithm-support vector machine. *Journal of Hydrologic Engineering,* 21(2).

[17] Yang, X.S. (2010). A new metahurestic Bat-Inspired Algorithm studies in computational Intelligence *Springer Berlin*, *284*, 65–74.

[18] Yaseen, Z.M., Allawi, M.F., Karami, H., Ehteram, M., Farzin, S., Ahmed, A.N., Koting, S.B., Mohd, N.S., Jadfar, W.B., Afan, H.A. and El-shafie, A. (2019). A hybrid Bat-Swarm Algorithm for dam-reservoir operation. *Neural Computing and Applications*, 31, 8807–8821.

[19] Zarei, A., Mousavi, S.F., Gordji, M.E. and Karami, H. (2019). Optimal reservoir operation using bat and particle swarm optimization and game theory based on optimal water Allocation among consumers. *Water Resources Management*, *33*, 3071–3093.

Barriers to E-Waste Recycling Units in Sustainable Management of E-Waste

Namrata Jain[1] and Santosh Dhar[2]

Shri Vaishnav School of Management,
Shri Vaishnav Vidyapeeth Vishwavidyalaya, Indore, Madhya Pradesh
E-mail: [1]namratajain@svvv.edu.in; [2]deanresearch@svvv.edu.in

ABSTRACT: India is among the top three generators of e-waste in Asia and is the fifth biggest producer of e-waste in the world after US, China, Japan and Germany. Among these nations US, Japan and Germany are at an advantage from the technological per se whereas for countries like India and China a proper system of e-waste management is yet to evolve. Management practices and policy level initiatives in developing countries like India and China are at an embryonic stage. In developed countries producers are responsible for managing e-waste through the concept of extended producer responsibility (EPR) however due to the wide cultural differences and also because the producer's lobby being strong in India it is not practically possible to implement the EPR in the developing countries like India the same way as it has been implemented in US or Japan. The major responsibility of e-waste recycling in India lies with e-waste recyclers operating in organized sector. A number of reports have been published regarding the hazards associated with unorganized processing of e-waste. However, hardly any study has been conducted to identify the problems of e-waste recyclers in organized sector that actually process e-waste in a scientific and environmentally safe manner.

The present study is an attempt to understand the issues and challenges from the perspective of e-waste recyclers working in the organized sector in India. With this objective in mind field visits have been made to 20 registered e-waste recycling units across India and case studies were developed on them. A thorough analysis of the case studies developed and in-depth interaction with promoters of the units (recyclers) lead to identification of ten major challenges. The cumulative effect of all these challenges indicates that there is an existential threat to the vast majority of the small recyclers, including the larger ones that have invested huge amount. The issues demand quick remedial actions so as to ensure that e-waste recycling units in organized sector in India do not turn sick in the next few years.

Keywords: E-waste, Recycler, Recycling, Unorganized Sector, Waste.

INTRODUCTION

India is among the top three generators of e-waste in Asia as per 2014 estimates. Though the country is among the major Asian producers there is no formal management of e-waste (Wath *et al.*, 2011) exists in India. Moreover, there is a lack of accurate data on e-waste generation, disposal or imports (Jain and Sharma, 2013). There are only estimations of e-waste generation either by NGOs or government agencies. India with 1.7 million tonnes e-waste per annum is the fifth largest generator after US, China, Japan and Germany. Among all the continents, Asia is the largest generator, generating around 16 million tonne with 3.7 kg per inhabitant per year (Balde *et al.*, 2015).

Scientific recycling of e-waste is crucial to minimize its adverse impact on health and environment and maximize the welfare of workers engaged. Efficient recycling of e-waste can create positive impact on economy, society and environment. But in India, more than 90 percent of e-waste processing is done by unorganized sector who has taken the business from their ancestors and passing on to new generations.

However, after the initiatives taken by the Government of India e-waste recycling units in the organized sector are gradually coming into existence. This makes it necessary to investigate the status of these organized e-waste recycling units. Furthermore, e-waste is relatively a new waste stream when compared with municipal solid waste, bio-medical waste for which proper system of management is yet to evolve in India. Failure of prior rules to effectively manage hazardous wastes for instance, Batteries Management and Handling Rules 2001 warrants a more meticulous investigation in managing e-waste. There is a strong need for conducting studies on e-waste recyclers in organized sector in Indian context because hardly any study has been done or documented which focuses on problems faced by them. Understanding the perception and identifying the problems of e-waste recyclers working in the organized sector would throw light on the areas that need to be worked upon to lay down the foundation for developing an effective e-waste management system in India.

REVIEW OF LITERATURE

Life and environment is endangered across the world because of negative impact of e-waste. It has been reported by (Jackson, 2010) that US Environmental Protection Agency has declared e-waste concerns among the top six newly announced global priorities. Amfo-Out *et al.* (2013) reported that presence of toxic substances such as mercury, cadmium, lead, arsenic, chromium, brominated flame retardants (BFRs), polybrominated biphenyls (PBBs) and polybrominated diphenyl ethers (PBDEs) has made e-waste as an environmental threat (Appendix Table 1). Despite of health and environmental concerns unorganized sector holds a quite big pie because the sector is advantageous from the monetary incentive per se (Perry *et al.*, 2007) but quite disadvantageous in the long-term (Siqueira *et al.*, 2016). Studies conducted by

Greenpeace in India and China revealed presence of toxic chemicals and heavy metals in soil and local rivers around e-waste recycling scrap yards (Brigden *et al.*, 2005). The matter of concern was that the amount of some of these chemicals found were thousands of times higher than typical levels both in inside and outside the environments. Lack of awareness about threats associated with e-waste is a major problem in developing countries (Liu *et al.*, 2009).

Disposing e-waste through land fill or incineration is also hazardous. Improper management of landfills leads to leakage of chemicals, metals, vaporization of metallic mercury and dimethylene mercury. Despite of many threats associated with improper handling of e-waste there is lack of knowledge about management of e-waste management as the adverse impacts of such issues cannot be seen or realized immediately (Ciocoiu *et al.*, 2011).

The concern is more for developing countries as these countries are not adept from the technological per se and then dumping of e-waste from developed nations adds to their plight. For instance, it has been reported that US exports its e-waste to India as sending e-waste to India is a cost-effective alternate than processing e-waste in US itself. Illegal imports along with domestic generation is one the reasons that contributes to exponential growth of e-waste in developing countries (Zoeteman *et al.*, 2010). Although, transboundary movement of e-waste has become a common phenomenon across the globe yet it is vague whether such an act would be classified as waste crimes. Enforcement of waste regulations is ineffective in developing countries whereas in developed countries waste regulations have been tightened that results in dumping of waste from developed to developing (Baird *et al.*, 2014).

METHODOLOGY

Qualitative research methods are gaining popularity over the past few decades. Since the present investigation involved comprehending live experiences of e-waste recyclers operating in India, issues and challenges faced by them, qualitative method was used. In the opinion of Bryman and Bell (2011) qualitative methods are useful when the purpose of research is to develop an in-depth understanding of the perception of respondents which is difficult to assess using purely quantitative methods. Moreover, qualitative methods are helpful when little is known or if there is uncertainty about a phenomenon (Cronholm and Hjalmarsson, 2011). Another advantage of qualitative approach is that the method gives freedom to participants to narrate their lived experiences in the form of story which they may not share in survey (Haq, 2014). Keeping these things in mind the approach used was qualitative so that e-waste recyclers could better share their problems in detail.

Further, case method was used as a tool for data collection from e-waste recyclers. The reason behind using the case method as a tool for data collection is that Flyvbjerg (2006) stated that case method is an effective means to conduct research as it takes the researcher close to real-life situations. According to Yin (2003), this method is particularly useful when a phenomenon is complex and broad, available knowledge is not sufficient, a holistic/in-depth investigation is required and when a phenomenon cannot be studied outside the context in which it occurs. It is regarded as particularly useful where research and theory are at their early and formative stages. Considering the nascent stage of e-waste recycling units in India the use of qualitative approach and case method is completely justified.

E-waste recyclers operating in India constitutes the population for the study. E-waste recycling units are spread across 12 states. The sampling frame indicated presence of 97 recyclers located in these 12 states. A representative sample of 20 recyclers from six states was drawn using purposive sampling technique and case studies were developed on each of them. The participants were selected purposefully because Creswell (2003) asserted that in such studies the participants need to be selected purposefully so that it would help the researcher to identify the problem. Field visits to all 20 recycling units were made as per the prior appointment during the period of 2014–2017 and 20 case studies were developed. The sample size of 20 case studies was adequate as Eisenhardt (1989) suggested to develop four to ten cases in such studies. In order to derive the findings of the study all these 20 case studies were subjected to SWOT analysis.

RESULTS AND DISCUSSION

Findings were derived after analyzing 20 case studies that were developed on various e-waste recyclers located in different parts of the country. The installed capacity of visited 20 recycling unit varied from 300 MTA to 12,000 MTA. These units were located in the states of Maharashtra, Karnataka, Madhya Pradesh, Rajasthan, Uttarakhand and Chhattisgarh. Out of these 20 recycling units around 50 percent have been in operation for the last two to five years. 18 units had on an average not more than 10 employees. There were two units with around 100 employees and only one unit with more than 500 employees. A thorough analysis of the case studies developed and in-depth interaction with recyclers lead to identification of following issues and challenges in e-waste management.

Inadequate Collection

Inadequate collection of e-waste is one of the major problems reported by e-waste recyclers in India. E-waste recycling units are facing acute shortage of e-waste availability for recycling. In fact, majority of the units operating in India were not receiving even 50 percent of their installed capacity. This was despite the fact that the country generated around 18.5 Lac MTA of e-waste annually estimated to reach at 30 Lac MTA by 2018 as per study by Assocham and Frost and Sullivan (http://www.assocham.org/retrieved on December 30, 2016). In Indian context, the situation is quite alarming as this was around six times the total installed capacity of all recycling facilities of the country, which was around 2.96 Lac MTA, as per 2014 statistics(http://www.cpcb.nic). Unavailability of waste as a raw material for in food waste and waste paper recycling units have been reported by (Livingston *et al.*, 2016).

Underutilization of Resources

Due to inadequate collection the resources of the e-waste recycling units remained underutilized. In view of the unavailability of sufficient raw material to recycle, the recyclers had idle capacities at their setups which had adverse financial implications. The sum of installed capacities of these 20 recycling units was 57,560 MTA. Out of which the capacity utilization was merely 20,230 MTA. In other words, capacity utilization was only 35.15 percent. 80 percent of capacity remained underutilized in more than 50 percent of units. In order to run the businesses, there should be proper capacity utilization as unused installed machineries and infrastructure undermined the productivity of workforce. Baldwin *et al.* (2013) contended that underutilization of production capacity leads to decline in workforce productivity and 50 percent of slowdown in overall productivity growth.

Technical Constraint

For Indian e-waste recyclers, technical constraint is adding another burden. Employing scientific methods for precious metal recovery demanded technical know-how and expertise. Findings of the study revealed that 70 percent of visited recyclers did not have any engineering or chemical background. Remaining 30 percent of the recyclers with technical or chemical background no doubt were at an advantage than others who lack such knowledge. Nonetheless, e-waste processing in India in organized sector did not demand any such credentials. Baring a few e-waste recyclers, most of the unit owners were lagging in technical competencies and know-how. As per Asian Productivity Organization (2007) solid waste management too lack technical competence. This calls for the training and development programs to enrich technical knowledge of recyclers and to equip e-waste recycling units technically so as to improve the returns obtained at different stages while processing e-waste.

This reflected the need to take actions to make e-waste recyclers known not only about the materials but also the properties of materials found inside the electric and electronic equipment. Knowledge of internal composition of material was a perquisite for e-waste processing (Chancerel *et al.*, 2009). This is because computer server boards a kind of e-waste for instance contained niobium capacitors. These capacitors could explode if the workers at units dismantled it casually. Moreover, the batteries removed had to be stored in drums filled with sand else collision might lead to fire. Thus, to avert any untoward accident workers engaged in handling e-waste needs to be trained. Askari *et al.* (2014) too stated that there is lack of knowledge regarding e-waste storage and disposal at 75 percent of e-waste processing units. This lack of knowledge results in inefficient processing of e-waste. As per Reintjes (2016) inefficient processing of waste materials resulted in loss of precious resources thereby affecting financial benefits as well.

Financial Constraint

Indian e-waste recyclers face financial constraint. Establishing state-of-art recycling unit for optimum recovery with minimum loss of resources and adverse impact on environment is a capital-intensive project. Advanced handheld analysers for metal analysis are capable of offering results within seconds. These could help recyclers in improving returns by analyzing and testing scrap for composition and grade. Though, such equipment are quite expensive (Schluep *et al.*, 2009).

Challenges associated with funds and then prevalent scenario of underutilization discouraged Indian e-waste recyclers to modernize operations and adopt latest technologies for efficient recycling. Findings revealed that there is a need for financial assistance for e-waste recycling units in the country. Lack of financial resources for managing municipal solid waste had also resulted in its inadequate management (Siqueira *et al.*, 2016). This is one of the major reasons that despite their willingness, Indian e-waste recyclers were not able to organize technical enhancement training programs for workers. Not only quantity recovered, quality of the material recovered is also one of the important parameters in waste recycling from financial and resource conservation per se. Nonetheless, in the absence of financial support it would be difficult for e-waste recyclers to improve e-waste processing methods.

Unorganized Sector

Wide prevalent unorganized sector in India is posing a threat to recyclers working in the organized sector. Thousands of workers engaged in unorganized sector need not to invest in infrastructure or on logistics. Apart from ineffective processing of e-waste, unorganized sector also raises other socio-economic issues, such as child labor and environment pollution. In order to evade from pollution control board authorities these workers keep on changing their sites of operations periodically. Unorganized units are important competitors for organized units (Wilson *et al.*, 2006). Being economically weaker and marginalized social groups, these workers are casual towards health and safety aspects too. However, in the opinion of Lundgren (2012) family obligations and meager job opportunities in organized sector made them to prefer unorganized sector.

Involvement of child labor in unorganized sector is quite high (WHO, 2011). Large numbers of children are processing e-waste without any fear of its hazardous content as they are quite ignorant. The same was affirmed while interacting with a child at one of the unorganized recycling site in the state of Karnataka who believed that a banana or carbonated cola drink clears the stomach and wipes off the ill-effects, if any, in e-waste processing. This showed the gross ignorance on the part of the child labor. During the processing many chemicals get accumulated in their bodies because of the immature systems in children that prevent the effective excretion of toxic materials (Tinmaz and Demir, 2006). Even low levels of lead, mercury, cadmium and other heavy metals could result in severe irreversible neurological problems. The challenges due to unorganized sector is not confined to India only but has been there in many developing nations like China, Turkey and Vietnam (Chi *et al.*, 2011).

In Indian context as well, the unorganized sector holds quite big pie. And hence, corrective measures need to be taken with great care. It is vital to keep a check on their activities and at the same time workers from unorganized need to be assured of job security. As per reports of Labour Bureau, India created 9 lakh jobs in the year 2011, that dropped to 4.19 lakh in 2013 and subsequently to 1.35 lakh in 2015 (Times of India, October 17, 2016). In such a scenario, where generation of jobs is getting tougher, if unorganized sector is banned from processing e-waste then it would be adding to the existing plight of unemployment.

Mindset of Consumers and Lack of Awareness

Mindset of consumers in India is another challenge for recyclers. Understanding the attitude and behavior of consumers towards waste disposal is one of the major pre-requisite for setting up any system of waste management. In the opinion of Welsch and Kuhling (2009) one of the major contributors to the environmental problems is the behavior of human. However, merely change in attitude alone would not lead to the desired behavior from environment per se but it would be certainly the first step on the ladder. Lack of awareness on the part of consumers has been reported in many studies. For instance, Jain and Dhar (2017) conducted a study and found that that none of the consumer was aware of existence of any e-waste recycling unit at state or national level and hence never disposed e-waste with recycler. This was despite the fact that e-waste regulations made it mandatory for consumers to dispose e-waste with recyclers. The situation is alarming as 85 percent of respondents were not aware that the government has enforced any such regulations way back in May 2012. One of the reasons that could be attributed towards the casual approach of consumers while dealing with e-waste is that they could not see the immediate detrimental impact due to improper management of e-waste. Afroz *et al.* (2013) also found low awareness of consumers regarding negative impacts of e-waste. There is a need for international cooperation to raise awareness that e-waste has become one of the major threats to environment and health (Alabaster *et al.*, 2013). Consumers in India expect lucrative incentives while disposing e-waste. It is then quite prudent to plan rewards accordingly. Nonetheless, Bolderdijk (2015) asserted that until and unless consumers were not personally convinced about importance of waste recycling, the incentives might not bring in the desired results.

Studies suggest that measures like repetitive communication through advertising, emphasizing personal benefits, organizing awareness campaigns on mass scale can initiate behavioral changes (Vasileva and Ivanova, 2014). Behavioral change was the most sought of as it would make citizens of country to voluntary contribute in issues pertaining to environment. Consumers of developed nations with high per capita income, high status of living would not bother in paying extra fees for recycling or taxes but in India any additional monetary burden matters to a common man. Consumers are trying to evade from responsibilities because of the financial reasons. Unorganized sector offers more incentives than organized sector and hence people are interested in disposing e-waste to unorganized sector. The need is to identify ways that could help in bridging the gap of financial incentives received from e-waste recycler and that from other possible sources (unorganized sector/outlets).

Tedious Approval Procedures

E-waste recyclers in India found the approval procedures for obtaining e-waste recycling licenses quite tedious. Recyclers found it tough to get through the statutory norms due to highly bureaucratic and lengthy procedures. Approvals to setup and operate were not granted within the stipulated time frame of 90 days for authorization and 90 days for registration. The application processing in majority of e-waste recycling units visited took very long time ranging from one to four years. Repeated visits to different departments for approvals were mandatory and, in the process, it dampened the spirits of the applicants. Recyclers were at a loss to understand the expectations of concerned officials and ran from pillar to post.

It was expensive to purchase a property in an industrial area and hence more than 50 percent of e-waste recyclers had to operate in rental premises. In case recyclers wanted to change the place of operation they had to take a fresh approval which was a cumbersome process. Due to low understanding of regulatory requirements made small and medium size units more susceptible to bureaucratic rigidity. Gifts were considered a way to avoid bureaucratic procedures or to put mistakes out of sight (Lecuna, 2016).

It is imperative to take initiative for reducing the bureaucracy in Indian context. De-bureaucratization program has resulted in positive results in Chile, New Zealand, Australia, Canada, and Singapore. In World Bank's ranking, India is at 150th rank for starting a business and at 130th rank in the ease of doing business in contrast to New Zealand which is on the top position. Reducing length of procedures up to 20 to 40 percent and payment reductions up to 50 percent had significant impact on the number of registrations of entrepreneurial units (Klapper and Love, 2010).

Sustainability

Sustainability is other challenge for e-waste recycling units in India. With the passage of time advance technologies made it possible to manufacture electronic devices with less content of precious metals. It was reported by Raval and Oza (2014) that due to technological developments in electronic industry, content of precious metal in older devices were more than their existing counterparts. Consequently, profit margins of e-waste recyclers have been affected. Moreover, most of the equipments in e-waste did not have potential to even return the cost of processing. According to Widmer *et al.* (2005), only those electronic equipment that contained gold and copper could help in reclaiming the cost incurred for e-waste processing.

Slack periods were a common phenomenon in waste recycling units (Joseph, 2007). Those recyclers who have alternate sources of income are not affected. But 71 percent of e-waste recyclers under study did not have any other business and were dependent completely on the operations of recycling units. While working in organized sector recyclers had to bear many costs for their survival. During their establishing years, few e-waste recyclers recruited full time employees, but irregular operations forced them to switch to contractual labors as they could not afford paying regular salaries to their employees in the wake of meager revenues.

Recycling units in Japan and US too faced similar kind of problems. Japanese recycling units had to switch over to temporary workers (Bo and Yamamoto, 2010) whereas in California low prices for scrap made 30 percent of recycling units out of business. *Waste Management*, known as one of the top waste processor in US had to shut about 20 percent of its processing facilities nationwide in the last two years (Nash, 2016). Generation of revenue is a prerequisite for sustainability of any business.

Legislative and Administrative Constraint

Legislations play a crucial role in regulating prevailing systems in a democratic society. Regulations might benefit the society on a broader scale but at the same time it could result in creating negative impact on individual units (Bozeman, 2000). Moreover, framing of effective polices would be a tough task for countries that did not have well proven record of regulating environment (Kuehr and Magalini, 2013). These findings suggest that situation is bit challenging for India as Dey (2009) reported that the *Eco-Mark* initiatives taken by the Government way back in the year 1991 and *Battery Management and Handling Rules* in *2001* have failed.

India enforced e-waste management and handling rules in 2012 so as to initiate a system for e-waste management in India. Nonetheless, unaddressed legislative gaps have laid back its effective enforcements. As a result, the problems of e-waste recyclers remain unaddressed in India. For instance, the rules did not define any mechanism through which unorganized sector could be checked. Recyclers from unorganized sector entered in organized sector in India after availing licenses. Thereafter, licenses were misused to procure e-waste and such trades go unnoticed. Even in the organized sector, some recyclers have reverted back to the traditional system of e-waste processing after getting approvals as there was no periodic review from the monitoring authorities to check their day to day operations. Any system devised to rehabilitate unorganized sector is missing in Indian context. Moreover, traditional processing of e-waste is not termed as illegal. This demands careful balancing of interest of both organized as well as unorganized sector.

The e-waste management rules in India lay emphasis on producers for collection and channelization as a part of extended producer responsibility (EPR) like in developed countries. But recyclers find it difficult to remain completely dependent on collection centers or producers for operating their units. Implementing EPR is difficult in developing countries because it would be difficult to track down and assign financial accountability to small producers who are producing goods after importing or assembling (Kojima *et al.*, 2009).

In India, ambiguity in penal actions on violation of e-waste management rules has resulted in casual attitude amongst the consumers. One of the reasons that violators often go unpunished was because of lack of powers vested to pollution control boards (Agarwal, 2005). Officials of pollution control board could only initiate prosecution against violators in courts and do not have power to punish them. Lack of resources and underdeveloped legal systems are responsible for ineffective implementation of environment regulations (Jain, 2013b). Systems in developing countries should provide more autonomy to the State Boards. According to Jain and Dhar (2017) in order to have, evidence-based decision making it was imperative to infuse scientific mindset among officials by promoting research activities. In India, as per e-waste management and handling rules, consumers were instructed to dispose e-waste with recyclers but bulk consumers, such as IT companies do not have defined policies for e-waste disposal.

Ethical Constraint

Recycling of e-waste poses an ethical challenge to recyclers in India. However, ethical business decisions are quite complex and have mixed outcomes in the form of social benefits and social costs as are financial revenues and expenses. Due to complexity of decisions, at times e-waste recyclers had to overlook some considerations and some may be sidestepped because of high costs involved. According to Kuratko and Rao (2014), decisions of entrepreneurs involve economic-tradeoff wherein at times units earn profit but others in society may suffer. This makes ethics to be a judgment call and continue to remain a major issue for entrepreneurs during the new century because unethical view of one entrepreneur may be ethical for other. Business should not be considered as a means for wealth creation only these should also create more value for stakeholders. E-waste recyclers are not only the beneficiaries of their business rather their units have to create positive impact on society and environment as a whole.

CONCLUSION

E-waste recycling in organized sector is at its nascent age in many developing countries especially in India. With the result, many of the e-waste recyclers are novice in the organized sector and are unacquainted with the professional expertise expected of them. Lack of awareness regarding disposal of e-waste and expectations of monetary incentives is creating collection issue before recyclers. One of the ways to facilitate them is granting subsidies. Government should grant subsidies to assist e-waste recyclers at initial stage and later when the units pick up the pace the subsidies can be withdrawn. Government could initiate training and skill development programmes. Even, device loans could be granted to assist recyclers in procuring machineries in initial years so that they can sustain themselves in the competitive organized sector. It is equally important to assist them on financial and legal front in these initial years as the sector helps to keep the social fabric intact.

Educating people regarding the need of proper disposal of e-waste is must. A series of parallel actions need to be taken to address the issues associated with e-waste management. Developments in organized sector should be made to bring in welfare and to result in betterment for the society rather than giving rise to social and environmental issues or serious repercussions.

REFERENCES

[1] Afroz, R., Masud, M.M., Akhtar, R. and Duasa, J.B. (2013). Survey and analysis of public knowledge, awareness and willingness to pay in Kuala Lumpur, Malaysia—A case study on household WEEE management. *Journal of Cleaner Production, 52,* 185–193.

[2] Agarwal, V.K. (2005). Environmental laws in India: Challenges for enforcement. *Bulletin of the National Institute of Ecology, 15,* 227–238.

[3] Alabaster, G., Asante, K.A. Li, J.H., Sly, P. and Zeng, E.Y. (2013). The Geneva declaration on e-waste and children's health. World Health Organization: Geneva.

[4] Amfo-Out, R., Bentum, J.K. and Omari, S. (2013). Assessment of soil contamination through e-waste recycling activities in Tema community one. *Environment and Pollution, 2,* 66–70.

[5] Asian Productivity Organization (2007). Solid waste management: issues and challenges in Asia. ISBN: 92-833-7058-9. Tokyo, Japan.

[6] Askari, A., Ghadimzadeh, A., Gomes, C. and Ishak, M.B. (2014). E-waste management towards and appropriate policy. *European Journal of Business Management, 6,* 37–46.

[7] Atiemo, S.M., Ofosu, F.G., Aboh, I.K. and Kuranchie-Mensah, H. (2012). Assessing the heavy metals contamination of surface dust from waste electrical and electronic equipment (e-waste) recycling site in Accra, Ghana. *Research Journal of Environmental and Earth Sciences, 4,* 605–611.

[8] Baird, J., Curry, R. and Cruz, P. (2014). An overview of waste crime, its characteristics, and the vulnerability of the EU waste sector. *Waste Management and Research, 32,* 97–105.

[9] Balde, C.P., Wang. F., Kuehr, R. and Huisman, J. (2015). The global e-waste monitor 2014. United Nations University, IAS – SCYCLE, Bonn, Germany.

[10] Baldwin, J.R., Gu, W. and Yan, B. (2013). Export growth, capacity utilization, and productivity growth: evidence from the Canadian manufacturing plants. *Review of Income and Wealth, 59,* 665–688.

[11] Bo, B. and Yamamoto, K. (2010). Characteristics of e-waste recycling systems in Japan and China. World Academy of Science, *Engineering and Technology, 62,* 500–506.

[12] Bolderdijk, J.W. and Steg, L. (2015). Promoting sustainable consumption: the risks of using financial incentives. Handbook of Research on Sustainable Consumption, 328–342.

[13] Bozeman, B. (2000). Bureaucracy and red tape. New York: Prentice Hall.

[14] Brigden, K., Labunska, I., Santillo, D. and Allsopp, M. (2005). Recycling of electronic wastes in China and India: workplace and environmental contamination. Greenpeace International, Amsterdam.

[15] Bryman, A. and Bell, E. (2011). Business Research Methods. 3rd ed., Oxford University Press.

[16] Chancerel, P., Meskers, C., Hageluken, C. and Rotter, V.S. (2009). Assessment of precious metal flows during preprocessing of waste electrical and electronic equipment, *Journal of Industrial Ecology,* 13:791–810.

[17] Chi, X., Streicher-Porte, M., Wang, M.Y. and Reuter, M.A. (2011). Informal electronic waste recycling: A sector review with special focus on China. *Waste Management, 31,* 731–742.

[18] Ciocoiu, N., Dobrea, C. and Tartiu, V. (2011). The role of consumer behaviour in e-waste management system in Romania. *Review of International Comparative Management,* 12, 208–214.

[19] Creswell, W.J. (2003). Research design: Qualitative, quantitative and mixed methods approaches. Sage Publications Ltd., London.

[20] Cronholm, S. and Hjalmarsson, A. (2011). Experiences from sequential use of mixed methods. *Electronic Journal of Business Research Methods, 9*, 87–95.

[21] Dey, D. (2009). Managing e-waste in India: Challenges initiatives and concerns. Presented for discussion at the IEEE Forum on November 05, 2009, Jadavpur University, Kolkata.

[22] Eisenhardt, K.M. (1989). Building theories from case study research. *Academy of Management Review, 14*, 532–550.

[23] Flyvbjerg, B. (2006). Five misunderstandings about case-study research. *Qualitative Inquiry, 12*, 219–245.

[24] Haq, M. (2014). A comparative analysis of qualitative and quantitative research methods and a justification for use of mixed methods in social research. Annual Ph.D Conference, University of Bradford Business School of Management.

[25] Jackson, L. (2010). EPA cites the e-waste as one of six global environmental priorities. Hudson Valley Business Journal.

[26] Jain, N. (2013 b). Strategizing e-waste recycling. *Waste Recycling India, Cover Story on E-waste Recycling*, 1, 46–47.

[27] Jain, N. and Dhar, S. (2017). E-waste Awareness: A Study of Indore City. Paper presented at Shodh-2017, Conference for Doctoral Students, Innovative Practices in Science, Technology, Humanities and Management: Contemporary Perspective, Indore City.

[28] Jain, N. and Sharma, A. (2013). E-waste: an emerging global threat. *Clean India Journal*, 9, 61–63.

[29] Joseph, K. (2007). Electronic waste management in India—issues and strategies. In Eleventh International Waste Management and Landfill Symposium, Sardinia.

[30] Klapper, L.F. and Love, I. (2010). The impact of business environment reforms on new firm registration. World Bank Policy Research. Washington: World Bank (Working Paper).

[31] Kojima, M., Yoshida, A. and Sasaki, S. (2009) Difficulties in applying extended producer responsibility policies in developing countries: case studies in e-waste recycling in China and Thailand. *Journal of Material Cycles and Waste Management, 11*, 263–269.

[32] Kuehr, R. and Magalini, F. (2013). UNU and WHO Survey on e-waste and its health impact on children. Final Report. United Nations University Institute for Sustainability and Peace–Sustainable Cycles.

[33] Kuratko, D.F. and Rao, T.V. (2014). Entrepreneurship A South Asian Perspective. Cengage Learning: Delhi.

[34] Lecuna, A. (2016). Corruption and Bureaucracy in entrepreneurship. In United States Association for Small Business and Entrepreneurship. Conference Proceedings. United States Association for Small Business and Entrepreneurship.

[35] Liu, Q., Li, K.Q., Zhao, H., Li, G. and Fan, F.Y. (2009). The global challenge of electronic waste management. *Environmental Science and Pollution Research*, 16, 248–249.

[36] Livingston, E., Mergo, C., Crain, S. and Sines, M. (2016). Commercial food waste collection assessment. *Bio Cycle*, 26–27.

[37] Lundgren, K. (2012). The global impact of e-waste: Addressing the challenge. International Labour Office, Programme on Safety and Health at Work and the Environment (Safe Work), Sectoral Activities Department (SECTOR) Geneva: ILO: 2–5.

[38] Nash, J. (2016). California's recycling industry is in the dumps. *Bloomberg Businessweek.*

[39] Perry, G.E, Maloney, W.F., Arias, O.S, Fajnzylber, P., Mason, A.D. and Saavedra-Chanduvi, J. (2007). Informality: Exit and exclusion. The World Bank, Washington DC.

[40] Raval, N.K. and Oza, M.P. (2014). E-Waste problem - present status, challenges faced in its management and future: A study of Gujarat region. *Journal of Research in Humanities and Social Sciences, 2,* 31–36.

[41] Reintjes, M. (2016). Handheld analysers: Essential tools for unlocking scrap's secrets. *Recycling International, 6,* 18–23.

[42] Schluep, M., Hagelueken, C., Kuehr, R., Maglini, F., Maurer, C., Meskers, C., Mueller, E. and Wang, F. (2009). Recycling from e-waste to resources, sustainable innovation and technology transfer industrial sector studies. Paris, France: EMPA, Umicore, UNU.

[43] Siqueira, ACO., Webb, J.W. and Bruton, G.D. (2016). Informal entrepreneurship and industry conditions. *Entrepreneurship Theory and Practice*, 40:177–200

[44] Tinmaz, E. and Demir, I. (2006). Research on solid waste management system to improve existing situation in Corlu town of Turkey. *Waste Management, 26,* 307–314.

[45] Vasileva, E and Ivanova, D. (2014). Towards a sustainable consumer model: the case study of Bulgarian recyclers. *International Journal of Consumer Studies, 38,* 475–484.

[46] Wath, S.B., Dutt, P.S. and Chakrabarti, T. (2011). E-waste scenario in India, its management and implications. *Environmental Monitoring and Assessment, 172,* 249–262.

[47] Welsch, H. and Kuhling, J. (2009). Using happiness data for environmental valuation: issues and applications. *Journal of Economic Surveys, 23,* 385–406.

[48] Widmer, R., Oswald-Krapf, H., Sinha-Khetriwal, D., Schnellmann, M. and Boeni, H. (2005). Global perspectives on e-waste. *Environmental Impact Assessment Review, 25*: 436e458.

[49] Wilson, D.C., Velis, C. and Cheeseman, C. (2006). Role of informal sector recycling in waste management in developing countries. Habitat International, *30,* 797–808.

[50] World Health Organization (2011). Summary of principles for evaluating health risks in children associated with exposure to chemicals. Retrieved from http://www.who.int/ceh/health_risk_children.pdf, on June 09, 2016.

[51] Yin, R.K. (2003). Case study research, design and methods. 3rd ed. Newbury Park, Sage Publications.

[52] Zoeteman, B.C., Krikke, H.R. and Venselaar, J. (2010). Handling WEEE waste flows: on the effectiveness of producer responsibility in a globalizing world. *The International Journal of Advanced Manufacturing Technology, 47,* 415–436.

APPENDIX

Table 1: Substances Found in E-Waste and Health Hazards

Chemical	*Found in*	*Health Hazards*
Antimony	CRTs, Printed Circuit Boards, etc.	Hazardous when inhaled or when it comes in contact with skin and eye. Causes damage to the blood, kidneys, lungs, liver and nervous system.
Arsenic	Transistors	Soluble inorganic arsenic is acutely toxic. It can cause chronic arsenic poisoning, skin injuries, gastrointestinal problems, cardiovascular disease and cancer.
Barium65	CRTs	Damages heart, liver and spleen. Short-term exposure can lead to weakening of muscles and swelling in brain.
Beryllium	Motherboards of computers	Can cause lung cancer.
Cadmium	Chip resistors and Semiconductors	Harmful for kidney and lever.
Chlorofluorocarbons (CFCs)	Refrigerators and Coolers	Damages the ozone layer and is a potent greenhouse gas. It leads to coughing, sore throat, difficulty in breathing, and eye redness, unconsciousness, irregular heart-beat.
Cobalt	Rechargeable batteries and coatings for hard disk drives	Toxic to lungs and skin irritant.
Copper	Used as a conductor	Toxic to lungs and mucous membrane. Highly hazardous when inhaled and in case of ingestion.
Dioxins	Released during open air burning of electronics	Highly toxic and can cause cancer. It interferes with hormones, damages immune system and creates problem for reproductive systems.
Gallium	Integrated circuits	Toxic to lungs and mucous membranes. Severe over-exposure can result in death in case of over exposure.
Hexavalent Chromium	Corrosion protection of untreated and galvanized steel plates	Causes asthma, cancer, damages kidneys, liver and DNA.
Indium	LCD screens	Less investigated substance regarding to environment. Causes eye irritation, creates problems in respiratory tract. It may have long-term effects on the kidneys.

(Contd...)

(Table 1 contd...)

Chemical	Found in	Health Hazards
Lead	Solder of printed circuit boards, glass panels and gaskets in computer monitors	Damages nervous systems, cardiovascular, renal and blood systems. Damages kidneys. It affects brain development of children.
Lithium	Rechargeable Batteries	Highly toxic as it can be excreted in maternal milk. Hazardous in case of ingestion and inhalation.
Mercury	Relays, switches and printed circuit boards	Hazardous for nervous, digestive and immune systems. Damages lungs and kidneys. Inhalation of mercury vapour may be fatal.
Nickel	Rechargeable batteries	Have carcinogenic effects. Harmful for kidneys, lungs, liver, respiratory tract.
Phthalates	Used to soften plastics	Harmful for endocrine, reproduction, nervous and immune system. It leads to liver cancer.
Polybrominated diphenyl ethers (PBDEs) used in brominated flame retardants (BFRs)	Plastic housing of electronic equipments and circuit boards to reduce flammability	BFRs disrupt endocrine system functions. It leads to high cancer risk. It may effect on the levels of thyroid stimulating hormone and cause genotoxic damage.
Polychlorinated. biphenyls (PCBs)	Insulating material in electronic products	Harmful for reproductive and immune system.
Polyvinyl Chloride (PVC)	Cabling and computer housing plastics contain PVC for its fire-retardant properties	On burning it releases dioxins. It leads to reproductive and developmental problems. Damages immune system and interferes with regulatory hormones.
Silver	Wiring circuit boards, etc.	Accumulated in human organs on repeated exposures which damages health. Harmful in case of eye contact, ingestion and inhalation. Severe over-exposure can result in death.
Thallium	Batteries, semiconductors, etc.	Harmful for to kidneys, nervous system, liver heart, and may cause birth defects. Highly toxic in case of ingestion and inhalation. Fatal in case of over exposure.
Tin	Lead-free solder	It disturbs gastrointestinal tract. It produces irritation in case of skin and eye contact, ingestion and inhalation.

Source: Lundgren, 2012.

Bloom's Taxonomy—A Universal Measuring Tool to Assess the Learning Outcomes of an Architecture Design Project

Rupali H. Gupte[1] and Ujwala Chakradeo[2]

[1]Smt. K.L. Tiwari College of Architecture, Shreeprastha, Nallasopara (W), Maharashtra

[2]Smt. Manoramabai Mundle College of Architecture, Seminary Hills, Nagpur, Maharashtra

E-mail: [1]archrupaligupte@yahoo.com; [2]uchakradeo@gmail.com

ABSTRACT: The profession of architecture is a service to humanity and society at large. A socially sensitive and sustainable approach becomes one of the most important aspects in this profession. As per Under Graduate B. Arch course (UIA), architecture education should be able to produce good world citizens who are intellectually mature, ecologically sensitive and socially responsible. The initial stage of understanding basics of architecture education is Stage-1 i.e. at the end of 3rd year of UIA. The outcomes of the learning is gained in each semester and is reflected in the Architecture Design (AD) project which the learner produces at the end of each term. This final output is graded as per the work produced under variable measuring criteria of concept, ideas, design, technical details, digital representations, quantum & quality of work etc. The varied grading system leaves negligible scope to gather on what was lacking in the learning process of the student. The final design should be a basis for measuring the learnings achieved by the learner under specific criteria of educational goals. Specific educational learning outcomes are needed on the basis of which the design output could be analysed. Blooms Taxonomy has developed a common language for teachers to assess learning outcomes under specific learning domains. The present paper intends to analyse and evaluate with the help of pilot study, the parameters of Bloom's taxonomy which can be used for assessing the AD projects at the end of Stage-1 of UG B. Arch course.

Keywords: Architecture Education, Bloom's Taxonomy, Council of Architecture (COA), Optimum Learning Outcomes, UIA.

INTRODUCTION

Architecture Institutes play a major role in transmitting the required knowledge through their learning and teaching objectives to ensure optimum learning in Architecture education. Learning outcomes need to be holistically planned in curricula and strategized efficiently in order to achieve the purpose of Architecture education. The sole purpose of Architecture is to serve humanity and society at large. Architecture education has evolved in creativity and technology achieving new paradigms and hence the responsibility of being socially relevant in the profession needs to be deep rooted. Educational institutes have been educating young architects with the required knowledge, skills and values to handle this responsibility. Architectural learning should be able to optimise the knowledge, skills and values required for serving the society. Learning theories have provided a strong base and guided the teaching and learning methodologies. Teaching pedagogies and learning theories can ensure the learning outcomes required from students. Development of creative skills, analytical understanding, decision making capacity are mandatory for producing competent, critical minded and ethical professionals.

The goals of architecture education, learning theories, learning outcomes and social sensitivity are intensely interwoven in the journey of undergraduate architecture course. The UG course in architecture being a higher education course comes under the parameters of higher education learning goals. The transformation from basic learning outcomes to specialized and mastered learning outcomes is required. In the total duration of five year UG B.Arch course, UIA and Council of Architecture (COA) has divided the course into 2 stages: Stage-1 (First to Third Year) which is termed as the "generalist" stage and Stage-2 (Fourth and Fifth year) which is the "specialist" stage. Understanding the goal of architectural education and achieving it in an optimum way needs to be the sole purpose of architecture institutes. As per UIA, architecture education should have two basic purposes; to produce competent, creative, critical minded and ethical professional designers/builders and to produce good world citizens who are intellectually mature, ecologically sensitive and socially responsible.

UIA has further stated that the first 3 years in the architect's education requires rigorous and very careful programing. Architecture students need to acquire the capabilities of design, knowledge and skill to fulfil an architect's role. It thus, becomes a crucial responsibility of architecture institutions to assure whether these goals are transmitted to the students during the course.

Understanding the Goals of Architecture Education in Stage-1 *(as per UIA)*

Architect is defined as a "generalist" in stage-1 who should be capable of integrating the following capabilities of design, knowledge and skill as follows:

Design i.e., ability to engage imagination, think creatively, innovate and provide design leadership; ability to gather information, define problems, apply analyses and critical judgment and formulate strategies for action; ability to think three-dimensionally in the exploration of design; ability to reconcile divergent factors, integrate knowledge and apply skills in the creation of a design solution. ***Knowledge*** **i.e.,** studies related to cultural and artistic; social; environmental; technical; design and professional. ***Skills i.e.,*** ability to act and to communicate ideas through collaboration, speaking, numeracy, writing, drawing, modelling and evaluation; ability to utilise manual and electronic graphic and model making capabilities to explore, develop, define and communicate a design proposal; understanding of systems of evaluation that use manual and/or electronic means for performance assessments of built environments.

Architecture should be considered as a service accessible to the whole community. It could act as a mediator of social tensions and should be considered as a resource, one of the instruments which contribute to the balance of the society. The objectives of architecture education can be summarised under the following 2 categories:

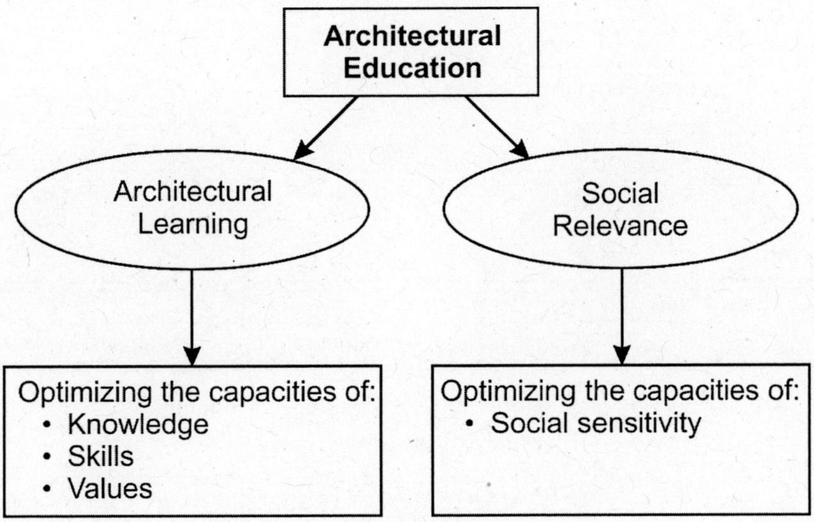

Fig. 1: Architecture Education Goals

(*Source:* Self)

The values of Architectural learning majorly form the emotion-based learning of morals and ethics towards society, environment and profession. The lens of sustainable development forms the core value towards developing social sensitivity of the learner. It becomes necessary to understand if learners are achieving all the three aims of architecture learning i.e., knowledge, skills and values. The present study has been undertaken to find a common tool that can scrutinize and measure the output produced by students in all three parameters. Specifically, these learning outcomes need to be achieved successfully by the end of stage-1 (Third year B.Arch) which is the threshold to enter stage-2.

THEORIES FOR MEASURING OPTIMUM LEARNING OUTCOMES

Educationists and philosophers have developed theories and parameters to assess the learning outcomes. Bloom's taxonomy (1956) of educational objectives explains certain detailed parameters which have been predominantly used in education.

These educational learning objectives of cognitive (knowledge based); affective (emotion based); psychomotor (action based) can be classified in sets of 3 hierarchical models/domains, depending on their levels of complexity.

Bloom's taxonomy defines and distinguishes different levels of human cognition i.e., thinking, learning and Understanding (Bloom, 1956).

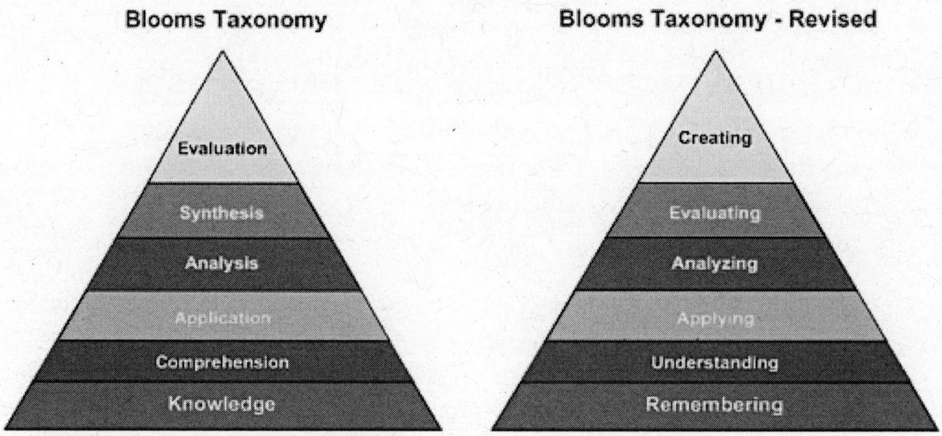

Fig. 2: Cognitive Levels of Bloom's Taxonomy
(*Source:* blogs.edweek.org)

According to Muhammed *et al.* (2017) and Anderson *et al.* (2001), the learning outcomes expected in *cognitive domain* are knowledge which involves the ability to recall information; comprehension which refers to understanding and interpreting the data; application which means using knowledge in a new situation; analysis helps students to understand the difference between facts and opinions; evaluating means making own judgements based on a set of guidelines and creating refers to putting information together and creating a new version in an innovative way.

The learning outcomes expected in *affective domain* are receiving information wherein a person becomes aware of the feelings and emotions; responding to the situation involves the active participation of the people; valuing is the ability to see the worth of something; organization means to organize values into matters of great importance; characterization that refers to the ability to internalize values.

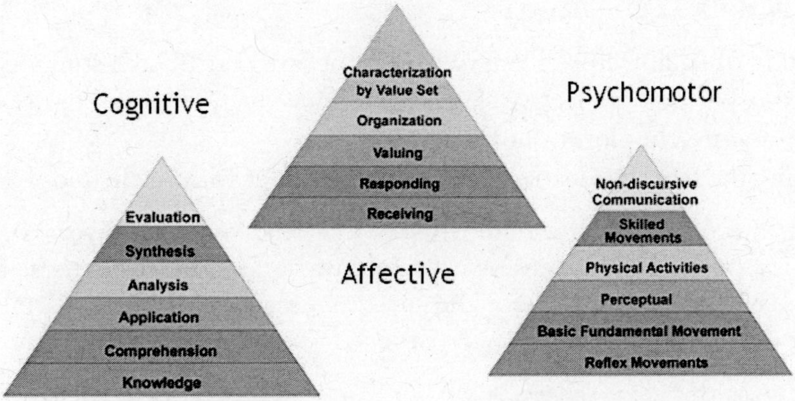

Fig. 3: Cognitive, Affective and Psychomotor Domains
(*Source:* educationaltaxonomy.weebly.com)

The learning outcomes expected in *psychomotor domain* are perception where a person applies sensory information to activity; set where a person is ready to act on the given opportunity; guided response refers to one's ability to follow a behaviour; mechanism- is a person's ability to convert responses into a habit; complex clear response is a person's ability to perform complex patterns of action; adaptation means to adapt one's behaviour in case of special events; origination means to form new ways or patterns for a situation.

BLOOM'S TAXONOMY AND ARCHITECTURE EDUCATION

Bloom's taxonomy defines different levels of learning stages as detailed above. Architecture education expects a compilation of all these stages in the final output. The final output at the end of each semester is the AD project that the learners produce in UG course. This project is the optimum learning outcome gained by the student in the entire semester. Hence, this project needs to be the base of understanding whether the student has acquired the required knowledge in all the expected parameters of knowledge, skills and values. Thus, the domains of Bloom's taxonomy can be evaluated for assessing architecture education learning outcomes as cognitive – knowledge based; psychomotor – skill based; affective – value based.

The AD projects can be framed and assessed as per the expected learning outcomes on the basis of Bloom's taxonomy. The taxonomy can thus be used as a tool to understand the achievements and shortcomings of the learners work in specific categories. In order to assess the learning outcomes achieved at the end of stage-1, a pilot study was conducted on Third Year B.Arch Design projects using Bloom's taxonomy as a measuring tool.

METHODOLOGY

- Pilot study of Architecture Design Projects of 3rd Year B.Arch students.
- Analysis of critical reflective learning achieved by learner under cognitive, affective and psychomotor domains.
- Evaluating the reflective learning achieved by learner with the help of Likert Scale.

Step 1: Architecture design assignments of 20 students of 3rd year B.Arch were considered for pilot study. The design project was a 50 bedded General Hospital at Nallasopara (w), Palghar dist. Since the site was near the institute, it could be easily accessed for detailed analysis and society interventions throughout the duration of the project.

As per bloom's taxonomy the following parameters were considered for assessing the final output of all students under each learning domain:

Cognitive Domain: Knowledge gathered, analysed, applied and evaluated with respect to:

- Case study & Data collection
- Site analysis
- Climatic analysis
- Zoning of spaces
- Concept & Bye-Laws
- Building Services
- Construction technology
- Space planning

Affective Domain: Emotion/value-based learning. Evaluation was done by observing the response of the learner in understanding the value of design with respect to different users of the society, ecology and environment sensitivity. Organization and consideration of these values in to priorities while planning.

- User centric prioritization to comfort and planning w.r.t staff, doctors and patients in various sections of OPD, Casualty, waiting areas and open spaces.
- Environmental values.
- Social and community values.

Psychomotor Domain: Skill based origination was considered. The communication skill, model making, personal grooming and computer skills with respect to the development of learner's locomotive/body skills were prioritized.

- Innovative skills for presentation
- Hand-drafting

- Rendering
- Cad drafting/computer skills
- Views
- Model
- Communication Skills
- Personality skills

Assessment of the learning achieved under Cognitive, Affective and Psychomotor domains on Likert Scale was conducted for each design project as follows:

Table 1: Example of Assessment of AD Projects on Likert Scale

Analysis of Sem- VI Architecture Design Project on basis of Blooms Taxonomy (Learning Domains)						
Project - 50 Bedded General Hospital at Nallaspara (W), Palghar District.						
Cognitive Domain - Knowledge based (Evaluation)						
	Name of student	**1**	**2**	**3**	**4**	**5**
1	**Abhishek Patel**	**Very poor**	**Poor**	**Fair**	**Good**	**Excellent**
	Case study & Data collection					
	site analysis					
	climatic analysis					
	Zoning of spaces					
	Concept					
	Building Services					
	Construction technology					
	Space planning					
Average cognitive understanding - Fair						
Affective domain - emotion/ value based (Characterization)						
	Name of student	**1**	**2**	**3**	**4**	**5**
1	**Abhishek Patel**	**Very poor**	**Poor**	**Fair**	**Good**	**Excellent**
	User centric prioritization to comfort & planning w.r.t staff, doctors, patients and vehicles					
	OPD					
	Casualty					
	General hospital					
	waiting areas					
	open spaces					
	Environmental values					
	social and community values					
Average Affective understanding - Poor						
Psychomotor domain - Skill based (Origination)						
	Name of student	**1**	**2**	**3**	**4**	**5**
1	**Abhishek Patel**	**Very poor**	**Poor**	**Fair**	**Good**	**Excellent**
	Innovative skills for presentation					
	Hand- drafting					
	Rendering					
	Cad drafting/ computer skills					
	Views					
	Model					
	Communication Skills					
	Personality skills					
Average Psychomotor understanding - Fair						

The summary of all the assessed results were concluded as follows:

Table 2: Summary of Pilot Study

Summary of Likert scale anaysis	COGNITIVE DOMAIN					AFFECTIVE DOMAIN					PSYCHOMOTOR DOMAIN				
	Very poor	Poor	Fair	Good	Excellent	Very poor	Poor	Fair	Good	Excellent	Very poor	Poor	Fair	Good	Excellent
Number of Students	0	3	6	8	2		11	3	5	0	0	2	9	2	6
Total percentage of students scoring above average in each category	**Cognitive**			Total 10/19 = **53%**		**Affective**			Total 05/19 = **26%**		**Psychomotor**			Total 08/19 = **42%**	

RESULTS AND DISCUSSION

Findings from pilot study: Under Cognitive and Psychomotor domains it was observed that architectural learning as per the parameter of Bloom's Taxonomy was achieved by 50% of learners, by scoring above average and highest in their projects. Under affective parameter however it was found that only 26% could score "good". 58% learners were found to be Poor and none could achieve highest in this category.

The results show architecture design projects could achieve the highest/optimum parameter under cognitive and psychomotor domains. However, the optimum affective learning lacks amongst learners. Specifically, in affective domain the society interventions are completely absent, while the environmental and ecological considerations are below average. It should be noted that the required learning outcomes under each category can be amended depending on the project brief and the skill sets taught by the institution. This decision needs to be taken independently by the institutions at the beginning of the academic term.

Some reseasrchers have pointed that bloom's hierarchy is a very linear, straightforward view of how humans comprehend information. Constructivist teaching has suggested that teachers need to spread higher-order thinking skills throughout a task rather than begin with the imparting of knowledge. Moreover, it is unilateral and also considers single subject and also is individualistic i.e., group discussions and interventions are lacking (http://teachercommons.blogspot.com/2008/04/bloom-taxonomy-criticisms.html).

Architecture design project being multi-lateral (integration of all subjects) it does not cater to the drawback of linear and unilateral projects. Neither does the design projects lack group discussion or higher-order thinking skills as there are intense task-oriented exercises that the students delve in during the entire course before attempting the final design projects. Hence, we can consider this taxonomy as an appropriate tool for assessment of Architecture Design Projects.

CONCLUSION

There are complexities observed in assessment pattern due to varied assessing parameters that are utilised for conducting architecture Design Juries by different institutions. Having a universal measuring parameter can help in an overall consideration of the knowledge gained by the learner. The pilot study produced in the research paper was conducted at the Sem–VI level to assess whether the students have achieved the required learning that is needed while moving from the generalist stage to the specialist stage-2 level of UG B.Arch course. The achievement of educational goals can also be assessed at earlier academic semester levels and further action can be strategized. This assessment outcome will help institutions to understand the strengths and weaknesses in specific areas/subjects/pedagogies of transmitted knowledge during the course.

Institutes can reflect critically on the weaknesses observed and formulate future educational enhancement initiatives in those specific areas to overcome these realised gaps. Students will equally be able to self-assess their weaknesses in focused areas and work towards overcoming them. Architecture education being a multi–disciplinary profession, demands all-round holistic educational goals. Blooms Taxonomy can be an optimum tool to formulate assessment parameters and help institutions in achieving their goals towards shaping intellectually mature, critical minded, skilled, ecologically sensitive and socially responsible architects for the future.

ACKNOWLEDGEMENT

We thank Smt. K.L. Tiwari College of Architecture for providing and sharing the architectural Design projects of Sem-VI students.

REFERENCES

[1] Anderson, L.W. (Ed.), Krathwohl, D.R. (Ed.), Airasian, P.W., Cruikshank, K.A., Mayer, R.E., Pintrich, P.R., Raths, J. and Wittrock, M.C. (2001). A taxonomy for learning, teaching, and assessing: A revision of Bloom's Taxonomy of Educational Objectives (Complete edition). New York: Longman.

[2] Bloom, B., Englehart, M., Furst, E., Hill, W. and Karlworth, D. (1956). Taxonomy of educational objectives: The classification of educational goals. Handbook I: Cognitive domain, Longmans, Green, New York, Toronto.

[3] Council of Architecture (2020). Minimum standards of Architecture Education. Online: www.coa.gov.in.

[4] Muhammed, C.T., Salima, P. and Rabia, I. (2017). Article Bloom's Taxonomy: Assessment and Teaching—Learning Process. *Journal of education and Educational Development,* 3(2).

[5] UIA and Architectural education reflections and recommendations (2002). Document prepared by the UIA architectural education commission (Version 16). Paris, France: International Union of Architects.

Coopetition as a Business Strategy in Indian SMEs for Sustainable Development and its Impact on Financial Performance

Rajesh Kothari[1], Priyanka Jain[2], Sunita Sharma[3] and Vidhu Mathur[4]

ICFAI University, Jaipur, Rajasthan

E-mail: [1]vc@iujaipur.edu.in; [2]priyankajain@iujaipur.edu.in; [3]sunitasharma@iujaipur.edu.in; [4]vidhuk.mathur@iujaipur.edu.in

ABSTRACT: Coopetition is portmanteau in nature as it derives its significance from both cooperation and competition simultaneously. It is a phenomenon where at the same time firms are involved in cooperative and competitive relationships. They share their complementary resources and capabilities with each other to create synergies. Although, it is a common business strategy followed by larger firms; but it has been reported that small and medium firms (SMEs) can gain competitive advantages too, if they pursue coopetition from strategic perspectives. The objective of the present study is to determine the attitude of SMEs towards coopetition as a business strategy for sustainable development and its implication on financial performance.

To accomplish the purpose an exploratory study was conducted. The data was collected using a structured questionnaire based on pre-tested scale items, from 284 SMEs operating in Rajasthan state belonging to different sectors. Structural equation modeling (second order) is employed for the data analysis. Findings revealed a positive attitude of SMEs towards coopetition as a business strategy and trust is considered as the most imperative factor in relationship with competitors followed by commitment and mutual benefit dimensions. The statistics shows the overall model fit and findings indicate a significant and a strong positive relationship between coopetition and financial performance.

Keywords: Average Variance Extracted, Composite Reliability, Coopetition, Financial Performance, Small and Medium Enterprises.

INTRODUCTION

Mutable factors generate challenges and threats in the global environment that leads to strategic changes in the business fraternity. The dynamic, hostile, and complex environmental conditions are constantly posing threats to the survival. To cope up with the competitive pressures and risk firms are demanded to be proactive, innovative, aggressive, adaptive and flexible with their strategies. For their existence firms are struggling hard and are adopting different types of competitive strategies. On the one hand these strategies are somehow helping the firms in upgrading their proficiencies in terms of products and processes but on the other side they are generating a scenario of competitive rivalry by acting as a source of competitive advantage (Dadfar *et al.*, 2013).

However, small and medium enterprises (SMEs) are more exposed to the environmental changes as compared to the large firms due to their peculiar characteristics. They face tremendous challenges in their endeavour of pursuing entrepreneurial opportunities. Their inadequate operating resources in terms of limited finance, competitor's aggressive expeditions, limited product/service line (Gnyawali and Park, 2009), lack of support from distributors and suppliers and a niche customer base (Bengtsson and Johansson, 2012) often subjecting them to face significant fluctuations in demand. Due to the constraints of resources and capabilities small firms are not able to compete and innovate (Akdoğan and Cingöz, 2012) and henceforth either they lose the struggle of their existence or they are out of the game (Parker, 2000).

Therefore, to tune themselves with such difficult external conditions firms are seeking new ways of conducting business for their survival. A collaborative relationship with competitors may be a feasible strategy for leveraging resources (Parker, 2000). Kanter (1994) states that cooperative associations can produce "collaborative advantage" as they are a type of corporate asset and can be a source of enhancing firm's market position (Dyer and Singh, 1998). When collaboration integrates and synthesizes competition and cooperation simultaneously then it is termed as "coopetition" (Levy, 2003). It is defined as a dynamic process in which competing firms not only cooperate with each other in coordination of their activities for achieving mutual goals, but concurrently they compete with each other as well as with other firms for seeking competitive advantage (Zineldin, 2004).

Generally, large and multinational companies are seeking competitive advantage through the development of coopetitive portfolio and enhance their strategic positions in the market place (Luo, 2007). Akdoğan and Cingöz (2012) suggested that coopetition strategy is equally beneficial for small and medium firms (SMEs) which have scarce resources. Deployment of the coopetition strategy is a kind of strategic alliance for SMEs which enables them to avail benefits in terms of innovation, technological development, new market exploration, research and development activities and scale of economies in terms of cost (Kock *et al.*, 2010).

Hence forth, the purpose of the present study is to determine the attitude of small and medium firms towards the coopetition as a business strategy for sustainable development and its impact on financial performance. In this context, the literature associated with coopetition strategy is thoroughly reviewed and a hypothetical model is proposed. Following the scale of Morris *et al.*, (2007) coopetition is studied as three dimensional in nature comprised of mutual benefit, trust and commitment and it is postulated that it affects performance of firms. As there is a dearth of studies dealing with SMEs attitude towards coopetition; the study will add significant knowledge and could be useful to mitigate the gap.

REVIEW OF LITERATURE

Concept of Coopetition

Coopetition has been defined as a means of value creation (Padula and Dagnino, 2007; Brandenburger and Nalebuff, 1996). It has also been defined as a process of developing a dyadic or network coopetitive relationship between the business activities through cooperation and competition (Bengtsson and Kock, 2000; Gnyawali and Park, 2011; Ritala, 2012). In such type of relationship for the promotion of a novel idea firms cooperates through joint initiatives and at the same time competes in market (Bengtsson *et al.*, 2010).

Some researchers pointed out that coopetition between firms are only feasible when they have partial convergent interests for creating new values (Bonel and Rocco, 2007) and hence they coined this interdependence among different firms as a "coopetitive system of value creation". If the competing firms are sharing a relationship either on one or more levels of value chain then it is termed as "dyadic coopetition", whereas when more than two firms are cooperating and competing simultaneously at one or more levels of value chain then it is called as "network coopetition" (Dagnino and Padula, 2002).

Coopetition is a complex phenomenon as it integrates two different paradigms, viz. cooperation and competition (Akdogan *et al.*, 2015). Both paradigms have their own ideologies. Cooperative paradigms believe that to gain competitive advantage it is essential for the firms to establish business networks of relationships, strategic alliances and follow cooperative interdependences across firms (Yami *et al.*, 2010). Whereas, focus of competitive paradigm is on inter firm rivalry and a firm's motive is to achieve abnormal profits in order to gain competitive advantage. Although, both the patterns explains only a partial view of reality therefore, in today's environment following the dictum of Charles Darwin "Survival of the fittest" it is mandatory for the firms to pursue both cooperation and competition concurrently (Chai and Yang, 2011). Consequently, an alternative concept "coopetition" has emerged as an alliance between competition and cooperation.

Coopetition is strategically advantageous for the firms if they are able to maintain a balancing act between cooperation and competition (Ganguli, 2007). The prime motive of firms behind coopetition is the use of supplementary resources which they received from each other's cooperation. It not only enables the firms to learn from each other's valuable experiences but also help them in enhancing their own skills through the proper utilization of competencies (Walley, 2007). These symbiotic relationships not only improvise the financial results of the firms but also reduce the costs associated with different innovative processes (Luo, 2007). Coopetitive firms are acting as a resource pools and with their capabilities they are able to get them positioned at a better place and can avail the economies of scale (Tomski, 2011).

The prerequisite for the coopetition is the commitment and a level of trust that can create a congenial atmosphere for the firms so that they can have mutual benefits (Zineldin, 2004). As such it is a difficult process because coopetition is a kind of symbiotic relationship where two or more firms join together to create certain benefits for them through interaction, communication, cooperation and sharing. Hence, it is quite difficult to be decisive on the part of each other's approach. Therefore, there are certain preconditions for developing such a mutually beneficial business relationship (Zineldin, 2004) which are as follows:

- Willingness of the two or more firms to engage in an interactive exchange relationship.
- Each party must have some valuable possession that the other party wants.
- Each party must be ready to give up their valuable belongings in order to receive in return of the something valuable from other party.
- There must be a free communication and interaction between the parties.
- For a sustainable long term relationship parties should follow ethical values and norms.
- Each party must have a right or a freedom to agree or disagree with the terms and conditions of exchange.
- Each party must be aware about the pros and cons of the relationship.

Therefore, firms who are intent to be in coopetitive relationship should follow the above stated preconditions and must be willing to share resources and information (Morris *et al.*, 2007).

Dimensions of Coopetition

Conceptually coopetition is bi-dimensional in nature i.e., competitive and cooperative dimensions. Luo (2005) treated these two dimensions separately and independently. He further stated that cooperation has sub-dimensions which include technological association, subunit form and strategic interdependence. Whereas, sub dimensions of competition include market overlap, local responsiveness and capability retrogression. Contrary to this Morris *et al.* (2007) stated that two independent and heterogeneous behaviours and ideologies cannot lead into a coopetitive relationship until or unless they are intricately interwoven. They considered coopetition as three dimensional in nature as to generate a synergistic relationship and termed them as mutual benefit, trust and commitment.

Success of a symbiotic relationship depends upon its extent of mutual benefits to both the parties but in a meaningful way. Otherwise, pursuing of any relationship without benefit is instrumental in nature. It further depends upon the mutual dependence of partners in a relationship (Svensson, 2002). Benefits can derive from both competition and cooperation as they are mutually exclusive but collectively exhaustive in nature. The exclusivity is based on the fact that in a coopetitive relationship competitive side involves contradictory interests whereas cooperative side involves compatible interests (Bengtsson *et al.*, 2003).

Viability and prosperity of any long-term relationship depends upon trust (Farrelly and Quester, 2003). It raises and creates a comfortable level of mutual confidence between the firms regarding the usage of shared resources, information and not to malign the image in market or to deceit the partners on competitive aspects of this coopetitive relationship. Trust is more about balancing self-interest against mutual interest (Gnyawali and Madhavan, 2001).

Commitment is defined as the willingness to go on a valued relationship. It strengthens through the process of mutual adaptation, strategic alliances, adjusted expectations, operations, interactive sessions, collaborative agreements, communication approaches and internal processes (Garaffo, 2002). Organizational learning, sharing of resources and ongoing knowledge development through cooperation insists them for such kind of adaptation.

The underlying philosophy of coopetition is that organizational activities are aimed for the establishment of mutually beneficial relationship with competitors. Successful long-term relationships are based on trust and deep commitment is required for its maintenance to avail mutual gains (Sargeant and Lee, 2004). A high level of commitment is only possible when parties have an essence of trust in each other which makes them to adapt and act accordingly to the requirements of the relationship (Zabkar and Brencic, 2004). Mutual benefit too influences the level of commitment. It has been reported that when firms are having higher opportunities for greater benefits then they show a deep commitment. Likewise, trust has a positive impact on mutual benefit, which in turn affects success of a relationship. Hence forth, coopetition is a kind of a joint effort to gain mutual benefits which depends upon the interaction of these dimensions.

THEORETICAL FRAMEWORK AND RESEARCH OBJECTIVE

Strategic alliances like coopetition are quite common in larger firms and are well-researched by the scholars (Dagnino and Padula, 2002; Luo, 2007). However, the literature on coopetition as a business strategy in SMEs has been calling for research. SMEs are not like the large firms, there are significant characteristic differences (Morris *et al.*, 2007). Large firms are characterized by formal and well-defined controlled systems, availability of credit resources, technological advancement and organized structures; whereas, SMEs are characterized by the informal structures, less organizational capacity, looser control systems, less documentation and fewer tax advantages (Beaver, 2002; Castka *et al.*, 2004).

Due to the scarcity of resources in terms of finance, human capital and technological advancement sometimes SMEs are not able to materialize the opportunities available in the market. Lack of competencies makes them vulnerable and they are not even able to sustain themselves in the presence of market uncertainties. It has been reported that actually such factors increase the likelihood of coopetition in SMEs (Gnyawali and Park, 2009). Coopetition strategy helps the SMEs in leveraging the benefits through the combination of cooperation and competition with their partners (Eikebrokk and Olsen, 2005). Through the access of complementary capabilities it produces synergistic effects in terms of organisational learning (Bouncken and Kraus, 2013); economies of scale, new product development (Nasution *et al.*, 2011); wider continuum of complementary resources; technological convergence and exploration of new market (Kock *et al.*, 2010). This coopetitive portfolio not only enables the SMEs to create value through the sharing of valuable possessions and capabilities but also accelerates their performance through the reduction of costs and uncertainties (Kossyva *et al.*, 2012).

The extensive literature in the perspective of coopetition provides a framework to proceed in the direction. Therefore, in this context authors proposed the hypothetical model (Figure 1) and have employed structural equation modelling, with the research objective of studying coopetition as a business strategy in SMEs and its impact on their financial performance.

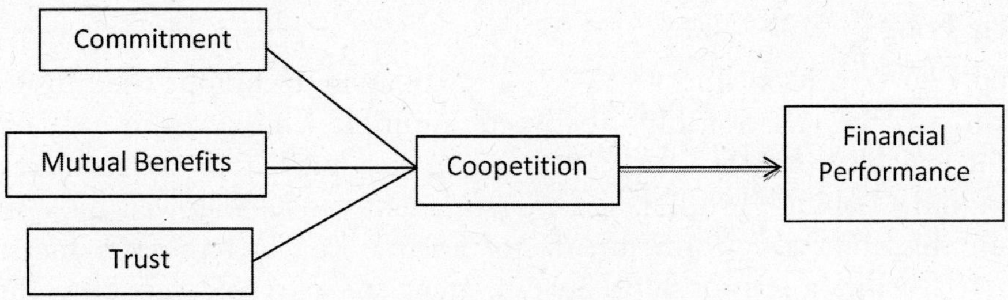

Fig. 1: Proposed Model
(*Source:* Author's Own Representation)

The study proposes the following hypothesis:

H1: There is a significant relationship between coopetition and financial performance.

RESEARCH DESIGN AND METHODOLOGY

Sample and Data Collection

A structured questionnaire was used for the survey, and data was collected either through electronic mail or through the telephonic interview which were conducted with the owner—managers of the small firms. Out of 600 questionnaires 579 were completed in all respect and were included for further analysis. Moreover, out of 579 responses only 284 SMEs were found to be actively using coopetition as a business strategy.

Scale Items

A structured questionnaire was employed for the purpose of this research. The scale adapted was based on the dimensions proposed by Morris *et al.* (2007) namely trust, commitment and mutual benefit. These dimensions were assessed by 16 items or variables. Four variables refer to commitment, four variables to trust and five items to mutual benefits. Financial performance was measured with three variables namely sales growth (Ploetner and Ehret, 2006), profit (Yusuf and Saffu, 2005) and competitive position (Jarvis *et al.*, 2000). To resolve the difficulties of obtaining reliable profit and sales figures from SMEs, previous researches have used reports based on relative changes over a period of time (Morris *et al.*, 2007). Therefore, respondents were asked to report the changes in the above stated variables over two years. A Likert scale of five points, ranging from "1 = strongly disagree" to "5 = strongly agree" has been used to measure each item (total sixteen). With reference to proposed number of points, Netemeyer *et al.* (1996) stated that neutral response may be a valid answer for some items therefore, scale should include a mid-point.

Research Tool

Structural Equation Modelling (SEM) is a multivariate technique used for empirical estimation of the relationships between multiple independent and multiple dependent variables (Smith, 2004). It is a two-step procedure as recommended by Anderson and Gerbing (1988) i.e., a measurement model followed by a structural model. In this context confirmatory factor analysis (CFA) represents measurement model that specifies a relationship between latent and observed variables. Unlike the measurement model, the structural model is a hypothetical model and is used for examining the extent of the association between constructs. It is a statistical method that relates constructs to one another and provides parameter values (path coefficients) for framed hypothesis while considering the standard errors (Hair *et al.*, 2006).

RESULTS OF DATA ANALYSIS

Measurement Model

IBM AMOS 21 software was used to perform CFA. The analysis focused on one second order latent variable i.e. Coopetition (COP); four first order latent variables viz. Commitment (Com), Trust (Trus), Mutual benefit (MB) Financial Performance (FP) and 16 observed variables. In the present study as the used data has met down the postulations of univariate and multivariate normality therefore, MLE is used and the constructs (COM and FP) are jointly analysed in a measurement model.

In the measurement model, for each construct the degree of variance is examined by squared factor loadings. Various model fit indices are used to assess the model fit such as CMIN/DF, the comparative fit index (CFI; Bentler, 1990), Tucker-Lewis coefficient (TLI; Bollen, 1989), goodness-of-fit index (GFI; Joreskog and Sorbom, 1989), adjusted goodness of fit index (AGFI), root mean square error of approximation (RMSEA; Browne and Cudeck, 1993), and root mean square residual (RMR). The threshold for CMIN/DF should be less than 3.0 (Hu and Bentler, 1999) or less than 2.0 in a more restrictive sense (Byrne, 1989). However, CMIN is affected by sample size and normality of the data (Schumacker and Lomax, 2004; Tabachnick and Fidell, 2001). Therefore, the CMIN test should be used in combination with other indices. Values of CFI, TLI, AGFI and GFI should be over 0.90. Moreover, RMSEA should be lower than 0.05 to indicate a close fit of the model in relation to the degree of freedom. These fit statistics are evaluated to determine whether the predetermined model best explain the relationships between the observed and latent variables or not.

The proposed measurement model showed that all regression weights are significant ($p < 0.001$). The absolute fit statistics showed a chi-square of 151.744 with 100 (df) is significant ($p = .001$) [CMIN/DF = 1.517] with RMSEA = .043, TLI = 0.971, RMR

= 0.06 and CFI = 0.976. This suggested that the model is acceptable, moreover other fit indices viz. AGFI = 0.920 and GFI = 0.941 are also supportive. The results suggested that the model fitted adequately to the data.

All factor loadings for variables measuring the same construct are statistically significant and are greater than 0.60, which confirmed the convergent validity of the model. Moreover, covariance among the factors (FP and COP) are significant ($p < 0.001$) as shown in Table 1. Given that the model fitted the data adequately specification is not required.

Table 1: Covariance Matrix for the Measurement Model

	Estimate	*S.E.*	*C.R.*	*P*
FP ↔ COP	.685	.092	7.412	***

***P < 0.001.

Source: Author's Own Representation.

To test the convergent validity, composite reliability (CR) and average variance extracted (AVE) is calculated. Bagozzi and Yi (1988) recommended that CR should be equal to or greater than .60 and AVE should be equal to or greater than .50. It can be concluded that the measures used within this research are within the acceptable levels supporting the reliability of the constructs. After analysing the measurement model for unidimensionality, reliability, convergent validity and construct validity, the next step is the analysis of the structural model. Table 2 displays the summary results of CFA.

Table 2: Summary of Confirmatory Analysis

Variable Label	*Final Standardised Loadings*	*Squared Multiple Correlation*	*Average Variance Extracted (AVE)*	*Composite Construct Reliability (CR)*
COM1	0.774	0.599	0.57	0.75
COM2	0.692	0.478		
COM3	0.76	0.577		
COM4	0.791	0.625		
Trus1	0.727	0.528	0.55	0.73
Trus2	0.703	0.494		
Trus3	0.74	0.547		
Trus4	0.78	0.608		

(Contd...)

(Table 2 contd...)

Variable Label	*Final Standardised Loadings*	*Squared Multiple Correlation*	*Average Variance Extracted (AVE)*	*Composite Construct Reliability (CR)*
MB1	0.697	0.485	0.56	0.80
MB2	0.713	0.508		
MB3	0.786	0.617		
MB4	0.786	0.617		
MB5	0.75	0.562		
Fp1	0.806	0.649	0.58	0.70
Fp2	0.792	0.627		
Fp3	0.683	0.466		
Model Fit: Chi Square = 151.744 (df = 100), p = .001, RMSEA = 0.043, AGFI = 0.920, RMR = 0.060, GFI = 0.941, TLI = 0.971, and CFI = 0.976				

Source: Author's Own Representation.

STRUCTURAL MODEL

Structural Equation Modelling (SEM) is employed in this research to study the relationship between coopetition and financial performance. To evaluate the structural model, goodness-of-fit indices are examined to assess if the hypothesized structural model fitted the data. As the assumptions underlying structural equation modelling are met, the coefficient parameter estimates are examined along with the overall model fit indices to test the relationship between the two latent constructs (COP and FP). The evaluation of the structural model is discussed below (Figure 2).

In testing the hypothesized model, result presented in table 3 indicate that the hypothesis H1 is statistically significant and in the hypothesized direction. H1 is significant at 0.001 probability level.

Table 3: Hypothesis Testing using Standardised Estimates

Hypothesized Path	*Standardised Estimates*	*z-Value*	*Supported*
H1: COP → FP	0.806	7.457*	Yes

*p < 0.001.

Source: Author's own Representation.

The analysis result of direct influence between COP and FP generates path coefficient 0.806 which is significant at 0.001 probability level. The result support the hypothesis

(H1), which states there is a significant relationship between COP and FP of SMEs. Positive path coefficient indicates a *direct positive relationship* between COP and FP and the relationship is unidirectional.

The indices for goodness-of-fit demonstrate that this model fits the data adequately (Chi-square = 151.744, df = 100, p = .001). The GFI = 0.941, AGFI = .920, RMSEA = .043, CFI = .976, TLI = .976, RMR = .060 and CMIN/DF = 1.517. The R^2 for the model came to 0.65 (Table 4). The structural model is depicted in Figure 2.

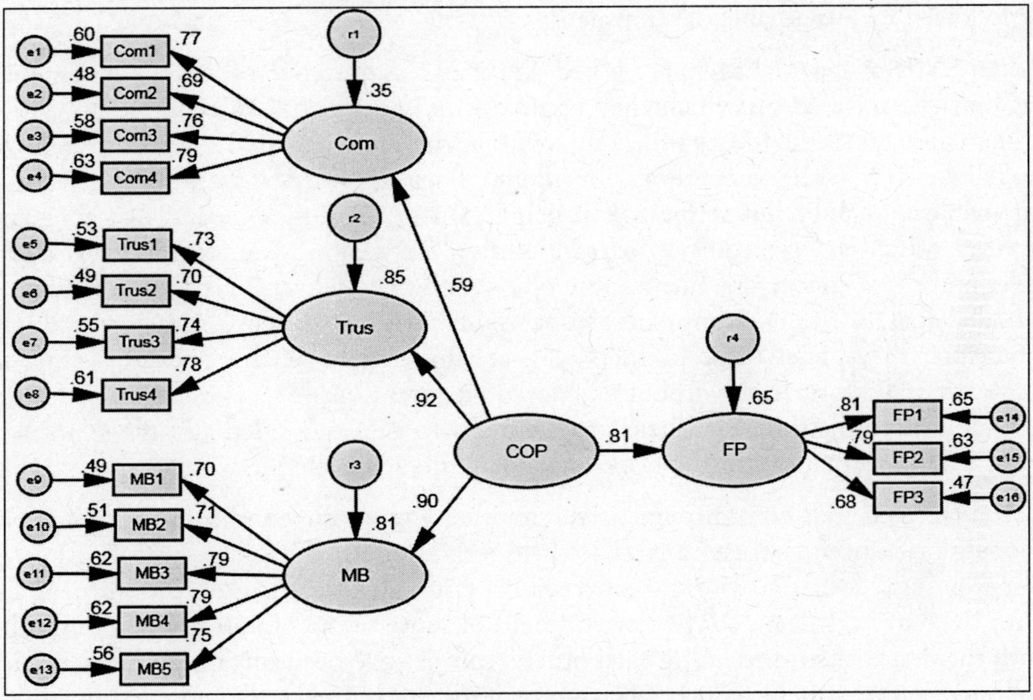

Fig. 2: Structural Model

Table 4: Structural Equation Result: Direct Relationship

	R^2
COP → Financial Performance	0.65

Source: Author's Own Representation.

The results indicate a significant and a strong positive relationship between coopetition and financial performance which is similar with the findings of Morris *et al.* (2007). The model explained 35% of the variance in commitment (COM), 85% of the variance in trust (Trus), and 81% of the variance in mutual benefit (MB).

FINDINGS AND IMPLICATIONS

Findings of the study suggested that coopetition is not a usual phenomenon among small and medium firms because from a very large sample only 49% SMEs are found to be actively engaged in a coopetitive relationship. Although, others are not having any negative perception about collaboration but they reported it a very risky venture. They are not willing to face the unique challenges which are associated with such activities such as mistrust, structural dissimilarities, leakage of information and betrayal on account of partnership. Therefore, they don't find coopetition a tempted strategy to be followed for sustainable development.

When SME owner/managers are asked about the importance of various parameters or dimensions based on which they entered into coopetition. In reply of the above statement most of the SMEs stated that trust is the most important aspect or a factor in relationship with competitors for them. They specified that although trust is intangible in nature but it has the capability of generating a feeling of safety and security which is a prerequisite for maintaining a symbiotic relationship. It is like a stake on one of contingent futures, the one which may deliver benefits. They further revealed that in the environment of uncertainty, risk of opportunism is very high. Therefore, they prefer those partners who are honest and reliable and are willing to share internal information without any deceptive intentions. The essence of this feeling further assured them that neither parties will try to gain one-sided advantage nor will misuse the information for their personal goals and achievements.

SMEs believed that commitment is the another important condition to implement coopetition. Once this trust based shared vision is established it evokes a strong sense of intention and focus; as a result expectations got transformed into commitment for both the parties. It leads to the development of sense of obligation and responsibility with the desire of strengthening each other's competitive positions in the market. This collective commitment ignites the momentum of mutual adaptation, adjustment followed by the resource allocation according to each other's characteristics and requirements. Such type of commitment fosters camaraderie, caring attitude and confidence in both the parties and they are willing to go together through the hard and soft times and hold out for the fruits of success.

They further elaborated that this committed and trusted association leads to the mutual benefit. Due to the combination of supplementary resources and skills they are able to obtain more benefits than by acting alone. These rewards are materialized in the form of sharing of cost, access of more human capital, sometimes even great bargaining power over suppliers, innovative products and services and partaking of technical know-how.

After knowing the attitude of SMEs towards the various dimensions of coopetition it was asked that how they correlate it with financial performance. Do they find any substantial increase in profit or sales after adopting coopetition as a business strategy? Findings revealed that coopetition has a significant impact on the performance. It not only strengthens their competitive position in the market but also leveraged their sales growth and profit margins. Due to the sharing of complementary resources they are able to curtail down the operative costs which otherwise reduces their revenues. Moreover, their enhanced bargaining power over suppliers and distributors allows them the access of raw materials at competitive prices. Not only this; exchanged ideas, experiences and knowledge mitigates the financial and managerial risks on their decisive part. Their joint marketing activity reduces the expenses on advertisements and sales promotion. This cooperative endeavor enables them to take larger orders from their customers and make them deliver services and products to them on time, henceforth increasing their sales growth.

PRACTICAL IMPLICATIONS

Results suggested that coopetition in SMEs is not as common as compare to SMEs of other countries where it is a usual phenomenon (Akdogan & Cingoz, 2012). However, those who are in this coopetitive relationship they valued the trust (Akdogan *et al.*, 2015; Chai & Yang, 2011; Zineldin, 2004) most followed by commitment and mutual benefit dimensions and ultimately have a positive and significant impact on performance. The findings are in the congruence with previous researches (Kossyva *et al.*, 2014; Morrie *et al.*, 2007).

SMEs have a strong conviction that although trust is imperceptible thereafter also it acts as an economic lubricant. It fosters an environment of commitment and assurance; promotes open and fair communication; reduce the transaction costs between parties through the sharing of resources. It enables new forms of collaboration and extending business accomplishments and generates mutual benefits in terms of enhanced competitive positions. These intrinsically interlinked or interwoven dimensions produce synergistic effects and have a positive impact on financial performance. In particular, SMEs agreed with the notion that the coopetition is not merely a philosophical concept. It is a matter of strategic perspective where cooperation and competition both are characterized by high levels of mutual trust and social commitment. It facilitates or paves the path for open exchange and sharing of information and resources. However, its success depends upon the magnanimity towards one another.

REFERENCES

[1] Akdoğan, A.A. and Cingöz, A. (2012). An Empirical Study on Determining the Attitudes of Small and Medium sized Businesses (SMEs) Related to Coopetition. *Procedia—Social and Behavioral Sciences, 58*, 252–258.

[2] Akdogan, A.A., Dogan, Ö., Nuri and Cingoz, A. (2015). Coopetition as a Business Strategy: Determining the Effective Partner Selection Criteria Using Fuzzy AHP. *International Review of Management and Business Research, 4*(1), 137–151.

[3] Anderson, J.C. and Gerbing, D. (1988). Structural Equation Modelling in Practice: A Review and Recommended Two-Step Approach *Psychological Bulletin, 103*(3), 411–423.

[4] Bagozzi, R.P. and Yi, Y. (1988). On the evaluation of structural equation models. *Journal of the Academy of Marketing Science, 16*(1), 74–94.

[5] Beaver, G. (2002). *Small Business, Entrepreneurship and Enterprise Development*. Harlow: Financial Times/Prentice Hall, (Pearson)

[6] Bengtsson, M. and Johansson, M. (2012). Managing Coopetition to Create Opportunities for Small Firms. *International Small Business Journal.*

[7] Bengtsson, M., Eriksson, J. and Wincent, J. (2010). *Coopetition: New Ideas for a New Paradigm, In Coopetition: Winning Strategies for the 21st century* USA: Edward Elgar Publishing Inc.

[8] Bengtsson, M., Hinttu, S. and Kock, S. (2003). *Relationships of Cooperation and Competititon between Competitors*. Paper presented at the 19th Annual IMP Conference.

[9] Bentler, P.M. (1990). Comparitive Fit Indexes in Structural Models. *Psychological Bulletin, 107*(2), 238–246.

[10] Bollen, K.A. (1989). *Structural Equations with Latent Variables*. New York:: Wiley.

[11] Bonel, E. and Rocco, E. (2007). Coopeting to Survive; Surviving Coopetition. *International studies of Management and Organization, 37*(2), 70–96.

[12] Brandenburger, A. and Nalebuff, B. (1996). *Co-opetition*. New York: Currency Doubleplay.

[13] Browne, M.W. and Cudeck, R. (1993). *Alternative Ways of Assessing Model Fit*. Newbury Park: Sage.

[14] Byrne, B.M. (1989). *A primer of LISREL: Basic applications and programming for confirmatory factor analytic models*. New York: Springer-Verlag.

[15] Castka, P., Balzarova, M. and Bamber, C. (2004). How Can SMEs Effectively Implement the CSR Agenda? A UK Case Study Perspective. *Corporate Social Responsibility and Environmental Management, 11*(3), 140–149.

[16] Chai, Y. and Yang, F. (2011). Risk Control of Coopetition Relationship: An Exploratory Case Study on Social Networks "Guanxi" in a Chinese Logistics Services Cluster. *The International Journal of Interdiciplinary Social Sciences, 6*, 30–39.

[17] Dadfar, H., Dahlgaard, J.J., Brege, S. and Alamirhoor, A. (2013). Linkage between Organisational Innovation Capability, Product Platform Development and Performance. *Total Quality Management, 24*(7), 819–834.

[18] Dagnino, G.B. and Padula, G. (2002). *Coopetition Strategy a New Kind of Inter-firm Dynamics for Value Creation.* Paper presented at the Second Annual Conference- Innovative Research in Management, Stockholm, Sweden.

[19] Dyer, J. and Singh, H. (1998). The Relational View: Cooperative Strategy and Sources of Interorganizational Advantage. *Academy of Management Review, 23*(4), 660–679.

[20] Eikebrokk, T.R. and Olsen, D.H. (2005). *Co-opetition and e-Business Success in SMEs: An Empirical Investigation of European SMEs.* Paper presented at the 38th Hawaii International Conference on System Sciences, Big Island, Hawaii.

[21] Farrelly, F. and Quester, P. (2003). The Effects of Market Orientation on Trust and Commitment: The Case of the Sponsorship Business-to-Business Relationship. *European Journal of Marketing, 37*(3/4), 530–553.

[22] Ganguli, S. (2007). Coopetition Models in the Context of Modern Business. *The ICFAI Journal of Marketing Management, 6*, 6–16.

[23] Garaffo, F. (2002). *Types of Coopetition to Manage Emerging Technologies.* Paper presented at the EURAM: Second Annual Conference, Innovative Research in Management.

[24] Gnyawali, D. and Madhavan, R. (2001). Cooperative Networks and Competitive Dynamics: A Structural Embeddedness Perspective. *Academy of Management Review, 26*(3), 431–449.

[25] Gnyawali, D. and Park, B.J. (2009). Co-opetition and Technological Innovation in Small and Medium-sized Enterprises: A Multilevel Conceptual Model. *Journal of Small Business and Management, 47*(3), 308–330.

[26] Gnyawali, D. and Park, B.J. (2011). Co-opetition between Giants: Collaboration with Competitors for Technological Innovation. *Research Policy, 40*(5), 650–663.

[27] Holmes, S.P. (2001). *Introduction to Structural Equation Modelling using LISREAL*. Perth.

[28] Hu, L. and Bentler, P. (1999). Cutoff Criteria for Fit Indices in Covariance Structure Analysis: Conventional Criteria versus New Alternatives Structural Equation Modelling, *6*(1), 1–55.

[29] Jarvis, R., Curran, J., Kitching, J. and Lightfoot, G. (2000). The Use of Quantitative and Qualitative Criteria in the Measurement of Performance in Small Firms. *Journal of Small Business and Enterprise Development, 7*(2), 123–134.

[30] Joreskog, K. and Sorbom, D. (1982). Recent Developments in Structural Equation Modelling. *Journal of Marketing Research*, 404–416.

[31] Kanter, R. (1994). Collaborative Advantage. *Harvard Business Review, 72*(4), 96–108.

[32] Kock, S., Nisuls, J. and Soderqvist, A. (2010). Co-opetition: A Source of International Opportunities in Finnish SMEs. *Competitiveness Review: An International Business Journal, 20*(2), 111–125.

[33] Kossyva, D., Sarri, K. and Georgopoulos, N. (2014). Co-opetition: A Business Strategy for SMES in Times of Economic Crisis. *South-Eastern Europe Journal of Economics, 1*, 89–106.

[34] Levy, M., Loebbecke, C. and Powell, P. (2003). SMEs, Co-opetition and Knowledge Sharing: The Role of Information Systems. *European Journal of Information Systems, 12*, 3–17.

[35] Luo, Y. (2005). Toward Coopetition within a Multinational Enterprise: A Perspective from Foreign Subsidiaries. *Journal of World Business, 40*(1), 71–90.

[36] Luo, Y. (2007). A Coopetition Perspective of Global Competition. *Journal of World Business, 42*(7), 129–144.

[37] Morris, M.H., Kocak, A. and Özer, A. (2007). Co-opetition and Small Business Strategy: Implication for Performance. *Journal of Small Business Strategy, 18*(1), 35–55.

[38] Nasution, H.N., Mavondo, F.T., Matanda, M.J. and Ndubisi, N.O. (2011). Entrepreneurship: Its Relationship with Market Orientation and Learning Orientation and As Antecedents to Innovation and Customer Value. *Industrial Marketing Management, 40*, 336–345.

[39] Netemeyer, R., Boles, J. and McMurriam, R. (1996). Development and Validation of Work Family Conflict and Family Work Conflict Scales. *Journal of Applied Psychology, 81*(4), 400–410.

[40] Padula, G. and Dagnino, G.B. (2007). Untangling the Rise of Coopetition: The Intrusion of Competition in a Cooperative Game Structure. *International Studies of Management and Organization, 37*, 32–52.

[41] Ploetner, O. and Ehret, M. (2006). From Relationships to Partnerships-New Forms of Cooperation between Buyer and Seller. *Industrial Marketing Management, 35*(1), 4–9.

[42] Ritala, P. (2012). Coopetition Strategy—When is it Successful? Empirical Evidence on Innovation and Market Performance. *British Journal of Management, 23*, 307–324.

[43] Sargeant, A. and Lee, S. (2004). Trust and Relationship Commitment in the United Kingdom Voluntary Sector. *Psychology and Marketing, 21*(8), 613– 635.

[44] Schumacker, R. and Lomax, R. (2004). *A Beginners Guide to Structural Equation Modelling* New York: Lawrence Erlbaum.

[45] Smith, D. (2004). Structural Equation Modelling in Management Accounting Research: Critical Analysis and Opportunities. *Journal of Accounting Research 23*, 49–86.

[46] Svensson, G. (2002). The Measurement and Evaluation of Mutual Dependence in Spesific Dyadic Business Relationships. *Journal of Business and Industrial Marketing, 17*(1), 56– 74.

[47] Tabachnick, B. and Fidell, L. (2007). *Using Multivariate Statistics* (5th ed.). New York: Allyn and Bacon.

[48] Walley, K. (2007). Coopetition: An Introduction to the Subject and An Agenda for Research. *International Studies of Management and Organization, 37*, 11–31.

[49] Yami, S., Castaldo, S., Dagnino, G.B., Roy, F.L. and Czakon, W. (2010). *Introduction-Coopetition Strategies: Towards A New Form of Inter-Organizational Dynamics?. In Coopetititon: Winning Strategies for the 21st Century*: Edward Elgar Publishing Limited.

[50] Yusuf, A. and Saffu, K. (2005). Planning and Performance of Small and Medium Enterprise Owners in a Country in Transition. *Journal of Small Business Management, 43*(4), 480–497.

[51] Zabkar, V. and Brencic, M.M. (2004). Values, Trust and Commitment in Business to Business Relationships. *International Marketing Review, 21*(2), 202–215.

[52] Zineldin, M. (2004). Co-opetition: The Organization of the Future. *Marketing Intelligence and Planning, 22*(6/7), 780–789.

Defining Sustainable Construction Materials and Technology for Sustainable Development

Deepak Kumar Sharma
School of Planning and Architecture, Poornima University, Jaipur, Rajasthan
E-mail: 2016archdeepak4502@poornima.edu.in

ABSTRACT: India is facing severe environmental problems in the construction sector due to rapid urbanization. Increased housing demand is leading to consumption of electricity, services, resources and has increased the carbon footprint. Cities are facing environmental problems such as climate change and environmental degradation. The solution lies in the use of renewable material. Green technology encompasses a number of innovations that aim to minimize harmful impacts on the environment and create new ways of achieving sustainable growth. Sustainable growth is what meets today's needs without undermining future generations' ability to meet their needs. The definition of sustainable development that has evolved over the past two decades is explored and the enhancement accomplished by the use of sustainable materials and technologies for construction is discussed in this paper.

Human culture is an integral part of the natural world and for human society to thrive, the environment must be preserved and sustained. This vision is embodied through sustainable development by outstanding designs by environmental managers which promotes the use of those values in day-to-day life. An alternative solution to conventional building must be used for sustainable development. The new approach must take into consideration the effect on the natural and cultural resources of the local, regional and global ecosystems of any material and technology option.

Keywords: Sustainable Development, Sustainable Materials, Sustainable Technologies, Urbanization.

INTRODUCTION

The Annual Report on Sustainable Development Goals provides an overview of current land reform efforts, highlighting areas of progress and areas where more action is needed to ensure that no one is left behind (Kotkar and Salunkhe, 2017). The world is gradually being urbanized. Quite half of the world's population has been living in urban areas since 2007 and this proportion is anticipated to extend to 60 per cent by 2030. Cities and metropolitan areas, which contribute about 60 percent of the world's GDP, are powerful housing hubs. They still account for about 70% of worldwide carbon emissions and over 60% of resource use. Rapid urbanization ends up in an increase within the number of slum dwellers, insufficient facilities and utilities and heavy loads (such as waste disposal and water and sanitation systems, roads and transport), worsening pollution and concrete sprawl that's not expected.

Sustainable development means the use of natural and physical resources that enable individuals and communities, without sacrificing the capacity of future generations to meet their needs, to ensure their social, economic and cultural well-being (Lacasse, 1999). In the course of achieving sustainable growth, the construction industry is required to face certain challenges. It uses a large quantity of natural and physical resources and thus has a direct effect on the environment (Acciona, 2019). In order to meet the needs of continuous construction, the existing framework of the building, engineering processes, manufacturing technologies and construction techniques need to be changed. Systematic approaches are required to overcome control constraints, the lack of creativity and efficient production technology, and the convergence of construction technologies in order to solve the problem of complexity. The promotion of sustainable development gives greater independence to the created environment and to the building industry. It is a well-known fact that the construction industry has played a significant role in many nations' social and economic growth. Statistics indicate that the construction industry usually accounts for over half of the national expenditure and accounts for at least 10% of our country's G.N.P (Gross National Product). For example, in the European Union, buildings account for more than 40 percent of total energy expenditure and the construction industry is expected to generate about 40 percent of the total waste generation. Sustainable construction growth and new things, globally, play a major role in resource utilization.

Sustainable development utilizes building materials which are locally accessible and energy-efficient. It offers the living people ability to live a complete life cycle in safe, comfortable conditions in all buildings. The life cycle consists of processes for material processing, building planning, design, development, service and storage. The aim of sustainability is to ensure that resources are used efficiently; viz. energy, water, and construction materials have a slight effect on the building environment. It is possible to divide the structure into three sizes: (Patil and Patil, 2017)

1. Economics
2. Social
3. Environmental.

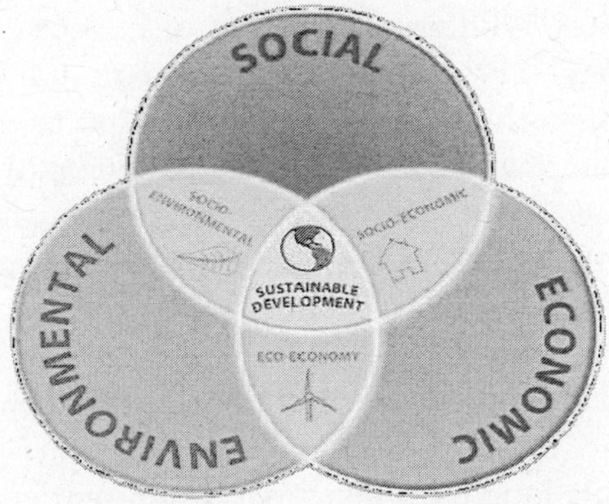

Fig. 1: Conceptual Level Representation of Sustainable Development

Social sustainability highlights changes in the quality of human life, including society, health education and globalization, as well as in the human environment and the land at each of the project phases. High efficiency, longevity, consistency and mixed use of the structure are required for technical sustainability. This paper discusses sustainable development principles, materials and innovations in building after shortlisting some construction materials.

Sustainability in construction is about everything to follow proper practices according to the selection of building materials, their resources and building methods and construction philosophy, so that they can improve performance, reduce project load, reduce waste and be environment friendly, with regard to environmental, economic and cultural values (Stevulova *et al.*, 2018). Selection of building materials that control all life cycle impacts such as extraction, total extraction, waste recycled bio-Geo sphere and recycling waste. Building materials also strongly influence the life force, user comfort and durability. By upgrading existing stocks through the use of modern developments or the creation and use of new energy-saving technology, countries with developed economies are in a position to devote greater attention to construct buildings that are more sustainable, while the developed countries concentrate on social equality and economic stability.

REVIEW OF LITERATURE

Many researchers have reported that a lot of energy is used by the building industry and emits greenhouse gases. The energy intensity of building materials has decreased with the advancement of construction technologies and production methods, leading to a substantial reduction in the energy consumption of each manufacturing facility and the production of building materials.

Kotkar and Salunkhe (2017) did critical analysis of the current Sustainable Building Materials and Technology. They explored the concept and scope of self-sustainable construction and all the technical and economic aspects of sustainable buildings around the world. The emphasis was on natural sustainability characteristics, such as energy efficiency, conservation of water and greenhouse gas emissions, as well as technological solutions. According to them, method of testing the life cycle, typically used in a green building's environmental features, may also be a valuable social sustainability tool. All around the world, new measurement methods are rapidly emerging. But further research in these fields is required to help these new measurement methods to assist investors and engineers in decision-making. Public understanding of green building principles and its long-term benefits is important and in this context India, lacks knowledge. The government intervention is required to spread the awareness.

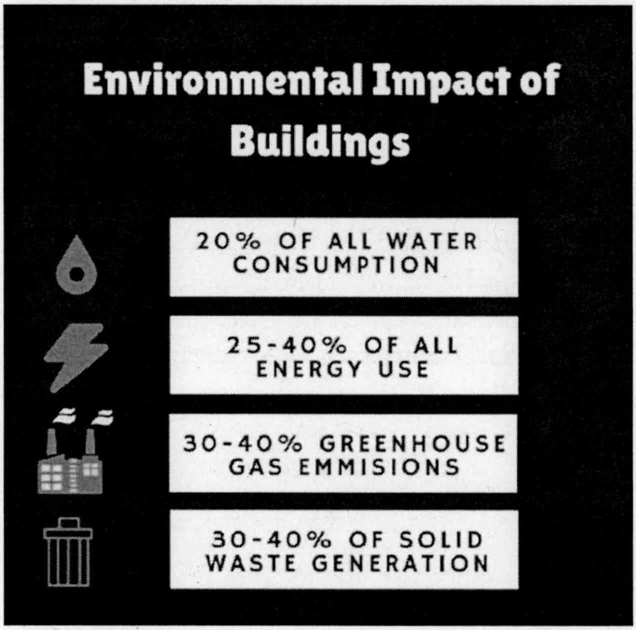

Fig. 2: Environmental Impact of Building

The environmental assessment of buildings has gained considerable significance in the construction industry along with the growing environmental consideration of building impacts. Tatari (2011) claimed that the built environment has a huge effect on the economy, culture and the environment. The model of implant techniques based on LEED categories was developed to estimate the cost of LEED certified green building costs. Researcher concluded that the expected future work requires the use of expanded data sets and a close review of LEED point dependency and its effect on forecasting. The present study focusses on how to improve upon sustainable building construction techniques. It also enumerates the benefits in terms of long-term cost savings of green buildings.

SUSTAINABILITY CHALLENGES FOR THE INDIAN BUILDING SECTOR

India has one of the world's fastest building markets. Over the last five years, new building costs have increased by 10 percent and landfills have doubled. Rapid urbanization is causing this rise in construction activity. Around 30 percent of the 221.1 million households in India are now concentrated in urban areas (UNEP, 2010). Demand for commercial construction has also risen sharply, fueled by the service sector boom, with total GDP rising by an estimated 53 percent in 2008 alone. The amount of office space under construction is projected to rise from 200 million square meters in 2009 to 890 million square meters by 2030, an increase of more than 70%. Several office buildings integrate the architecture of a standard glass wall and curtains that increase the Indian climate's need for very cold mechanical cooling. Latest energy efficiency studies of India shows that energy efficiency is poor by international standards. This has impacted and locked the Indian cities into highly competitive and efficient stocks.

Around 24 percent of the world's natural resources are used by the building industry. Traditional construction materials are all high-strength materials, including steel, concrete, aluminum and glass. At various points, a building uses a variety of materials and the range of materials used in the building can influence the functioning of its life cycle. The value of material selection, which makes low-energy materials look like building power, has been established by many studies. In the initial manufacturing process, the option of high-energy products can consume a lot of energy and contribute to a greater level of greenhouse gas emissions (Thormark, 2006).

Over their life cycle, building materials have an effect on both the structure and the natural environment. In the early stages of construction, it is necessary to select sustainable materials, produce sustainable building materials, and conduct market research. It is also proposed that the choice of building materials will impact the overall performance of the buildings, and from a life cycle perspective, sustainable building materials should be considered at a young age. From birth to grave, the life cycle of building materials is closely linked to the building's pre-use life stages, including the removal of materials, the manufacturing and transport process, and the specifications for storage and repair during construction.

LIFE CYCLE ANALYSIS

A product or organization's product life cycle involves the distribution, manufacture, usage and storage, repair and renewal, such as the demolition, reuse and disposal of such products. Applicants and designers are invited to consider, in the sense of sustainable development, the effects and consequences of each of these phases and their effect on the environment. Therefore, integrated solutions and methods for the selection, evaluation and interpretation of the effects of planning and design options for energy use, resource degradation and the development of natural hazards outside the life cycle of a built structure must be included (e.g. air, water and soil pollution). Presentations at this time and at similar times provide realistic examples of an integrated approach to the partial construction of items, as well as to urban renovation.

SELECTION OF SUSTAINABLE BUILDING MATERIALS

Careful selection of environment friendly building materials is an easy way for architects to begin to incorporate sustainable building principles into buildings. Traditionally, price has been a major factor in comparing similar items or items selected for the same job. The "off-the-shelf" price of a building item, however, only

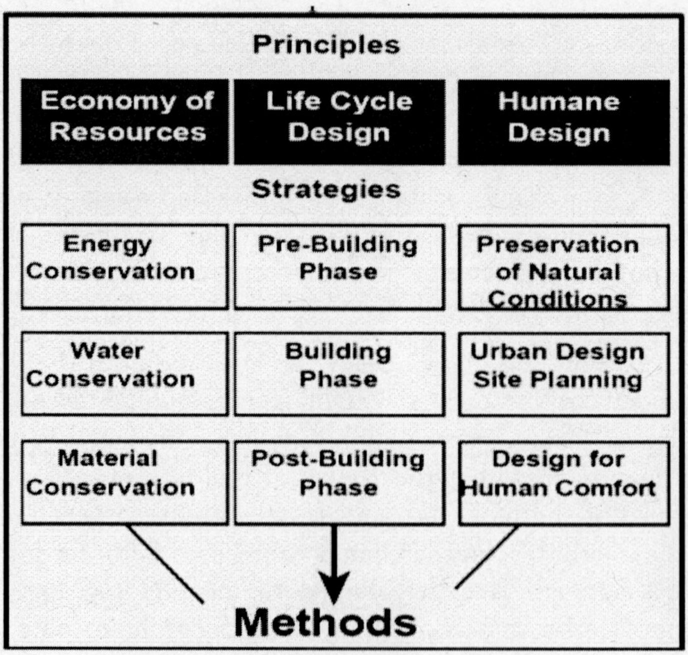

Fig. 3: The Three Principals of Sustainability

reflects the cost of manufacturing and transportation, not social or environmental costs. In architecture, there are three sustainability concepts:

1. **Resource Economy:** It is about reducing, reusing, and regenerating the natural resources that make up a building.
2. **Life Cycle Design:** It offers a means of evaluating the building process and its environmental effects.
3. **Human Design:** Concentrate on human relationships with the natural world. These policies will provide detailed understanding of the impacts of land use on the environment, domestic and global.

Each of these concepts involves a different set of learning methods that lead to a great deal of understanding of structural interactions in a very beautiful setting. This enables continuity to identify and evaluate those strategies that can be used by designers to decrease the effect of the systems they build on the environment (Yiming Song, 2018).

SUSTAINABLE BUILDING: CHANGING THE WAY WE LOOK AT CONSTRUCTION MATERIALS

The current housing design has many resources, making sustainable construction a challenge. While the types of housing and shelter vary from region to region, they share two common functions: protecting and demonstrating local context. Modern house design prefers inexpensive, easily assembled, and durable materials. Often, this leads to homes that are unsuitable for certain local challenges. That could include unstable

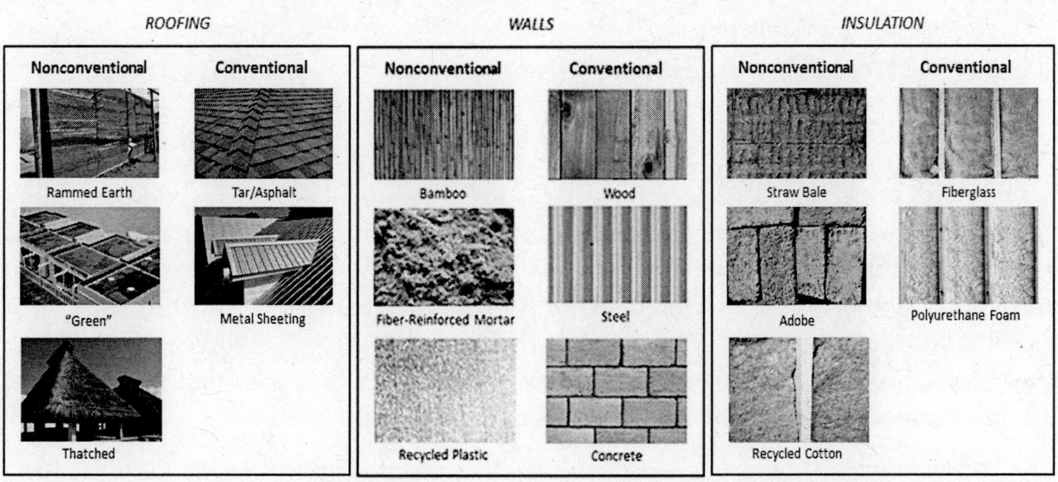

Fig. 4: Sustainable Construction with Unconventional Materials

housing in flood-prone areas or windowless buildings in tropical areas. To live in luxury and stability, we need to consider the context, history, and culture.

Sustainable construction solutions require environment friendly materials, reduce waste, and commitment to meeting the long-term needs of a growing community. A good way to deal with those situations is to build with non-traditional materials. These are materials that can be used instead of wood, tin, and concrete that is commonly used now. Contradictory practices such as those pictured below have evolved into local sources, long-standing cultural practices, and traditional knowledge. They often have the advantage of being environment friendly and are abundant in the area.

SUSTAINABLE BUILDING MATERIAL

In terms of set goals, sustainable construction materials can be defined as products with full functionality which takes into consideration the following:

1. Things that is locally manufactured and stored
2. Price and environmental effects of transport
3. Heating in thermal form
4. Requirements and health concerns of occupants
5. Financial production
6. Renovation of building materials for the foundation and demolished construction materials
7. The waste and impurities produced in the manufacturing process
8. The power needed in the manufacturing process
9. The use of renewable resources
10. The harmful pollutants that the product generates.

Lime

Lime is our principal building replacement for cement. It provides good air quality by carbon absorption and oxygen expulsion into the atmosphere. The cost of a lime is comparatively small compared to the cost of cement. Compared to cement production, the life cycle of lime construction is much longer. In contrast to cement production, the life cycle of lime construction is much greater. A Color Lime Plaster may be used to make lime concrete, mortar, and plaster or stucco depending on the combination of aggregate and water hydrated lime.

The application of lime is very easy to use, the outstanding quality of the lime mud to work. Its use requires the use of low power. Oily lime, as it is also called, shows a "buttery" consistency, a slope, very easy to use. Qualified professionals use lime mortars to make it easier to use, unlike other ineffective and less effective ones in its use, especially in cement mortar. During repair, energy consumption is reduced by the high durability of the limestone, if the application is successful and sufficiently resolved at the strength of the water and the strength of the structure. It does not require almost any care. In rare cases, hats and stockings may need to be cleaned with water.

Fig. 5: Lime Plaster

Fly Ash Bricks

Ash fly is one of the charcoal-burning process's natural products and is almost similar to volcanic ash. During the processing of FAL-G bricks, fly ash and gypsum ash can be wasted. The production of fly ash bricks should be encouraged; as it will indirectly save the high soil (commonly used in the production of clay bricks) needed for agricultural crop production and helps in keeping environment pollution free. There are following types of fly ash bricks:

1. Fly ash Lime/Gypsum Bricks
2. Clay Fly Ash Bricks
3. Sand Fly Ash Bricks
4. Red Mud-Fly Ash Bricks.

Fig. 6: Fly Ash Bricks

Eco-Friendly Tiles

The traditional flooring tiles are replaced by eco-friendly tiles and less energy is used in their manufacturing. In comparison with regular tiles, it is inexpensive. They are accessible with a selection of patterns according to consumer needs and are easy to set up. The consistency of the natural home environment is enhanced by these tiles. Compared to standard tiles, eco-friendly tiles are cheaper as these tiles are manufactured in the building so that their travel costs are minimized.

Fig. 7: Eco-Friendly Tiles

Environmental awareness and strict environmental laws imposed by government agencies drive the eco-friendly tile market. In addition, the growth in the number of end-user industries is due to the fact that the durability and low maintenance of clean tiles are fueling the market. However, the high cost of eco-friendly tiles hinders market growth. The use of renewable energy sources to power the equipment used to produce clean tiles has led to the mass production of tiles that do not cause minimal damage to the environment. This large product increases the chance of future market growth.

Bamboo

The Bamboo Plant is the world's fastest growing plant. It is a member of the grass family and is present in a number of climates, from cold mountains to tropical climates, in many regions across the globe. Like a natural cellulose fiber, micro-organisms and sunlight will rot 100 percent of the bamboo fabric in the soil, showing that bamboo is a natural source of environmental protection and even its waste does not have any adverse effects on environment. Bamboo offers bamboo items suitable for use as fabrics for roofing or roofing materials.

Ferro Cement

In comparison with reinforced concrete, Ferro cement has a very high tensile strength to weight ratio and superior cracking behavior. A variety of possibilities are provided for the solution of building construction with maximum reduction of electrical energy for prefabricated fibrocement cavity walls.

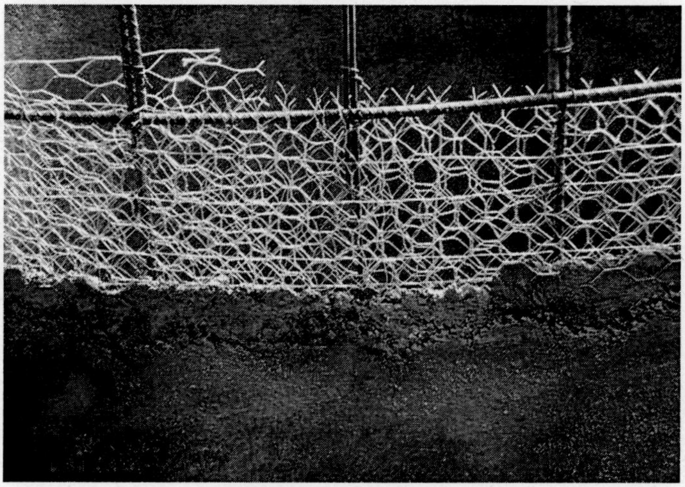

Fig. 8: Ferro Cement

SUSTAINABLE CONSTRUCTION TECHNIQUES

In order to keep up with this rising density, as green building has become a vital part of today's world, more and more construction technologies are being developed. These involve the use of appliances, toilets, and taps with low water, the re-use of gray water (water provided by sinks, showers, and washes), and the cessation of irrigation. Generated gray water should be used rather than discharged into a public sewerage system to irrigate the land area. 10 to 15 liters of flush toilets are created by the special water conservation toilets, with some fluid systems maintaining 90% water savings compared to traditional toilets. Composting Toilets reduce the amount of waste by 90%. It can rot and become a nutrient-rich fertilizer when human waste is combined with ample plant material (e.g. kitchen waste, garden waste, etc and when exposed to enough air.

All water pipes are insulated, both cold and humid. To avoid heat loss to the concrete, the bottom board is placed under the heater. The timers are mounted in a tank to shut it off automatically at night when there is no need for hot water. It is possible to use an ungrateful heater or a "demand" heater.

Solar power can be used to help mount the power input that is necessary. The panels absorb heat from the sun in this device and pass it through copper coils to a glycol solution. To add heat to the water tank, the coils go to the heating station. To minimize energy consumption, easy steps can be taken: fill the water tank, close the indoor/outdoor pipes, add water-saving devices, and lower the thermostat configuration.

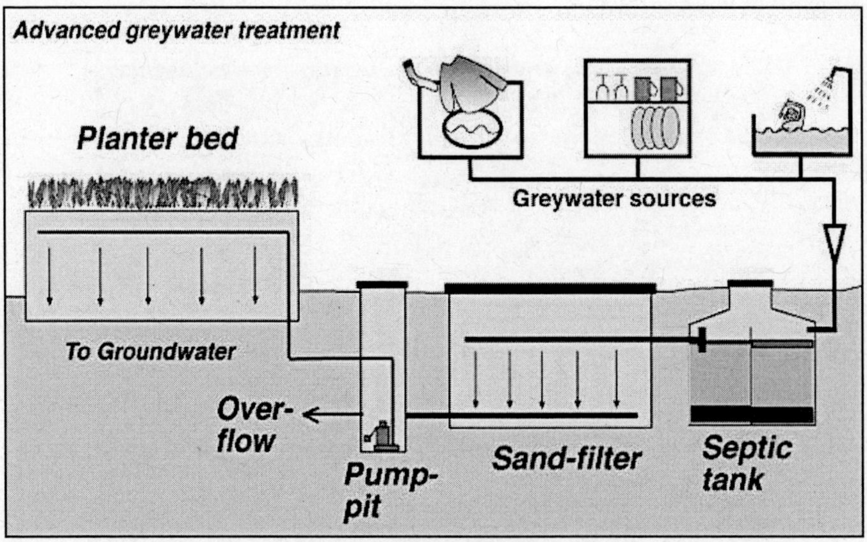

Fig. 9: Grey Water Reuse System

Solar Water Heating Systems: Horizontal plate collectors set to face the sun are used for most systems.

1. Closed Loop Systems
2. Thermo Siphoning
3. Open Loop Systems
4. Drain Back Systems
5. Batch Heater Systems.

Heating, Cooling, and Ventilation

A desire to use an integrated mechanical device is present in this new technique. This implies that as one device, space heating and cooling, water heating, ventilation, and heat return work together. Moreover, to maintain high indoor air quality, energy efficient homes need an air conditioning system. Space heating, water heating, solar storage, heat regeneration from gray water and partial cooling are provided by the mechanical system. Centered on a pump for heat transfer that transfers heat between a storage tank for ice water and a hot water tank. Heat is removed from the ice in winter and moved to a tank of hot water. The space's heating requirements are met by the fan coil unit.

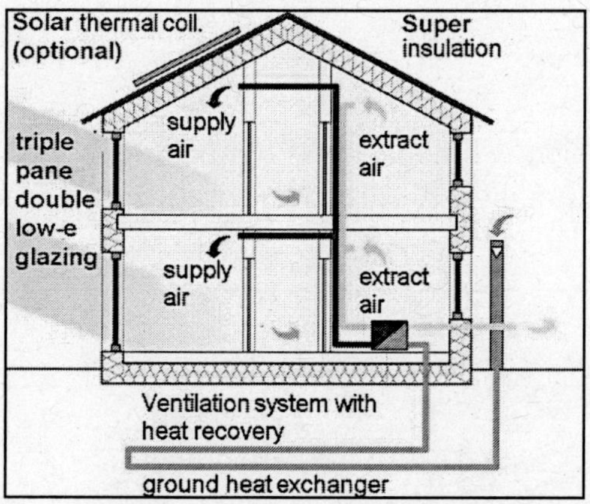

Fig. 10: Heating Cooling and Ventilation Systems

Indoor Air Quality

An exemplary plan to enhance the quality of indoor air by emission control has remained in effect. Sustainable ways of improving the quality of indoor air are:

1. Pick materials which are low-emission.
2. Plants as air cleaners for the climate.

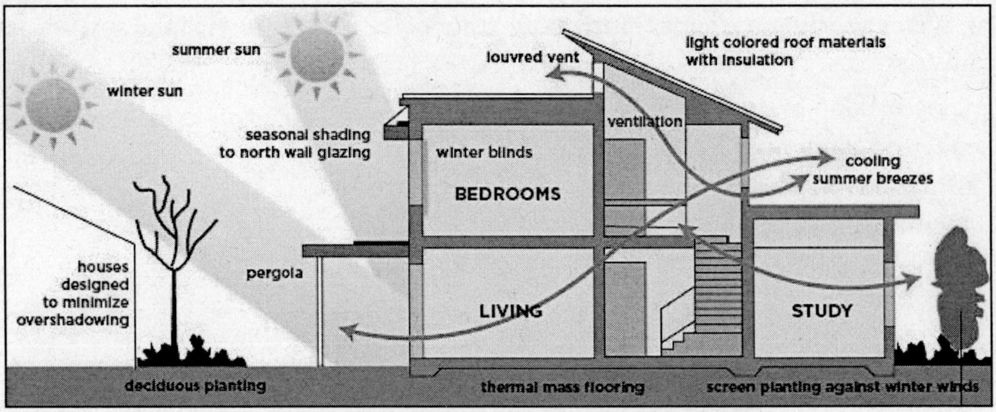

Fig. 11: Process of Improving the Indoor Air Quality

Use Sustainable Building Materials

In order to create a green house, the use of environment sustainable or eco-friendly goods can reduce the effects of environmental construction. It should be environment friendly for any aspect of the home, such as roofing materials, construction materials, cabinets, counters and floor coverings. Use items made from renewable, recyclable materials such as found wood, recycled plastic, recycled glass or natural products such as bamboo, cork and linoleum.

Cool Roofs

A cool roof is a roof which is built to hold temperatures lower than a typical roof in bright sunlight. More sunlight is absorbed by a cool roof surface and emits more heat than a so-called hot or dark roof.

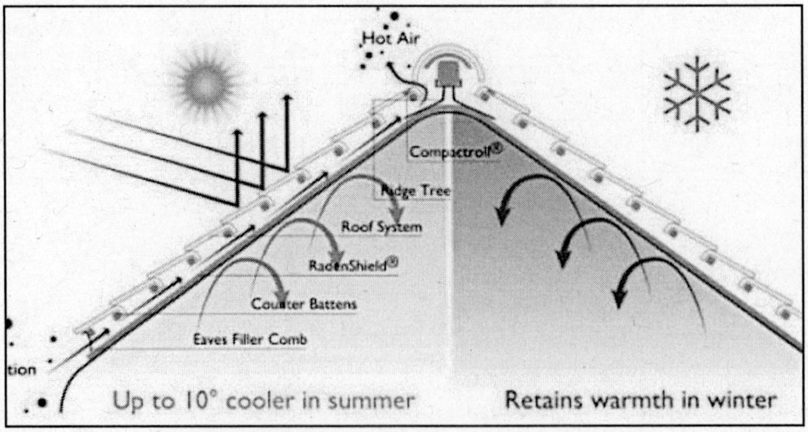

Fig. 12: Cool Roof System for Buildings

Zero-Energy Buildings

In order to work without an electric grid, zero-energy buildings are specially built and constructed to rely on renewable sources of energy, such as solar and wind power. Not only does this green system save electricity, but it also prevents excess heat from being emitted. In order to provide structural selection criteria and HVAC requirements, the zero-energy architecture uses solar cells and panels, wind turbines and bio fuels, among other things (Cameroon, 2020).

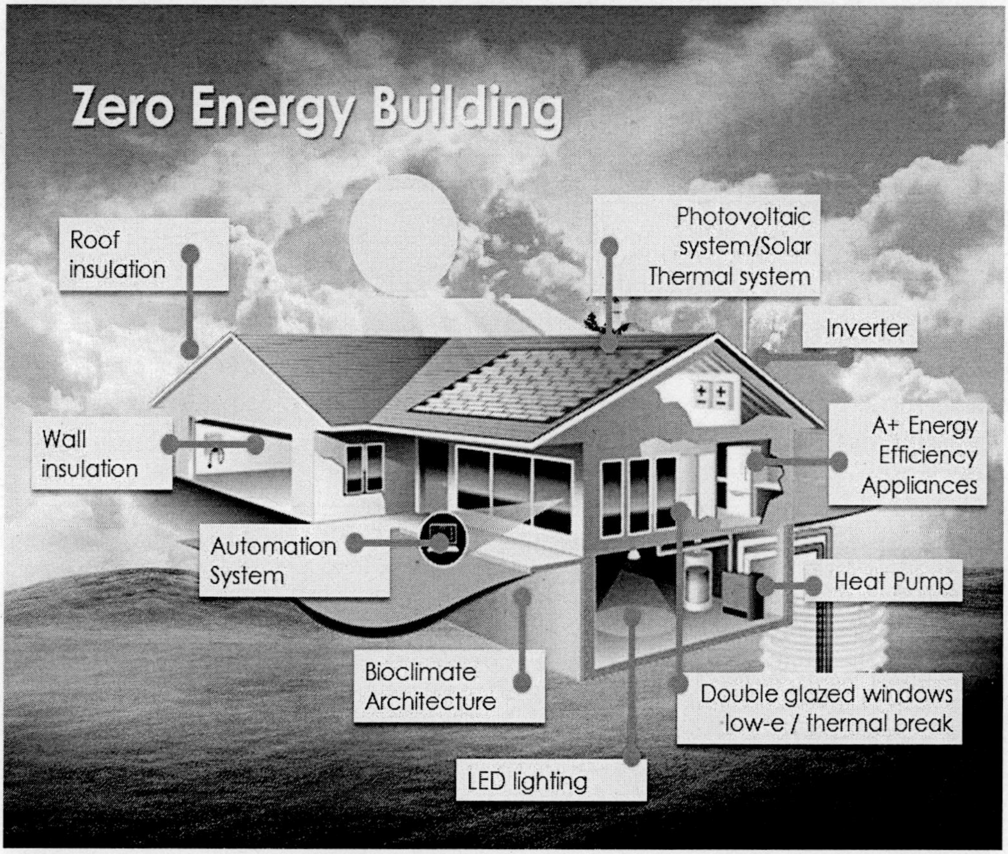

Fig. 13: Zero-Energy Building

CASE STUDY: TORRENT RESEARCH CENTRE (TRC)

The Research Center (TRC) 16 in Ahmadabad, Gujarat, discusses the above-mentioned school of thought and includes the use of common knowledge, common sense, creativity, trial and error; and the scientific decision to achieve a 'mera wala green' unique to the area and the structural role proposed (Palacios, 2007).

Fig. 14: Torrent Research Centre (TRC)

The TRC was completed and implemented in 1997 and has been reported as a specific example of a Passive Downdraft Evaporative Cooling (PDEC) climate response project. Notable architectural characteristics are:

- 72 percent (28–28.5°C as a temperature not exceeding the number of hours) of the central building achieved human comfort using PDEC.
- This building was able to create very low levels per meter of energy consumption.

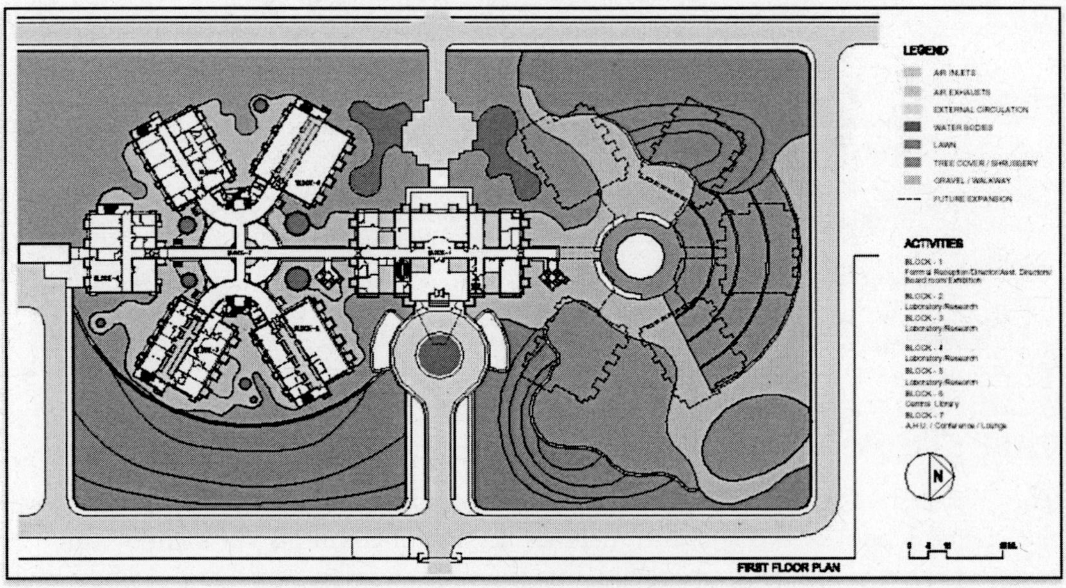

Fig. 15: Site Plan (Torrent Research Centre)

A range of factors such as customer dedication to environmental design, consistent environmental work goals, an organized approach to a variety of building team that remembers customer requirements, and responsive property management during deployment and service have a low power impact on the plant. The TRC house, situated in a group of buildings, has a range of research facilities that include pharmaceuticals and funding-related services.

MATERIALS

With good glazing design, full control of solar heat gain is achieved. Flexible windows are connected to the outside, not only horizontally with overhangs on the aircraft, but the air towers originating from the façade are also on the plane facing upwards. Buildings in the sun are fantastic. Hollow brick walls are built inside and out in reinforced concrete buildings, and concrete blocks do not even fill the roof pockets and are re-installed. On the roof and on both walls, with vermiculite used as protection. The exterior is white and the walls are finished with a mosaic finish from China on the roof (Palacios, 2007).

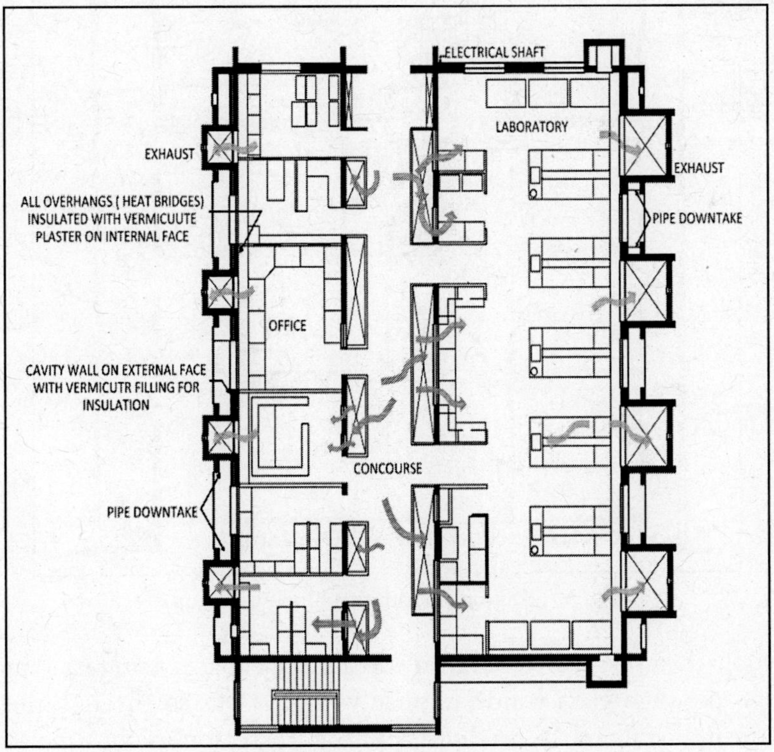

Fig. 16: First Floor Plan Laboratory Block Building 2

Techniques

The PDEC (Passive Downdraught Evaporative Cooling System) system is designed to work in severe weather conditions during the hot season, without temperatures approaching or exceeding 40°C in the late afternoon. On top of three large ventilation towers situated above the central tunnels of each laboratory building, the PDEC system pumps water through pipes with a pressure of 50 Pa to create fog (micronized).

The mist of fine mist cools the slow-moving air on either side of the walkway through the middle of the tunnel through the opening. Window hopper sets at each stage are designed to catch the flow.

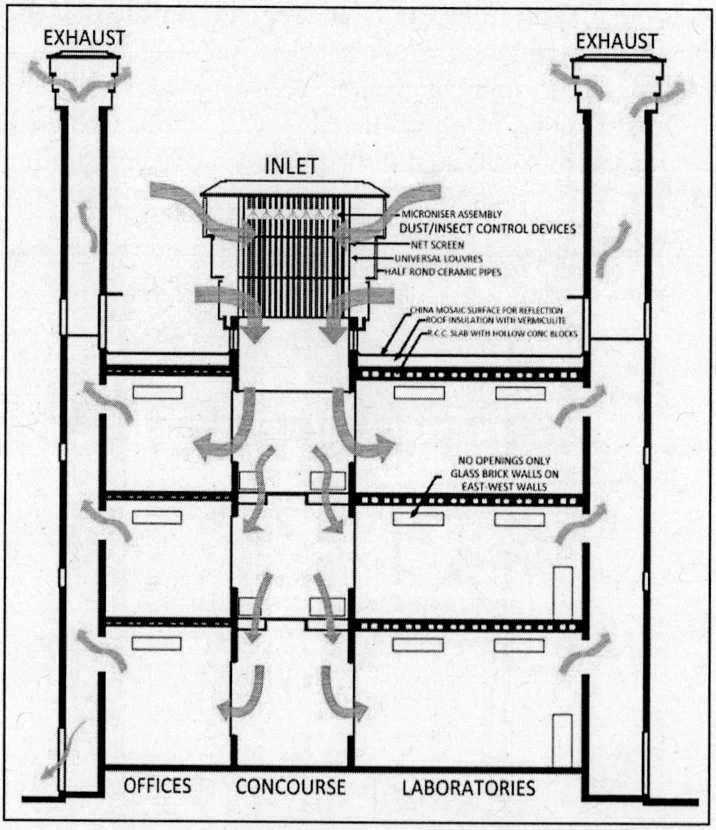

Fig. 17: Section Laboratory Block Building 2

Any of this cool air can be redirected into surrounding spaces using it. The air can then escape through the high glass windows once you have passed through the room, with spaces that attach directly to the air ducts. During the season, night time air time is also a possibility. Roof fans could be made to operate to provide more air movement in offices and laboratories during times of wet, humid rain if micronized usage was not suitable. The operating system is designed to regulate air inflow during the cool season, especially at night, to reduce heat loss by allowing users to change hopper windows and open spaces in their areas to meet their needs.

PARAMETER SELECTION OF SUSTAINABLE CONSTRUCTION TECHNIQUES

- Sustainable materials are generally natural materials with low energy consumption and low maintenance costs, which can be easily removed and reused during demolition.
- The combined consumption power of construction materials involves the original and repeated consumption of electricity. The first relates to the energy used during the construction era and the latter relates to the energy use needed during the performance phase, including modifications, improvements and repair processes during the active life cycle.
- Sustainable practices must protect the environment and reduce hazards of environmental degradation other than pollution or other pollutants during the life cycle that affect human health and well-being. Domestic environments currently have a major effect on users' health, well-being and performance, as individuals typically spend less than 90% of their time indoors. (P. Wargocki, 2011)
- Two sections are used as versatile parameters, one parameter is cooling technology and the other is chosen based on the component's efficiency in reducing the heat gain.
- Cool load essentially depends on two primary variables; internal heat gain and external heat gain. The advantages of internal heating primarily rely on the occupants, lighting and facilities used within the house. External heat gain depends on the various building materials.
- Some idle construction materials have a natural interaction and can be combined to create a special and potentially important comfort boost, minimizing the benefit of external heat and achieving greater energy efficiency. Via Passive Architecture, this can be done. The size or capability of the system will be determined by the estimated cooling load in each cooling system/strategy.
- In order to minimize cooling loads, the blend of non-abrasive materials and cooling design techniques complement each other. Passive design components help to minimize the external heat gain, to shape an envelope; structural design; direction of construction; location of the site and country considerations; after learning various design techniques.

CONCLUSION

Sustainable construction materials are those that are locally manufactured or purchased. Recycled and industrial waste includes this material. Sustainable materials have an occasional environmental effect and perform physically well. Compared to modern or conventional building materials, the assembly of such building materials requires little energy in manufacturing. The benefits of choosing sustainable building materials are that they not only function economically, but also minimize toxicity and thereby decrease the impact on the environment. Within the development of individual neighbors, sustainable building materials and technology should be used properly and contextually. The use of renewable materials and technology not only lowers transportation and manufacturing costs and carbon emissions, but also creates opportunities for members of the general public to improve jobs and skills.

FUTURE SCOPE

1. Automation technologies with high levels of control systems based on micro-processors lead to improved technical efficiency, such as solar panels, integrated HVAC and electrical systems.
2. A new evaluation of the use of agricultural waste instead of sustainable building materials would be considered in the light of the situation in India.
3. Non-conventional materials of sustainable construction built on a bio-reinforced bio-system can be considered.
4. An integrated design methodology is incorporated into a computer-based design method for the robust construction of building materials for a particular construction project. This includes the CAD model-based Life Cycle Analysis. Current technical constraints, however, do not provide a valid solution. The development of algorithms and the specifics of real-time analytics engines will fine-tune such tools. It will alter the architecture's current state.

REFERENCES

[1] Acciona (2019). Sustainability for all. Retrieved from https://www.activesustainability.com/construction-and-urban/ on October 10, 2020.

[2] Cameroon, J. (2020). Zero energy buildings. Retrieved from https://nssiitbblog.wordpress.com/2020/08/05/zero-energy-buildings/ on October 10, 2020.

[3] Frontczak, M. and Wargocki, P. (2011). Literature survey on how different factors influence human comfort in indoor environments. *Building and environment*, *46*(4), 922–937.

[4] Kotkar, A.V and Salunkhe, H. (2017). A review paper on green building. *International Journal of Advance Research in Science and Engineering*, *6*(7), 901–906.

[5] Lacasse, M.A. (1999). Materials and technology for sustainable construction. *Building Research and Information*, *27*(6), 405–408.

[6] Palacios, D. (2007). Case Study II: The Torrent Research Centre in Ahmedabad, by Abhikram. Retrieved from https://www.archidev.org/spip.php?article1115&lang=fr on October 12, 2020.

[7] Patil, K.M. and Patil, M.S. (2017). Sustainable Construction Materials and Technology in Context. *International Journal of Engineering Research and Technology*, *10*(1), 112–117.

[8] Stevulova, N., Baltakys, K., Estokova, A. and Sverak, T. (2018). Sustainable Building Materials and Technologies. *Advances in Materials Science and Engineering*, 2018.

[9] Tatari, O. and Kucukvar, M. (2011). Cost premium prediction of certified green buildings: A neural network approach. *Building and Environment*, *46*(5), 1081–1086.

[10] Thormark, C. (2006). The effect of material choice on the total energy need and recycling potential of a building. *Building and environment*, *41*(8), 1019–1026.

[11] UNEP (2010). The 'State of Play' of Sustainable Buildings in India. *Sustainable Buildings and Climate Initiative.* France.

[12] Yiming Song, H.Z. (2018). *Research on sustainability of building materials.* Nanjing 210096, China: IOP Conference Series: Materials Science and Engineering.

Demographic Effect on Factors of Offline Retailing

Suyog S. Dekhne[1] **and Rajeev K. Shukla**[2]

Shri Vaishnav School of Management,
Shri Vaishnav Vidyapeeth Vishwavidyalaya, Indore, Madhya Pradesh
E-mail: [1]suyog.dekhne@gmail.com; [2]directorsvsm@svvv.edu.in

ABSTRACT: Retail sector in India has undergone steep changes in recent years. This has happened mainly because of increase in use of internet and smart phones. Online retailing business is growing with growth in technology. Expansion of internet-based payment system; discounts, easy returns, convenience etc. are some of the reasons which turn the customers from offline to online system. In the present study the constituent factors of off-line retailing have been explored and subsequently impact of age, gender, and income on these factors were analyzed. Sales assistance, purchase involvement, retailer's sales motive, flexible transaction facility, product accessibility and entertainment values were found to be differentiating factors for off-line retailing.

Findings of the study revealed that there is no significant impact of age, gender, and income on sales assistance, and entertainment value factors of off-line retailing. Significant impact of age, and gender observed towards purchase involvement of customers, and sales motives of retailers. Age, gender, and income have significant effect on flexible transaction facility of retail stores. The study further revealed significant effect of gender on product accessibility at retail stores. However, no significant effect of age and income were observed towards product accessibility at retail stores.

Keywords: Age, Factors, Gender, Income, Retailing.

INTRODUCTION

According to Levy and Weitz (2016), 'Retailing consists of particular algorithmic trade activities that provide additional worth to a product or service given to consumers. It involves set of actions performed by a retailer under sales of goods and services to consumers. India is the promised land for global brands and Indian retailers. With an increase in the use of smart phones and fast spreading internet connections, online shopping is getting more popularity as buying products is now just a click away. Rosenbloom (2002) concluded that 'Internet retailing is the retailing business on the Internet'. Instead of wandering through stores and making impulse purchases, now shoppers use digital gadgets to search products and prices easily. Ability to shop anytime of the day or night, access to compare prices, huge discounts, more options, saving of time and fuel, easy access to consumer reviews, easy returns, free shipping, cash on delivery etc., are some of the reasons why people prefer to shop online.

Traditional way of shopping in India has been prevalent in India from decades. As per middle class value proposition, consumers prefer offline purchase in order to check and test the product and have its possession immediately after payment. But, because of the evolution of E-tailing, offline sale is declining and store traffic is going down, especially in peripheral shopping areas since online shopping takes over the role of providing a wide product range with various additional benefits. Show rooming has also come as an emerging way of shopping, through which customers check out products in the show rooms and then order the same product online. With the change in buying behavior of customers, offline retailers have to re-visit their marketing strategies to change their store offerings so that more customers can be attracted and sales will be increased.

REVIEW OF LITERATURE

Traditional retailing involves interaction of human with human and e-tailing involves human interaction with machines. Evanschitzky *et al.*, (2004) stated that traditionally customers consider store layout as important factor while purchasing, whereas browse and search functions, images are more important factor while purchasing online. Goswami and Mathur (2011) observed that consumers and merchants of metro cities such as Delhi and Mumbai were using internet in a large number that ultimately leads to increasing trend of online shopping in these metro cities.

Ghosh (2014) revealed that to overcome the retailer's problem to reach geographically dispersed Indian consumers, internet has given them convenience, easy online navigation, trustworthiness of e-commerce sites and brands, time, money, cost and energy saving. In a study conducted on 1,327 consumers, Joshi and Upadhyay (2014) stated that overall convenience, range and availability of products and lower prices are the reasons because of which people prefer online shopping. "Customers browse the products through physical stores to have a physical look at the product and buy it from an online store at a reduced price" (Saha, 2015). According to Sodi, (2014), there are certain unique advantages which attract customers towards online shopping; online pricing search; convenience of door step delivery and competitive prices. But they are relatively a disadvantage to traditional retailers. Ghosh (2014) also mentioned that, as compared to traditional shops, for Indian consumers who are conservative about online data and payment securities, easy payment options like cash on delivery is much more acceptable and reliable.

Krishna *et al.* (2015) found that benefits of online business were affecting the traditional retailing as online business provides wide range of benefits when compared with offline retailing business like easy shopping, time saving, updated information, cash on delivery and easy comparison etc. Even in case of off-line retailing, Goswami and Mathur (2011) have observed that big brand retailers are dominating the small ones adversely due to their wider investment capacities and it is becoming difficult for the small retailers to prove their existence in the market. Sodi (2014) statistically proved in his paper that, online shopping is a big threat for offline retailers as they are getting products on cheaper rates while traditional retailers are not. Saha (2015) revealed that, due to online shopping, offline retailers are facing considerable decline in their turnover and profit. In order to stand with the online stores who woes the customers with unbelievable discounts, the offline retailers have also started increasing their discounts but resulting in decreasing the profit margin.

OBJECTIVES OF THE STUDY

1. To identify the constituent factors of off-line retailing.
2. To analyze the effect of age, gender, and income of customers towards factors of offline retailing.

RESEARCH METHOD

Research Type: Present study is exploratory in nature and based on survey design.

The Sample: Purposive sampling method was used for the study. Sample size was 232.

Tools for Data Collection: Primary data was collected with the help of self-developed instrument consisting of sixteen statements and measured on five point Likert scale. Secondary sources of data were analyzed for defining and exploring the research problem.

Tools for Data Analysis: Factor analysis, One-way ANOVA. ANOVA was performed to find the effect of demographic profile of respondents (Independent Variables: Age, Gender and Income) on identified factors of offline retail market. The statistical data analysis was done using IBM SPSS Statistics 23.

RESULTS

Reliability of Instrument

Reliability of instrument was checked with the help of Cronbach's Alpha Coefficient. The alpha value came as 0.815 indicating a high reliability of scale for data collection (Table 1).

Table 1: Reliability Statistics

Cronbach's Alpha	*No. of Items*
.815	16

Table 2: Respondents Profile

		Percent
Age	20–30 years	27.8
	35–45 years	41.7
	50–60 years	30.5
Gender	Male	58.1
	Female	41.9
Income	₹ 10,000 to ₹ 25,000	28.1
	₹ 30,000 to ₹ 45,000	43.6
	₹ 50,000 to ₹ 65,000	28.3

Table 2 indicates demographic profile of respondents. It shows that 58.1 percent of respondents were male; 41.7 percent were in the age group of 35–45 years, and 43.6 percent respondents were in income group of ₹ 30,000 to ₹ 45,000 per month.

Factor Analysis

As a first step, the relevancy and appropriateness of analysis was found by KMO (Kaiser-Meyer-Olkin) Measure for Sampling Adequacy and Bartlett's test of Sphericity. KMO test was done to measure the adequacy of the data for factor analysis. While Bartlett's test of Sphericity compares the correlation matrix with identity matrix. It also checks for redundancy between variables that can be summarized with factors.

Table 3: KMO and Bartlett's Test

KMO Measure of Sampling Adequacy		*.798*
Bartlett's Test of Sphericity	Approx. Chi-Square	1213.436
	Df	120
	Sig	.000

Source: Primary Data.

Table 3 shows SPSS result of KMO and Bartlett's test indicating 0.798 and Sig 0.000 ($p < 0.01$). It means that collected data satisfy the assumption of factor analysis.

Table 4: Rotated Component Matrix

	Statements	*Components*					
		1	2	3	4	5	6
01	Sales executives provide prompt service to you as and when required.	.798					
02	Trained employees/executives can properly answer the questions.	.631					
03	Employees are always courteous towards customers.	.524					
04	The shopping ambience is important to you.		.801				
05	It gives homely feeling to shop from a particular retailer.		.765				
06	Retailer easily provides information about product you want to buy.		.663				
07	You found yourself very much involved in purchasing from a particular retailer.		.574				
08	It is tedious process to return the defective product.			.636			
09	Retailer makes false promises/claims to increase sales.			.537			
10	Retailer operates as per customers' schedule.				.785		
11	Retailer willingly handles returns and exchanges.				.621		
12	Retailer provides you different modes of payments.				.592		
13	You always get the product you search.					.721	
14	Your retailer frequently offers you the newly launched product.					.638	
15	You feel entertained during purchasing.						.695
16	It's always fun to shop from a particular retailer.						.584

Source: Primary Data.
Extraction Method: Principal Component Analysis.
Rotation Method: Varimax Rotation.

Rotated Component Matrix identifies and groups the different variables under identified components on the basis of their respective calculated communalities. A communality is a measure to which an item correlates with all other items. Higher communalities are always better.

Table 5: Total Variance Explained

Rotation Sum of Squared Loadings			
Factors	*Total*	*% of Variance*	*Cumulative %*
F1	2.958	12.379	12.379
F2	2.67	11.977	24.356
F3	2.475	10.755	35.111
F4	2.222	9.568	44.679
F5	1.856	8.316	52.995
F6	1.552	7.908	60.903

Extraction Method: Principal Component Analysis.

The principal component analysis, rotated component matrix and total variance (Table 5) indicates that total six components were extracted from sixteen statements based upon their factor loadings. These factors were named as Sales Assistance, Purchase Involvement, Sales Motive, Flexible Transaction, Product Accessibility and Entertainment Value.

To study the impact of independent demographic variables on factors of buying behavior in offline retail sector, Analysis of Variance (ANOVA) was conducted. The independent variables considered were gender, age and income while six extracted factors as dependent variables.

Table 6: Analysis of Variance (ANOVA) for Gender, Age and Income

Factors	*Gender*		*Age*		*Income*	
	F. Value	*Sig.*	*F. Value*	*Sig.*	*F. Value*	*Sig.*
Sales Assistance	1.830	.162	1.409	.246	1.698	.163
Purchase Involvement	3.466	*.033*	4.117	*.030*	2.383	.069
Sales Motive	4.563	*.011*	4.959	*.027*	1.526	.188
Flexible Transaction	4.870	*.008*	2.998	*.049*	5.012	*.005*
Product Accessibility	2.508	*.050*	2.402	.062	.465	.629
Entertainment Value	1.104	.355	1.180	.320	3.521	.029

Table 6 summarizes the ANOVA output over six extracted factors. Interpretation is discussed below:

1. **Sales Assistance:** Statements 01, 02 and 03 having factor loadings of 0.798, 0.631 and 0.524 respectively depicts the factor Sales Assistance. The ANOVA interpretation of dependent factor sales assistance over all the demographic components have been found insignificant. Thus, there is no significant impact of age, gender, and income of customers towards sales assistance factor of retail stores.
2. **Purchase Involvement:** From rotated component matrix table, statement number 04, 05, 06 and 07 having factor loadings of 0.801, 0.765, 0.663 and 0.574 respectively indicates the factor Purchase Involvement. The ANOVA output shows that, there is a significant impact of gender and age on purchase involvement.
3. **Sales Motive:** Retailers motive behind increasing its sales can be identified from the statements 08 and 09. Factor loadings for these statements are 0.636 and 0.537 respectively. The demographic variables gender and age shows significant impact on retailers' sales motive.
4. **Flexible Transaction:** Flexibility in transaction is one of the main factors responsible for declining offline retail sector. Factor loadings for the identified statements are 0.785, 0.621 and 0.592 respectively. ANOVA result shows that, there is a significant impact of gender, age and income of respondent on Flexible Transaction.
5. **Product Accessibility:** The Factor Product Accessibility has been identified from the statements 13 and 14 having factor loadings of 0.721 and 0.638 respectively. There is a significant impact of gender on product accessibility. While age and income are insignificant.
6. **Entertainment Value:** There is no impact of any independent variable on Entertainment Value.

DISCUSSION

Irrespective of age, income and gender of customers service assistance at offline retail stores was observed to be a key differentiating factor than online retail stores. Sales assistance, prompt service, trained employees, and courteous behavior of employees can make the difference for retail stores. Similarly, shopping as fun, enjoyment, and entertainment adds value to customers irrespective of gender, age, and income. Purchase involvement and sales motive factors were found significant for Gender and age, whereas it was non-significant for income. Purchase involvement in retail stores can be better facilitated by creating ambience of homely feeling, and by addressing the information search of customers. However, sales motives of retailers such as unrealistic claims on products and services, false promises, and avoidance of defective products return adversely affects customer goodwill.

Age, gender, and income have significant effect on flexible transaction facility of retail stores. Irrespective of age, gender, and income customers prefer flexible operating hours that matches their buying needs and transaction facility, retailers' willingness to exchange or return defective products. Gender has significant effect on product accessibility at retail stores. Availability of required products and new product arrivals at retail stores were perceived significant differently by male and female customers. However, no significant effect of age and income were observed towards product accessibility at retail stores.

Findings of the study was supported by Van *et al.*, (2002) that concerned for female and male customers were different for different products. Initially it was found that the brands of products sold online were male-oriented and it could be reason for late adoption of online platform among females. The difference in shopping approach of males and females can be attributed as females shop in a planned fashion and males are more impulsive shoppers (Zhang *et al.*, 2007). Alreck and Settle (2002) also observed that shopping satisfaction of females in offline convenience retail stores should be more emphasized as females have traditionally been and continue to be the principle buying agents for household items.

CONCLUSION

Online retailing has adversely affected the business of the traditional as well as organized retail stores. However, the present study has identified six factors of offline retailing as Sales Assistance, Purchase Involvement, Sales Motive, Flexible Transaction, Product Accessibility and Entertainment Value. Further, effect of gender, age, and income of respondents towards identified factors were analyzed. Findings of the study revealed no significant effect of age, gender, and income on sales assistance, and entertainment value factors of off-line retailing. Significant effect of age, and gender observed towards purchase involvement of customers, and sales motives of retailers. Age, gender, and income have significant effect on flexible transaction facility of retail stores. The study further revealed significant effect of gender on product accessibility at retail stores. However, no significant effect of age and income were observed towards product accessibility at retail stores.

REFERENCES

[1] Alreck, P. and Settle, R.B. (2002). Gender effects on internet, catalogue and store shopping. *Journal of Database Marketing*, 9(2), 150–162.

[2] Evanschitzky, H. Iyer, G.R., Hesse, J., and Ahlert, D. (2004). E-satisfaction: A re-examination. *Journal of Retailing, 80,* 239–247.

[3] Ghosh, S. (2014). Making business sense of the internet. *Harvard Business Review*, March-April, 126–135

[4] Goswami, S. and Mathur, M. (2011). Retail goes online—An Indian perspective. *International Journal of Management and Technology, 19(2), 01–11.*

[5] Joshi, P. and Upadhyay H. (2014). E-Retailing in India despite issues, customers satisfied with top retailers. Retrieved from http://consumeraffairs.nic. in/consumer/writereaddata/e-Retailingindia .pdf.

[6] Krishna, M.R., Pavan, K. and Gopal, V.K. (2015). Perception of retailers one-tailing. *International Journal of Advance Research in Computer Science and Management Studies,* 3(11), 199–202.

[7] Levy, U. and Weitz, S. (2016). A study of customer satisfaction in shopping malls: An empirical study. *Research Journal of Management Sciences, 4*(11), 10–18.

[8] Rosenbloom, B. (2002). "The ten deadly myths of e-commerce", *Business Horizons*, 45, 1–6.

[9] Roy, A. (2016). Growth and development of FMCG in India: A Study based on Impulse Buying Behavior. *Pacific Business Review International*, 8(7), 14–22.

[10] Saha, A. (2015). The impact of online shopping upon retail trade business. *IOSR Journal of Business and Management, 3*(4), 74–78.

[11] Sodi, J. (2014). E-tailing boom—impact on retailing. *Indian Journal of Applied Research, 4*(9), 106–107.

[12] Van Slyke, C., Comunale, C.L. and Belanger, F. (2002). Gender differences in perceptions of web-based shopping. *Communications of the ACM, 45*(7), 82–86.

[13] Zhang, X., Prybutok, V.R. and Strutton, D. (2007). Modeling influences on impulse purchase behaviors during online marketing transactions. *Journal of Marketing Theory and Practice, 15*(1), 79–89.

Designing Playful Employee Experience

Monika Sonta
Management in Networked and Digital Societies (MINDS)
Kozminski University, Poland
E-mail: msonta@kozminski.edu.pl

ABSTRACT: In times of organizational thirst for employee engagement and meaning through designing corporate stories, the aim of the present study is to explore and identify key sources (engines) of engagement during LEGO® SERIOUS PLAY® (LSP) corporate learning events of various types and size in Poland. The research was conducted using participant observation from the perspective of a certified facilitator. Eight training sessions (four LSP and four non-LSP workshops) have been analyzed using thematic analysis. A structure of thematic codes has been conceptualized and reflected as EPIC(s) framework.

The findings reveal the importance of the experience of emerging realities as a key generator of engagement; the significance of social collaboration and peer-to-peer interactions (experience of collective intelligence); the observable rise in engagement and willingness to contribute when real business situations, especially labelled as 'strategic issues' are discussed and the role of image-capturing ('snapshot experience') and creates an engaging learning experience. The findings are adaptable to the corporate practices aimed at empowering employees and are compatible with management models such as agile, human enablement and human-centered design in organizations. The 'learning experience' research is also culture- and context-sensitive, thus it can be replicated keeping the contextual contingencies in mind.

Keywords: Employee Experience, Employee Engagement Lego Serious Play, Organizational Events.

INTRODUCTION

Companies all over the world wrestle with how to better engage their employees in the workplace—this is the opening sentence about Employee Engagement from Salem Press Encyclopedia (2019). In times of Employee Experience mapping and work-life blend, the playful methods of learning are associated with greater engagement and are discussed as an alternative to traditional corporate training. The rising notion 'serious play' refers to learning activities that enable individuals to engage in playful way with the business intended output (Bonneu *et al.*, 2017). The theoretical background has been briefly introduced to propose the experiences and moments of the workshops that ignited the observable engagement in the room. These findings will be streamed into the EPIC(s) model.

The area of employee engagement can be researched and observed from various points of view—through the lens of theories of motivation, gamification, Human Resources and Organisation Studies. With such a wide possibility for theoretical reflection, the starting point of this discussion will be a niche work of Gauntlett (2007) who situated LSP method on the map of creative qualitative research. Thus, in this paper the concept of play in context of 'playful learning activity' and social constructivism that creates context for the discussion about employee experience will be focussed. The theoretical discussion will try to combine communicative constitution of organization in the context of qualitative organizational research. To narrow the complexity of this multidisciplinary topic, the multiple references to Gauntlett's not well-established, yet a refreshing concept on employee engagement research will be provided. To emphasize Gauntlett's concept, the four pillars of engagement; use of metaphors; concept of play; theory of flow and constructivism should be taken into consideration as the focal points to understand an 'engaging learning experience'.

THEORIZING 'PLAYFUL ACTIVITY'

According to Huizinga (1995), and his classic definition of 'play' in Homo ludens: "Play is a free activity standing quite consciously outside 'ordinary' life as being 'not serious,' but at the same time absorbing the player intensely and utterly". This definition is not accurate in context of playing in the business context due to two enforced elements:

1. Structure of the workshop—deliberate frameworks are set by the method and
2. Rules that frame the social interactions during the LSP workshop. Rules need to be added to emphasize the social character of playful experience as the whole workshop is based on socially agreed-upon regulations. In case of organizational events they play a role of social contract before the training and are imposed by the method that demands the agreement to certain behaviors, for example 'everybody builds, and everybody shares' rule.

On one hand, the challenge with the conceptualization begins with the interpretation: "Play is generally defined as an activity that participants engage in voluntarily and without coercion (Andersen, 2009; Huizinga, 1955). So, this interpretation: 'If participants are coerced or otherwise forced into an activity, it ceases to be playful" (Hinthorne & Schneider, 2012) makes Huizinga's approach to 'playing' inadequate to the business environment. On the other hand, play by definition requires order and flexibility (Hinthorne & Schneider, 2012) or is even treated as an order-creating activity. It is structured by rules or agreements among players, which may or may not be different from those that guide social interaction in ordinary life (Andersen, 2009; Huizinga, 1955; Brown, 2009). The various rhetoric of purposeful play (play as progress) and children's play as frivolity are repeated by Ashton and Giddings (2018).

Moreover, defining 'serious play' that leads to an identified purpose (Statler, Heracleous, Jacobs, 2011) that differs from 'just playing' that is conducted for pure enjoyment provides the new perspective. The definition of 'serious play' understood as AF goal oriented and concerned with outcomes as well as processes can be found in the academic paper of Andersen (2009) and Roos (2006).

The process of conceptualization of play in the business environments requires going beyond the ludic interpretation of play and adapting the perspective of Csikszentmihalyi's (1990) flow who defines the *flow experience* talks about the feeling of 'floating' beyond the output or being 'lost in the task'. Gauntlett adds to this "participants absorbed in the Lego building process are good examples of individuals 'in flow'".

Furthermore, in LEGO® SERIOUS PLAY® the element of social experience and collective intelligence is emphasized. The conceptual non-academic framework is suggested in Lego Serious Play brochure (2006) where social bonding and constructive competition is mentioned as the elements of the workshop experience. Moreover, the theories of Piaget's Constructivism, Papert's constructionism and learning by making and building knowledge are named as the background theories of business method of facilitation (Roos and Victor, 2004; Rasmussen, 2006). Here, the link to communication should be also mentioned to understand the concept in context of organizational capabilities as Sutton-Smith (1997) stated that "[p]lay is like language: a system of communication and expression".

The bridge between those two approaches can be found in Allegre's (2013) 'cocreative settings' which emphasized that the group flow experience is strongly associated with the individual flow which suggests that during 'playful experience' the engagement should be established and maintained both, at the individual and group level. In summary, the 'playful activity' in this paper is closer to the concept of 'serious play', *flow and social constructivism* than to the classic understanding of 'play' exposed in developmental psychology.

THEORIZING 'EMPLOYEE EXPERIENCE'

In conceptualization of Employee Experience the definition taken from coaching approach is used. Experience, according to group of researchers is defined as "an imprint of experienced events, situations, contacts, feelings or action in memory". In the introspective psychology approach, the timing of experiencing is emphasized as an imprint is experienced by a person in a given moment when specifying influence also states "Management has its end, influence stays' (Włodarski, 2010).

In the concept of Creative Explorations (2007) Gauntlett combines two elements of engaging experience namely, creativity through discovery and discovery thanks to self-reflection, stating that "[c]reativity often takes place where one perspective meets another, or where the insights of one paradigm have a playful engagement with the subject-area of another" (Gauntlett, 2007).

Analogically to experiencing *flow*, the self-reflection (individual experience) needs to be communicated to the group to gaining common understanding. The key element is linked to the collective intelligence transformed into collective memory and then, leads to organizational remembering.

Talking about time orientation, the experience is a past-oriented concept while organizational remembering is reoccurring, ongoing process of collective memorizing. Sanfuentes and Acuña (2014) discovered that "the ignorance of the past lessens the ability to face turbulent periods, because organizations are unable to connect new alternatives with preceding experiences". These findings confirm the results of several earlier studies (Kets de Vries and Balazs, 1997; Pollit, 2000). They defined 'organizational remembering' as 'the essential process whereby the heterogenous character of organizational practices and traditions can be negotiated and integrated'.

In LEGO® SERIOUS PLAY® the moment of sharing the stories is the place to talk about the past experience filtered by self-reflection and 'adapted' to the constructed metaphors. This distortion in the way of talking about past events helps to go beyond non-declarative responses. More reflexive stories lead to more reflexive micro-narratives. Still, the focus is on the shared mental model and streaming individual experiences into a social experience to create a common platform of shared interpretations of the events. The activity of participants "the knowledge becomes a common good" or common-pool resources that is additionally represented in the physical form of a brick model (Hofmolk, 2009).

Gauntlett (2007) in his creative explorations and LSP application in research links the description of the 'experience' to a captured 'scene' that constantly re-evolves in interpretations: "As the Nobel Prize-winning neuroscientist Gerald Edelman observes, we apprehend the world in each moment, as a 'unitary scene', although the scene may change continuously as we receive new stimuli or have new thoughts". According to Giddens (1984), human social activities are self-reproducing—'since these structures are reproduced through the actions of individuals', recursive and continuously recreated which also constitutes approach to this research.

METHODOLOGY

This paper is written with Durkheim' macro approach to sociology, stating that we can go beyond individual cases and should be able to discuss a broader context for social discoveries that makes findings about social existence. This is an evaluation study of an exploratory character (Stebbins, 2001) and employs participatory observation during the training sessions. The research adopts a qualitative approach using participation observation from the position of workshop facilitator who observes the participants to identify the character and sources of visible playful experience among participants of the developmental events.

The workshops took place between September, 2018 and May, 2019 in Poland in a corporate environment and discussed topics that can be clustered as Organizational Development, namely, Leadership; Identity; Company Values and Organizational Culture. Each event was treated as a separate field experiment (exploratory fieldwork) and the moments of the most visible engagement of the participants were identified. The other event in a pair was of similar expected results, however, the main method of work was not LEGO® SERIOUS PLAY®. To be able to compare results, in the chosen cases the number of participants is similar. The content of the workshop was ignored as the observation was focused on the employee experience and participants' reactions that are illustrations of the engaging moments of the workshops.

PARTICIPANT OBSERVATION FROM THE FACILITATOR'S PERSPECTIVE

In the participant observation, 'the researcher takes a role in a particular collectivity and is able to learn the functioning of the role-playing system and, especially to recognize the aspects of the role which he takes in the collectivity' (Mayntz *et al.*, 1985). The researcher's presence and participation are controlled and written in the role of facilitators. In LSP method we have the egalitarian collectives imposed with "everybody builds, everybody shares" rule, there is no observer in the room and there are no non-active participants. The observations were direct with the descriptions of the participants reactions as an output. The researcher followed the scheme of Observational Research Design established by Jemielniak and Ciesielska (2018) and the way of describing the most visible reactions and give them a direct description: "they leaned forward, spoke faster, smiled more, were more animated" (Bowden and Ciesielska, 2014).

The role of facilitator has been described by Yokakul and Zawdie (2010) as a network facilitator and the focus of this role is on 'knowledge management and social embeddedness', building social capital and trust and the main objective of actions to engage participants in knowledge sharing and exchange, igniting interactive learning, unleashing creativity and react to the dynamics within the evolving social network. The authors continue: 'network facilitators or leaders play a crucial role in promoting the development of entrepreneurship and social capital in the community. They act as 'gatekeepers', acquiring knowledge from outside the community and making it accessible for members to use and engage in knowledge sharing and exchange'.

For the sake of this observation the neutrality or even 'recommended invisibility' of the facilitator was intended. In all the cases, limited instructions were given in a non-judgmental way. In the "The Inner Game of Tennis" (1974) Timothy Gallwey, the coach of tennis, elaborated on correlation between the amount of instructions and the performance of his trainees. The result is that the instructions should be limited to a necessary minimum. The instructions work as the 'outer judge', however, our 'inner instructor' as Gallwey named it influence the results to a higher extent and leaves a more visible imprint and make the learning process not only more effective but also more 'desired' by a trainee. This approach was dictated by the willingness to making the individual experience stronger by offering more space for personal reflections that should give the experience of the 'impact' of the participant and employee-centric workshop design which is one of the assumptions of the playful learning experience design.

Furthermore, taking several roles by the researchers allows us to determine the meaning of a given role in a self-reflective and intersubjective way (Jemielniak, 2014) which was visible in the process of neutrality in identifying the moments with the highest number of reactions that suggest the engagement during the session and post-event self-reflection of the author when listening to recording of the workshop conversations.

CASE SELECTION

Criteria for case selection were based on the two factors:

- Type and size of the learning event, and
- Method of work during the learning event.

The method of research was participant observation. The precision of observation was confirmed by:

- Taking field notes during the event.
- Taking photos of the brick models.
- Recording audio with most crucial conversations of the event.

No.	*Company*	*No. of Participants*	*Type of the Learning Event*	*Method of Work*	*No. of 'Engaging Moments' Identified*
A1	FMCG	80	Mass-scale	LEGO® SERIOUS PLAY® with table facilitators	12
A2	Pharmaceutical	80	Mass-scale	Projective techniques with table facilitators	12
B1	Classified I	17	Communication workshop	LEGO® SERIOUS PLAY®	8
B2	IT (BPO)	18	Communication workshop	Process visualization	5
C1	IT (software house)	13	Qualitative Research (Exploratory)	LEGO® SERIOUS PLAY®	6
C2	Classified II	13	Qualitative Research (Exploratory)	In-depth interviews	4

The fact of the detailed observation was linked to the demand of preparing a summary report to the Client after the workshop which is in line with pracademic approach in action research, especially in the area of creative research methods. Roos and Victor (2004) represent the viewpoint that when it comes to LSP the gathered materials can be analyzed to gain both: academic understanding and practical value in the same time.

OBJECTIVES

The objective of this paper are:

- To explore the sources of engagement during the learning events.
- To find commonalities between creative and non-creative workshop, the experience from the events that use LEGO® SERIOUS PLAY® method.
- To compare the traditional methods of learning with the method of LEGO® SERIOUS PLAY®.
- To identify the elements that can engender engagement beyond the playful experience.

After the literature review linked to LEGO® SERIOUS PLAY® prepared in Billund in October 2018 by the LSP Research group led by Kristen Klassen the main conclusion is that apart from a few attempts to support practice by theory (Primus and Sonnenburg, 2018) most of research appears in a kind-of post-factum perspective.

The recordings from the sessions have been thematically coded. The moments of the most vibrant discussions during the workshop have been identified and streamed into the themes according to coding manual (Saldana, 2009). Due to the scale of the research and its geographical limitations, the findings are limited and cannot be treated as a universal concept, however, even here the confirmation of Gauntlett's (2007) main findings can be exposed:

- "Creative and visual research, methods give people the opportunity to communicate different kinds of information". These findings will be discussed in the strong connection to organizational communication.
- "Research participants need reflective time to construct knowledge"—this concept will be checked in context of self-reflection and identity exploring.

These conclusions are also supported by Allegre (2013) key findings about the role of metaphors, imagination, story-making and micro-narrative building that helps to facilitate a better understanding of core strategic business challenges. Still, the limitations and the question of the replicability of the research in different groups in various regions remains valid as the learning experience of the workshop participants is a highly context- and culture-sensitive issue. The findings presented below reflect the structure of thematic codes after analysis of the most engaging observable moments during the workshops conducted by the author.

KEY FINDINGS: INTRODUCING THE EPIC(S) CONCEPTUAL FRAMEWORK

The characteristic of 'playful experience' was based on categorization of mechanisms or phenomena that generated observable activation and engaged participants in a visible way. In most of the cases the moment of engagement involved: generation of impactful metaphors, unexpected moments of joy like 'Look what I've built!' (B1 workshop) or 'I didn't know that the tower can explain the story of your life' (B1 workshop), a wave of laughing, vibrant discussion, louder voice, or the moment of meaningful silence, questions asked directly to the speakers or direct statements like "We definitely need to discuss it after the workshop" (C1 workshop) talking about the corporate values. The moments of engagement were indicated by the facilitator and then confirmed by the replay of voice recording. During A1 and A2 workshops the table facilitators were present to indicate and write down the findings from the discussion. Those two sessions were not recorded. In those cases, the identification of the engaging moments took place from the perspective of the leading facilitator and field notes of the table facilitators.

The list of elements that make the LSP event an engaging experience with the highest level of saturation is as follows:

	Thematic Coding
E	Emerging realities/emergent situations/unexpected discoveries
P	Playful atmosphere
I	Images of physical models (capturing the scenes by taking photos, 'snapshot-like' environment)
C	Creation or Co-Creation as a collective experience
(S)	Stories (narratives)

E – Emerging Realities and Relationships

Concept of emerging strategies has been developed by Mintzberg (1994). In the LSP method emergent realities and systems view of life play an important role. Leveraging this concept to Communication Studies, during the workshops formal organizational structures and are replaced by the emergent relationships. This is close to Coreen's CCO (Communication Constitutes Organisation) Principle that sees Communication as Organizing and states that:

> "Organization emerges in the interplay of the textual world of ideas and interpretations and the practical world of an object-oriented conversation" (Cooren *et al.*, 2006). Those relationships—the experience of co-creation and co-orientation through interactions, emerge in conversation. The LSP framework enforces non-hierarchical platform for conversation, as the managers and their voices are equally vital to the voices of other participants. The space for actual talking is by rule, distributed equally among the participants, so this is the value of contribution to the discussion that stands for the quality of conversation. In such an environment, the criteria of the final conclusions emerge as a collective contribution, without the formal ownership of the idea. Additionally, the contributors, neglecting their formal position in the hierarchy, may become 'significant others' (Babbie, 2003) or social influencers as the rules of the importance are based on the contribution instead of personal visibility or formal roles.

The significance of the emergent character of events in LSP was also mentioned by other facilitators of the method. They observe and study phenomena grouped under the term "emergence," which management theorist Jeffrey Goldstein calls "the arising of novel and coherent structures, patterns, and properties, during the process of self-organization in complex systems" (Eberle, 2014).

In this vision of communication as a set of planned activities, the conversation needs to be framed in a deliberate way that leads to tangible outputs and "attributes success to rational planning" (Knudsen and Lemmergaard, 2014). In the emergent communication, the reality can be controlled only to a certain extent (Pfeffer and Salancik, 1978). It is still purposeful and intentional, however, not planned. According to Mintzberg (2017), first step in building organizational engagement is "to establish a sense of urgency". Thanks to the scenarios like "Playing Emergence", that are incorporated into the LSP method, during the workshop, the urgent challenges are expressed by the participants of the workshops and with the clear structure of summarizing and categorizing from the facilitator's side, the sense of urgency is visible on the spot. In this rather chaotic Communicative Bazaar Environment some structures that can frame conversation around organizational changes may emerge (Mintzberg, 2017), creating communicative opportunities.

The conversation that happens around the table with the bricks fits to the definition of 'strategic serendipity' (Knudsen and Lemmergaard, 2014) as it creates unexpected communicative opportunities. The illustration can be noticed in C1 workshop when two senior leaders in this company unexpectedly started taking about their concept to create more value-based company and purpose-driven company and the rest of the participants were surprised with the level of declarations about future actions. To explain it in the system view of life: "the process of communication changes from a linear structure, where messages are sent to target audiences, to hubs of communication, where surplus audiences disturb or advance messages (Jenkins *et al.*, 2013). What is more, so-called 'complexity shocks' can also be engaging elements than influence the workshop experience. *Free*-thinking and therefore *playful* kind of environment (Gauntlett, 2007). This 'not thinking' situation can be illustrated by one of the most frequently recurring comment in the first part of the workshop—'I didn't know that I need to introduce myself using this tower' (A1, B1, C1 workshops).

What also build an engagement was no expectations as the language (thinking through building) and unpredictability of the reactions created kind of tension. The participants were waiting for the next task, they had to be oriented in the new method of expression and remembering and reacting to the stories of people around them. To explore more and not to lose orientation in the situation, they had to stand the tension of not being able to control the environment. As the reality is not controllable by any of the stakeholders and the individual interpretation create the shared vision and understanding, the ideas developed in this way can be promoted much easier among stakeholder and this sense of immediate influence (Knudsen and Lemmergaard, 2014) is also a source of engagement. Fairhurst and Putnam (2004) tell about being in an ongoing state of forming and the experience of participant is that they take part in the formative activity.

P – Playful Participation through Contribution

Play makes us more interesting and better adjusted in social circumstances; it is education for the public self (Eberle, 2014). Participatory character of the workshop helps getting orientation and understanding of the situation and in the next step contribute through insightful stories. According to Cross-Cultural Development Strategy Model Wujec (2010), Communication, together with approach and modus operandi are elements of "[e]laboration of strategy". She claims that an identification of the situation and mutual cultural education in order to know and accept national or organizational culture is not sufficient to reach the level of a thorough understanding of the problem as a 'facilitated collaboration' is needed to achieve effective results. In this definition, the 'effectiveness' is equal to the quality collectively elaborated solutions. The observation from the B1 workshop suggests that the engagement was driven by the fact that through playing they generated ideas to their problems, they participated in the discussion on the ideas of strategic issues and as mentioned later 'discovered the pain points linked to the corporate culture'.

The type of participation that emerges during the LSP events is 'participation by collaboration' as it "forms groups of primary stakeholders to participate in the discussion and analysis of predetermined objectives set by Participatory Communication". Basing on participants reaction, the author situates the type of participation as Active, Horizontal, and Multifaceted Participation, however, due to limitations imposed by the structure of experience recommended by the method and the fact that participants cannot freely decide about participation (Tufte and Mefalopulos, 2009), it cannot be seen as a participatory development communication (PDC).

According to Resnick (2017), concept of Lifelong Kindergarten the building blocks of an engaging experience are: Projects; Passion; Peers and Play. Discussing the participation scheme during the LSP events 'Peers' and 'Projects' and 'Play' are usually incorporated into the workshop design while 'Passion' evokes in the conversation. This was visible especially in A1 workshop as the discussion was around the project in the organization and the fact that could talk instantly about project-related issues with their peers also involved in the project was igniting the engagement.

I – Image that sticks in your head and… you can share it

Image-driven communication—Sharing workshop experience through images

During the workshop the abstract concepts transform into the models and then, into stories. "In the modernistic tradition, persuasion and image management are the essence of strategic communication (Hallahan *et al.*, 2007). In this image-capturable reality the sense is created by:

1. Reflecting ideas through physical models (visualizing the abstract concept).
2. The feeling of creating a physical thing.
3. Creating a physical evidence of the discussion.

Those elements help creating memories that are easy-to-be-capture artifacts of a participants' experience.

Furthermore, likelability together with shareability level of these 'experiential snapshots' is high. According to (Rzycka, 2010), one of the most effective method is Word of Mouth Marketing understood as employee-to-employee recommendation through talking about their experience and effects of the training. In the case of LSP the difficulties in disseminating information is neutralized by bottom up spreading information through the photos of LEGO models. During all the sessions in LSP methods, most of participants were taking the photos of the model. The engagement grows with the instant comments from Facebook friends asking about 'What are you doing at work?' (happened during A1, B1 and C1 session). The experience of being a creative creature leaves an imprint enough to take and share the photo and then spread a word.

The images generated during the workshops had triple functions:

- *Reason-to-Talk:* The participants generated an interesting content to post.
- *Reason-to-Believe:* The participants could use the name of the method to 'label their experience'. Especially in the up to 20 participant workshops, participants ask about the detailed name of the method.
- Reason-to-Share.

Instant discussion in social media about the session impacted the level of engagement of many participants in a positive way.

Brick Models as Culture Artefacts

Sanfuentes and Acuña (2014) call organizational identity "an unknown, forgotten, and confusing place" thanks to 3D model abstract concepts are visualized and thanks to story sharing sessions, more acknowledged by the workshop participants. The focal point is not 'the abstract concept' but the rich context of the experience, as only the employees that take part in the workshop can understand the key findings to the highest nuances.

In the LSP methods, the context is at organizational level, the closest understanding is at group level (with the other participants) and individuals create the artifacts of the culture—they build a brick model. This kind of reproducing of meaning can be summarized by Czarniawska's quote: "the employees reproduce the sense and artefacts of daily work" Czarniawska, 1992) and form the basis for their identity and ideology. Oliver and Roos (2007) named it even straightforward, saying that the participants generate representations of their identities.

The model is seen as important symbolic element that represents the working practice and through this connection the moment of sharing stories is also a moment of reflexive and personalized learning becoming a part of shared interpretation and this construct organizational knowledge (Nolan, 2010). Additionally, this process is of iterative character which also generates engaging experience as: "[t]he best learning experiences go through alternating phases of immersion and reflection" (Resnik, 2017).

C – Creation as a Collective Experience

Creative activity seems to give people a special buzz (Gauntlett, 2007). Self-exploration that leads to creative discovery in a social space. This creative constructive tension is needed as [t]he goal of social constructivism is to identify how individuals and groups of people understand their co-created perceptions of social reality (Denzin & Lincoln, 2005), which is fluid and constantly changing through the interactions, refers to the notion of 'contribution' than 'co-creation' or 'co-creativity'. Andersen (2010) claims that creation of shared identity is a necessity to stay competitive in current fast-paced environment. He mentions the need to generate 'creative' inputs and be developed as the boundary spanning. In most of the workshops, the creative discoveries generated needs for further discussion.

When creative discovery does not take place, Allegre (2013) links the experience of creative confidence to the reframing of the situation as "Strategic thinking and creativity both entail the reframing of an organization's challenges and the generation of new ideas through the combination, adaptation or improvement of existing, ideas, processes or products. According to Dann (2018), the concept of creative discovery, co-creation has been mentioned by many researchers as a source of engagement. This is confirmed by the present research that the moments of discoveries, especially in A1 workshop were easy to notice through the faster and louder discussions. According to Gauntlett (2007), "creativity is much more commonplace' and "may include everyday ideas, writing, making, management, self-presentation and even creative speech and thought". The inevitable observation is that the presence of bricks generates curiosity and "[cu]riosity, a form of anticipation, leads to discovery, a dividend of play (Eberle, 2014).

S – Stories

The last element, did not receive the level of saturation equal to the previous ones, although it is worth mentioning as it embraces: creativity, image creation and shared identity. According to Gauntlett (2007), "*the stories we tell about ourselves* are crucially important to identity" and we need to adopt the ability to create narratives about ourselves as "the most important stories are those we tell about ourselves". The LSP workshop opens space for sharing individual micro-stories as during the short workshop (up to 2:30 hours) each participant speaks at least four times, so this is the individual's perspective that is shared with the contribution-approach way to gain a shared understanding.

Micro-narrative as a form of communication are closely linked to the expression of identity or verbal conceptualization of values: "It would be quite impossible for human beings to codify and to put in order such a complex and chaotic experience as reality. In this sense, the art of storytelling should be considered like a key tool for identity building, either individual or collective. At the same time, it should be seen as a way for organizing and sharing collective knowledge and personal experiences (Venditti *et al.*, 2017).

The workshop may change the perception of the social reality as typically, people do not play at work, so the participants observe others in a totally new playful business reality. This playful space creates a perception of 'total social immersion' and he value of the individual is based on the contribution, especially when we apply 'Shared Model' technique. The differentiation between 'play' and 'serious play' is an ownership and control over the structure is in hands of a facilitator not the primary stakeholders.

FUTURE PERSPECTIVES AND PRACTICAL IMPLICATIONS

Communication is emerging as framework of conversation encourage to individual self-reflection and the rules imposed create expectations of contribution to the shared vision. The feeling of creation accelerates the conversation as maneuvering through the stories and metaphors helps reaching unconscious statement that go beyond the declarative level, enabling the design of 'organizational stories'. The universalism of the method enhances the ability to integrate this experience with a broader context of professional development. The method is easily combined with most of the leadership models or coaching frameworks such as Universal Integrated Framework—a pragmatic model adapted by Passmore a Low (2009) and by Wujec (2010), showing the alignment with general communication methods and feedback mechanisms or even more specialized concepts such as Creative Leadership or creative fluidity, which is mentioned a dual pathway to creativity (Nijstad *et al.*, 2010).

RESEARCH LIMITATIONS

The main limitation of this research is related to the participant observation method only and the workshops findings are related to one country only. The further investigation should involve application of methods that are more advanced technologically for example emotion recognition software to be able to support the findings from participant observation with quantitative evidences or more tangible evidences linked to the learning outcomes. Through the observation, without searching for the deeper insights, it is not possible to clarify the blurred line between the engagement generated as a result of satisfaction on a surface layer—the brick building experience that is demanded by the context (Botte *et al.*, 2016) and the engagement that is part of the learning experience generated through social experience and self-reflection.

REFERENCES

[1] Andersen, P.H., Kragh, H. and Lettl, C. (2013). Spanning organizational boundaries to manage creative processes: The case of the LEGO Group. *Industrial Marketing Management, 42*(1), 125–134.

[2] Ashton, D. and Giddings, S. (2018). At work in the toybox: Bedrooms, playgrounds and ideas of play in creative cultural work. *The International Journal of Entrepreneurship and Innovation, 19*(2), 81–89.

[3] Babbie, E. (2003). Badania społeczne w praktyce. Warsaw: PWN.

[4] Botte, B., Imbellone, A., Marinensi, G., Medaglia, C.M. (2016). The Ludic and Narrative Components in Game Based Learning: A Classroom Training Experience". *Proceedings of the European Conference on Information Management and Evaluation,* 82–88.

[5] Bowden A. and Ciesielska M. (2014)Accretion, Angst and Antidote: The Transition from Knowledge Worker to Manager in the UK Heritage Sector in an era of Austerity in: Jemielniak Dariusz (Ed.), 2014, The Laws of the Knowledge Workplace. Changing Roles and the Meaning of Work in Knowledge–Intensive Environments, Gower Publishing Limited, England, 11–24.

[6] Cooren, F., Taylor, J.R. and Van Every, E.J. (Eds.) (2006). Communication as organizing: Empirical and Theoretical Explorations In the dynamic of text and conversation, Mahwah, NJ: Lawrence Erlbaum Associates.

[7] Csikszentmihalyi, M. (1990). Flow: The Classic Work on How to Achieve Happiness, London, Rider.

[8] Czarniawska, B. (1992). Exploring complex organizations: A cultural perspective. Sage Publications.

[9] Dann, S. (2018). Facilitating co–creation experience in the classroom with Lego Serious Play. *Australasian Marketing Journal*, Available online, 8 June 2018

[10] Denzin, N.K. and Lincoln, Y.S. (2005). Introduction: The Discipline and Practice of Qualitative Research, in The Sage handbook of qualitative research, Thousand Oaks, CA, Sage Publications Ltd., pp. 1–32.

[11] Eberle, S.G. (2014). The Elements of Play Toward a Philosophy and a Definition of Play. *American Journal of Play*, 214–233.

[12] Fairhurst, G.T. and Putnam, L. (2004). Organizations as Discursive Constructions. *Communication Theory*, 14 (1), 5–26.

[13] Gauntlett, D. (2007). Creative Explorations: New Approaches to Identities and Audiences, Taylor and Francis Ltd, London, United Kingdom.

[14] Geithner, S. and Menzel, D. (2016). Effectiveness of Learning Through Experience and Reflection in a Project Management Simulation. *Simulation and Gaming 2016*, *47*(2), 228–256.

[15] Giddens, A. (1984). The Constitution of Society, Cambridge: Polity.

[16] Hallahan, K., Holtzhausen, D., Ruler van, B., Vercic, D. and Sriramesh, K. (2007). Defining Strategic Communication. *International Journal of Strategic Communication 1*(1), 3–35.

[17] Hinthorne, L.L. and Schneider, K. (2012). Playing with Purpose: Using Serious Play to Enhance Participatory Development Communication in Research. *International Journal of Communication*, *6*, 2801–2824.

[18] Huizinga, J. (1995). "Homo Ludens: A Study of the Play-Element in Culture", Taylor and Francis.

[19] Jemielniak, D. and Ciesielska, M. (Eds.) (2018), Qualitative Methodologies in Organization Studies Volume II: Methods and Possibilities, Palgrave Macmillan.

[20] Jemielniak, D. (Ed.) (2014). The Laws of the Knowledge Workplace. Changing Roles and the Meaning of Work in Knowledge-Intensive Environments, Gower Publishing Limited, England.

[21] Jenkins, H., Ford, S. and Green, J. (2013). Spreadable Media: Creating Value and Meaning in a Networked Culture, New York: New York University Press.

[22] Knudsen, H. and Lemmergaard, J. (2014). Strategic serendipity: How one organization planned for and took advantage of unexpected communicative opportunities. *Culture and Organization, 20*(5), 392–409.

[23] Mayntz, R., Holm, K. and Hübner, P. (1985). Wprowadzenie do metod socjologii empirycznej Warsaw: PWN.

[24] Mintzberg, H. (2017). Transformation from the top? How about engagement on the ground?, available at: http://www.mintzberg.org/blog/transformation-from-the-top-how-about-engagement-on-the-ground, accessed: 20.062019, 1:51 p.m. CET.

[25] Nijstad, B.A., De, Dreu, C.K.W., Rietzschel, E.F. and Baas, M. (2010). The Dual Pathway to Creativity Model: Creative Ideation as a Function of Flexibility and Persistence. *European Review of Social Psychology*, *21*(1), 34–77.

[26] Nolan, S. (2010). Physical metaphorical modelling with LEGO as a technology for collaborative personalised learning. In Technology-Supported Environments for Personalized Learning: Methods and Case Studies, 364–385, IGI Global.

[27] Oliver, D. and Roos, J. (2007). Beyond Text: Constructing Organizational Identity Multimodally, *British Journal of Management*, 18, 342–358.

[28] Passmore, J. and Low, H. (2009). Cross-cultural and diversity coaching. In: Passmore, J. (Ed) Diversity in Coaching. London – Philadelphia: Kogan Page.

[29] Pfeffer, J. and Salancik, G. (1978). The External Control of Organizations a Resource Dependence Perspective. Harper and Row, New York.

[30] Primus, D.J. and Sonnenburg, S. (2018). Flow Experience in Design Thinking and Practical Synergies with Lego Serious Play. *Creativity Research Journal*, *30*(1),104–112.

[31] Rasmussen, R. (2006). When You Build in the World, You Build in Your Mind. *Design Management Review* 2006, *17*(3), 56–63.

[32] Resnick, M. (2017). Lifelong Kindergarten. Cultivating Creativity through Projects, Passion, Peer, and Play, The MIT Press, Cambridge, Massachusetts.

[33] Rzycka, O. (2010). Manager, Coaching, Coaching-based management—coach's insights (subjective approach), 176–182 in Czarkowska Lidia D. (Ed.), Coaching as a method of Developing Human Potential, Academic and Professional Press by Kozminski University, Warsaw.

[34] Sanfuentes, M. and Acuña, E. (2014). The Castaways of Life': A study of organizational remembering within the context of a Chilean Geriatric Hospital. *Culture and Organization*, 20*(4)*,288–306.

[35] Sutton-Smith, B. (1997). The Ambiguity of Play, Harvard University Press.

[36] Tufte, T. and Mefalopulos, P. (2009). Participatory Communication: A Practical Guide. World Bank Publications, The World Bank, number 5940.

[37] Venditti, S., Piredda, F. and Mattana, W. (2017). Micronarratives as the form of contemporary communication. *The Design Journal*, *20*(1), 273–S282.

[38] Włodarski, W. (2010). Admit model – management and influence domain, in Czarkowska Lidia D. (Ed.), Coaching as a method of Developing Human Potential, Academic and Professional Press by Kozminski University, Warsaw, 64–81.

[39] Wujec, B. (2010). Cross-cultural Coaching in Czarkowska Lidia D. (Ed.), 2010, Coaching as a method of Developing Human Potential, Academic and Professional Press by Kozminski University, Warsaw, 162–175.

Developing Communication Intelligence among Future Managers and its Predictive Value for Effective Corporate Performance

Reeta Raina
FORE School of Management, New Delhi
E-mail: rraina@fsm.ac.in

ABSTRACT: The new definition of human intelligence by Gardner that goes beyond the realms of psychology includes musical, interpersonal, spatial-visual, and linguistic intelligence, etc. that human beings are gifted with. However, in this article, it is proposed if Communication Intelligence could be an added dimension of human intelligence. Although different facets of Communication intelligence is already a part of Gardner's multiple intelligences for example verbal intelligence; Intra and Interpersonal communication and nonverbal communication but these and many other facets of Communication can be brought together under one umbrella that could be labeled as Communication Intelligence.

Keywords: Communication, Corporate Performance, Future Managers, Intelligence, Psychologist.

INTRODUCTION

The new interpretation of intelligence by Howard Gardner-psychologist at Harvard goes beyond the traditional definition of intelligence by psychologists that limit the understanding of the same. According to Gardner, people are endowed with varied kinds of intelligence that includes musical, interpersonal, spatial-visual, and linguistic intelligences. He theorizes that psychometric definition of intelligence limits it to mere intellectual capacity while as man possesses range of abilities and talents. The theory of multiple intelligence as proposed by Gardner manifests eight human intelligences or abilities (Cherry, 2019). These are:

- **Musicality** (music-al-ity) is "sensitivity to, knowledge of, or talent for music" or "the quality or state of being musical".
- **Spatial intelligence** is an area in the theory of multiple intelligences that deals with spatial judgment and the ability to visualize with the mind's eye.

- **Verbal intelligence** is the ability to understand and reason using concepts framed in words. More broadly, it is linked to problem solving, abstract reasoning, and working memory.
- **Logical-mathematical:** This area has to do with logic, abstractions, reasoning, numbers and critical thinking.
- **Bodily-kinesthetic:** The core elements of the bodily-kinesthetic intelligence are control of one's bodily motions and the capacity to handle objects skillfully. [6] Gardner elaborates to say that this also includes a sense of timing, a clear sense of the goal of a physical action, along with the ability to train responses.
- **Interpersonal:** In theory, individuals who have high interpersonal intelligence are characterized by their sensitivity to others' moods, feelings, temperaments, motivations, and their ability to cooperate to work as part of a group.
- **Intrapersonal:** This area has to do with introspective and self-reflective capacities. This refers to having a deep understanding of the self; what one's strengths or weaknesses are, what makes one unique, being able to predict one's own reactions or emotions.
- **Naturalistic:** This area has to do with nurturing and relating information to one's natural surroundings.
- **Existential:** Gardner did not want to commit to a spiritual intelligence, but suggested that an "existential" intelligence may be a useful construct.

Although, there has been lot of criticism both from the psychologists and academicians claiming that Gardener's expanded list of intelligence do not fall under the definition of human intelligence, rather these can be categorized as abilities, talents, or personality traits. Further, they dispute that there are no empirical evidences to support his theory. Irrespective of the fact that Gardner's theory of multiple intelligence has been criticized for short of empirical validation, but nevertheless, the educators especially many teachers have adopted multiple intelligences in their teaching philosophies and have worked to integrate Gardner's theory into the classroom. In fact, the theory is supposed to be enjoying considerable popularity with educators.

DIFFERENT FACETS OF COMMUNICATION

Gardner has also hinted at including few more intelligences to the list that represents the abilities and competencies of human beings, though these have not been as yet concretized. However, in pursuance to Gardner's current chain of thoughts, it can be recommended that Communication Intelligence could be seen as another dimension of human intelligence. Although, different facets of Communication intelligence are already a part of Gardner's multiple intelligences for example verbal intelligence; intra and Interpersonal communication and nonverbal communication but these and many other facets of Communication can be brought together under one umbrella that could be labelled as Communication Intelligence.

Communication is a wide subject that is constituted of set of skills like reading, speaking, writing and listening and at the other end of the continuum is its behavioral/psychological aspects of communication. And to date, communication is studied only in parts and not as an integrated subject that has a critical importance and application both in one's personal and professional life. A person who is good at speaking or writing skills may not necessarily be good at interpersonal skills. Similarly, a corporate who is given training in interpersonal communication may be lacking in self- awareness. He may not be aware of the perceptual errors he commits or he suffers from which can become a great hindrance in developing harmonious interpersonal relationship.

Poor Communication and its Impact

A glimpse into the Communication syllabus across World business schools especially in India indicates that teaching of Communication competency to our future managers suffers of tokenism. Most of the academicians and the corporate are of the view that Communication is a soft skill. Accordingly, the focus of the course in Communication will be majorly on honing their public speaking/writing/critical skills or teaching them interpersonal or intercultural communication. They fail to understand that these prospective managers will be in need of the combination of all these skills and knowledge together to manage people both at workplace or in their personal life. It is said that buildings or machines do not give trouble but it is people who are either themselves a problem or create one for others. Research suggests that many of the problems that occur in an organization may be attributed to failure of communication. Poor communication alone is a major contributor for most business and industrial organizations running at less than 12% efficiency. According to Hergie (2000) and Argenti (1998) if employees are not given adequate information nor allowed to contribute to the solution of problems, they may revert to being the cause of them, resulting in increased absenteeism, lower productivity, and grievances and so on. Research reveals that Communication is a glue that binds people together.

The contemporary scenario of the corporate Olympiad is fiercely competitive with uncertainties and ambiguities in the business world. The globalization has further added challenges to the process of communication. New managerial work involves communication and collaboration across functions, across divisions, and across companies and having the knowledge, skills, and sensitivity to mobilize people and motivate them to do their best (Kanter, 1998). Achieving success in today's workplace is closely tied to the ability of employees and managers to communicate effectively with each other and with people outside the organization. A close interaction between people from different cultures exposes their inadequacy and the inability to communicate with one another. In fact, an academic research prior to globalization indicate that people even from within the same culture faced problems in communication. Bernard Shaw did not make a comment in vain that "The greatest problem with communication is the illusion that it has been accomplished".

Lack of Understanding/Implementation of Communication by Leaders/Managers

Despite the importance of communication to successful organizational change or overcome crisis, the apex leadership has by and large failed in gauging the potential of communication in managing people centric issues as is evident from the findings of varied studies. Communication was till recently considered as a soft skill which has no impact on organizations. Even while hiring individual communication skills never was a major criterion for hiring. However, even if today, communication has been endorsed as a critical skill both by the academicians as well as practitioners, but studies unravel that the leaders/managers fail when it comes to implementing communication in its true spirit. They perhaps deep down are convinced that communication does not impact profits of the company. They, therefore, focus more on the nitty-gritty of business and are more task-focused than people-focused. They perhaps find communication conceptions like building of relationships, seeking of employees' opinions especially from people at the bottom of the pyramid, sharing of critical and timely information with them, and showing empathy as having only cosmetic value as compared to other organizational functions. The major impetus for leaders'/managers apathetic attitude towards communication could be attributed to their lack of training/understanding of the subject and its application in running of an organization. Secondly, it could be attributed to their lack of balance between task-focus and people-focus resulting in complete failure of the systems or limited success at every level.

Holistic Approach to Teaching of Communication

In the present diverse and challenging context, it is important to develop Communication Intelligence among our students who are to take up varied roles professionally in future. The word communication intelligence is to develop an intelligence that enables students/managers/leaders to use a wider range of communication tools significantly and contribute towards streamlining work communication. Communication Intelligence should be inclusive of communication skills like listening, writing and public skills besides it should develop the proficiency among students to understand the psychology of the recipient of information/message as well as be aware of the "context" in which the message is delivered. This may include the current political and social environment, or the broader culture for instance, the corporate culture or the national culture. Thus, Communication should be taught in its entirety and ensure that it sticks to the memory of the learners.

Shifting of Focus on Communication Intelligence

An initiative for developing Communication Intelligence requires a shift in focus, on having a radical rethink of 'business as usual' education is required so that our students are exposed to the perils of communication catastrophe as it is through education that the individuals and the future decision makers are empowered to face the complex and key challenges of the 21st century, including enabling change and collectively building effective organizations. Besides, it is suggested that children should be exposed to the communication education even before they start their school so that they become future agents of change (Davis, 2009; Scott *et al.*, 2012). It is imperative for all students to experience and be familiar with the work place culture long before they leave school (Torii, 2018). Post COVID has accelerated the transformation of jobs. Consequently, children need to be imparted digital and transferable skills, like collaboration, problem solving and communication, that future generation will need for successful careers. Beside the core skills of literacy and numeracy. Governments and educationists in India need to look into it to ensure smooth transformation.

REFERENCES

[1] Argenti, P.A. (1998). Strategic employee communications. *Human Resource Management, 37*(3–4), 199–206.

[2] Cherry, K. (2019). *Gardner's Theory of Multiple Intelligences.* Retrieved on December 05, 2020 from https://www.verywellmind.com/gardners-theory-of-multiple-intelligences-2795161.

[3] Davis, J. (2009). Revealing the research 'hole' of early childhood education for sustainability: a preliminary survey of the literature. *Environmental Education Research, 15*(2), 227–241.

[4] Hargie, O., Tourish, D. and Wilson, N. (2002). Communication audits and the effects of increased information: A follow-up study. *Journal of Business Communication, 39*, 414–437.

[5] Kanter, R.M. (1989b). The new managerial work. *The Harvard Business Review* 67, 85–92.

[6] Scott, G., Tilbury, D., Leith, S. and Deane, E. (2012). Turnaround leadership for sustainability in higher education: Final report. *Sydney and Canberra, Australia: University of Western Sydney and Australian National University, Sustainable Futures Leadership Academy.*

[7] Torii, K. (2018). Why school kids need more exposure to the world of work. Retrieved on December 06, 2020 from https://theconversation.com/why-school-kids-need-more-exposure-to-the-world-of-work-100590

Education Orientation and Store Atmospherics: An Empirical Study

Pooja Pirodiya[1], Rajeev K. Shukla[2] and Ajit Upadhyaya[3]

[1]Devi Ahilya Vishwavidyalaya, Indore, Madhya Pradesh

[2]Shri Vaishnav School of Management,
Shri Vaishnav Vidyapeeth Vishwavidyalaya, Indore, Madhya Pradesh

[3]Prestige Institute of Management and Research, Indore, Madhya Pradesh

E-mail: [1]poojapirodia@gmail.com; [2]directorsvsm@svvv.edu.in; [3]ajiteverywhere@gmail.com

ABSTRACT: Store atmosphere has the ability to make costumers feel pleasant, enjoy shopping and consequently make shopping a recreational activity. Elements of store atmospherics can be used as differentiating factors for success and failure of retailers in marketplace, which is characterized by intensive competition. It not only affects consumers cognitively but also emotionally. Atmospherics can be defined as an effort to design buying environments that produce certain emotional effect in the customer to increase purchase probability. In the present study, the effect of education on customers' perception towards factors of store atmospherics was analyzed. Findings of the study revealed education-wise significant difference towards ambience psyche, and peripheral motives related to store atmospherics. However, no significant difference was observed for design psyche of store atmospherics. The study further revealed that with advancement in educational qualification the dimensions of store atmospherics have received more importance by the customers. The higher educated group of respondents have rated relatively higher than lower education group of respondents to the dimensions of store atmospherics.

Keywords: ANOVA, Education, e-WOM, Retail Stores, Store Atmospherics.

INTRODUCTION

Retailing is an integral part of today's society. People considerably depend on retail stores to lead a comfortable life. It influences lives and enhances lifestyle. The exemplar shift among modern consumer socioeconomic, demographic and geographical proportions are driving a traditional small-scale retail outlet into an organized retail format focused to meet the evolving needs and likes of discerning consumers. Ever evolving lifestyle, higher rate of literacy, increasing number of working women, excessive urbanization, high rate of media penetration, growing young population, tendency to 'spend now' and favorable demographic patterns act as the key in the recent organized retail sector in India.

Store atmosphere can potentially make customers feel happy, enjoy shopping experience and consequently make shopping a recreational activity. It not only affects consumers cognitively but also emotionally. Term atmospherics was coined as quality of surrounding space; highlighting importance of place where the product is bought or consumed. Kotler (1974) described the surroundings in sensory terms and proposed four sensory dimensions: Visual dimensions- color, brightness, size and shape; Aural dimensions- volume, pitch, tempo; Olfactory dimensions- scent and freshness; and Tactile dimensions - softness, smoothness and temperature.

Efforts of retailers have shifted towards creating a happy, enjoyable experience for the shoppers from sole focus on product breadth, depth and quality. Experience within the store is paramount to the overall retail customer shopping experience. Retailers must always put the users first when rethinking an in-store experience. It simply not about designing aesthetically pleasing elements or integrating lux materials as a way to impress. A memorable retail experience is absolutely about how all components including sales associates, signage, and merchandise displays etc., work together to inspire, empower and benefit the customer. A store thus, becomes space with opportunities to stand apart from competitors. Retailers need to figure out way to keep their stores in the minds of consumers in an exceptionally favorable way. By enhancing the in-store atmosphere, a store may create an efficient consumption situation to induce the immediate buying behavior of consumers. Thus, growing body of knowledge towards this stream shows that by delivering better experiences to customers, retailers can exploit happy customers to feel emotionally attached and bonded with the retail store.

REVIEW OF LITERATURE

Donovan and Rossiter (1982) applied the Mehrabian-Russell environment psychology model in retail setting or store atmosphere with three basic emotional states: Pleasure, Arousal, Dominance (PAD). The study established a relationship between emotional state induced in a retail environment and statements of behavioral intentions in that environment. The result proposed that correct emotional combination of pleasantness and arousal created by store atmosphere can stimulate shopping behavior within the store.

Baker *et al.* (2002) found that the physical environment is critical in-service marketing mix and studied the relationship between store environment cues on consumer perceptions of store choice decision criteria such as perceived merchandise value and shopping experience costs. The study also tried to examine the mediating role of store choice criteria on the relationship between store atmospherics and store patronage intentions. Donovan *et al.* (1994) extended his earlier study with broader sample of shoppers during the shopping experience and recorded the effect of emotions on actual shopping behavior. The findings showed the effect of emotional factors of pleasure and arousal to cognitive factors such as variety and quality of merchandise, price specializing and value for money.

More specifically, the pleasure induced by store atmosphere seems to have strong aspect to influence customers spending extra time in the stores and spend more money than intended. Customers are considered to be critical agents for the recommendation of various stores and its products as they are the king for customer experience and e-WOM (electronic word of mouth) through social media usage. As self-image becomes congruent with the digital store image, the customers tend become loyal (Clottey *et al.*, 2008). Das *et al.* (2019) highlighted the hedonic aspect of happiness with the quality of life and pointed out that "nice feelings" is affected by price, quality, and reputation.

Bitner (1992) in a study developed the servicescape concept for understanding the relationships between the physical environment and the people (i.e., service providers and customers). The study emphasizes on the impact of physical environment on human beings. Servicescape consists of three dimensions: 1) ambient conditions; 2) spatial layout and functionality; and 3) signs, symbols, and artifacts.

OBJECTIVE OF THE STUDY

To analyze the effect of education on factors of store atmospherics for retail stores.

HYPOTHESES

$H_{0(1)}$: There is no significant difference in retail stores atmospherics factors on account of education.

$H_{0(1.1)}$:There is no significant difference towards Ambience Psyche of retail stores on account of education.

$H_{0(1.2)}$:There is no significant difference towards Design Psyche of retail stores on account of education.

$H_{0(1.3)}$:There is no significant difference towards Peripheral Motives associated with retail stores on account of education.

RESEARCH METHOD

- *Research Type:* Descriptive type of research based on survey design was used for the study.
- *The Sample:* Purposive sampling method was used for the study. Sample size was 300 and area of sampling were Indore and Mumbai Cities in India. Customers of retail stores were sampling unit for collection of data.

- *Data Collection:* Secondary sources were referred for conceptual understanding of store atmospherics of retail stores. Primary data was collected with the help of Store Atmospherics scale. The scale consists of thirty-six statements, measured on five-point Likert scale ranging from Strongly Agree (5) to Strongly Disagree (1).
- *Tools for Data Analysis:* One-way Analysis of Variance (ANOVA) was used for data analysis.

RESULTS AND DISCUSSION

Education Profiling of Respondents

The majority of the respondents who participated in the survey were post graduates accounting for 57 per cent of the sample size. 33 per cent of the respondents were graduates whereas 6 per cent were undergraduates and 4 per cent did not belong to any of these categories.

Table 1: Education Profile of Respondents

Undergraduate	19	6.33
Graduate	97	32.33
Post Graduate	172	57.33
Others	12	4.00
Total	**300**	**100**

Three dimensions of store atmospherics viz. Ambience psyche, Design psyche, and Peripheral motives of scale were used for data collection that comprises of in total 36 statements. In which, Ambience Psyche factor included aroma and fragrance theme of stores, lighting, music, cleanliness and hygiene, ambient temperature and air quality inside the stores. Ambience elements of store atmospherics can be used for designing stores in such a way that it could differentially communicate the brand personality and image of the retail stores. Design of lighting can be attributed to development of store theme. It can use different colors as well as controlled intensity of lighting in the range of dim or bright lighting as per pre decided store theme. Similarly, freshness and fragrances can be uniquely selected for the stores. Music themes such as classical, modern, and trendy or specific tune of instrumentals can be decided for the stores. Basic amenities can also be worked out to maintain cleanliness and hygienic conditions, appropriate ambient temperature, and air quality inside the stores.

Design psyche factor was related to store design, layout, store interior and functionality, signage and merchandizing. Store design provides base for experimenting with ambience elements. So, it should get more focus initially from retailers as strategic consideration. Store design can also facilitate proper layout of signage, merchandizing, and hassle-free approach for shopping in the store.

Peripheral motives related to window displays, product displays, trials and demo facility, store approach, external signs, neatly dressed and well- behaved sales persons. Peripheral motives of customers can be used as clues for promoting in-store marketing by attractive window dressing, product displays and in-store promotion by sales persons.

Table 2: Education-wise Mean and Standard Deviation Towards Factors Considered for Store Atmospherics

		Mean	*Std. Deviation*
Ambience Psyche	UG	1.5992	.44380
	Graduate	2.0262	.80539
	PG	2.1682	.86041
	Others	2.0449	.63471
	Total	**2.0813**	**.82370**
Design Psyche	UG	1.4306	.37094
	Graduate	1.7713	.75584
	PG	1.9218	.92878
	Others	1.7955	.57119
	Total	**1.8370**	**.84448**
Peripheral Motives	UG	1.4402	.33507
	Graduate	1.8407	.76219
	PG	2.0005	.89004
	Others	1.9545	.83993
	Total	**1.9115**	**.83226**

Findings of the study revealed education-wise significant difference towards ambience psyche, and peripheral motives related to store atmospherics. No significant difference observed for design psyche of store atmospherics (Table 3). So, hypotheses $H_{0(1.1)}$, and $H_{0(1.3)}$ were rejected. However, hypothesis $H_{0(1.3)}$ was not rejected.

Graduate and Post Graduate respondents have given significantly higher importance to ambience psyche and peripheral motive related attributes of store atmospheric than

Under Graduate respondents. It was also observed that Graduate and Post Graduate respondents have given relatively more importance to design psyche related attributes of retail stores than Under Graduate respondents (Table 2).

Table 3: Education-wise ANOVA towards Factors Considered for Store Atmospherics

ANOVA						
		Sum of Squares	*df*	*Mean Square*	*F*	*Sig.*
Ambience Psyche	Between Groups	6.025	3	2.008	3.020	.030
	Within Groups	196.840	296	.665		
	Total	202.864	299			
Design Psyche	Between Groups	4.813	3	1.604	2.278	.080
	Within Groups	208.420	296	.704		
	Total	**213.233**	**299**			
Peripheral Motives	Between Groups	6.093	3	2.031	2.991	.031
	Within Groups	201.013	296	.679		
	Total	**207.106**	**299**			

DISCUSSION

An in-store environment constitutes the man-made physical surroundings within the store in contrast to the social or natural environment. The atmosphere of a retail store space reflects the overall vibe and ambience that plays around the store. In the present study, three factors viz., ambience, design, and peripheral motives towards stores have been analyzed from education orientation of respondents. Under Graduate, Graduate, and Post Graduate qualification of respondents were considered three levels of education. Previous researchers have identified and highlighted the effectiveness of store atmospheric elements on in-store consumer psychology. Vanrompay *et al.* (2012) have observed that the cognitive, physiological, and affective responses towards elements of store atmospherics were not separate but interdependent and ultimately influenced the customer response in store atmospheric conditions.

Findings of the present study did not support the findings of Rhee and Bell (2002) that demographics do not appear to have a strong effect on store mobility, as education-wise significant difference observed towards ambience psyche and peripheral motives related attributes of store atmospherics. Similarly, Laroche *et al.* (2000) have also identified various differences in the manner in which men and women act in a retail store when they search for a gift. Various elements of store atmospherics such as visual, aural, olfactory, and tactile can be effectively used in marketing to influence consumer behavior for attention creation, affect creation, and message creation (Kotler, 1973; Vanrompay *et al.*, 2012). Thus, the factors of store atmospherics should get due consideration and should be utilized as a tool for creating desired image of the store.

CONCLUSION

Effect of education on customers perception towards store atmospherics was analyzed in the present study. Findings of the study revealed education-wise significant difference towards ambience psyche, and peripheral motives related to store atmospherics. No significant difference observed for design psyche of store atmospherics. The study further revealed that Graduate and Post Graduate respondents have given significantly higher importance to ambience psyche and peripheral motive related attributes of store atmospheric than Under Graduate respondents. Irrespective of education, design psyche related attributes of store atmospherics were perceived important for store patronage by the customers. The study further revealed that with advancement in educational qualification the dimensions of store atmospherics have received more importance by the customers. The higher educated group of respondents have rated relatively higher than lower education group of respondents to the dimensions of store atmospherics.

IMPLICATIONS

Store atmosphere act as a pivotal contributor to the customer experience, which is arguably one of the most significant elements of the retail business today. As a result, businesses need to seek strategies that will differentiate their brand from the competitors, and one way to do it is by providing pleasant and engaging shopping ambience. Findings of this study validate the notion that store atmospherics is interplay of a number of attributes. For providing superior store atmospherics, one should take an integrated view of the situations and work on multi-pronged strategies.

REFERENCES

[1] Baker, J., Parasuraman, A., Grewal, D. and Glenn B. (2002). The influence of multiple store environment cues on perceived merchandise value and patronage intentions. *Journal of Marketing, 66*(2), 120–41.

[2] Bitner, M.J. (1992). Servicescapes: The impact of physical surroundings on customers and employees". *Journal of Marketing, 56*, 57–71.

[3] Clottey, T., Collier, D. and Stodnick, M. (2008). Drivers of customer loyalty in a retail store environment. *Journal of Service Science, 1,* 35–48.

[4] Das, S., Nayyar, A. and Singh, I. (2019). An assessment of forerunners for customer loyalty in the selected financial sector by SEM approach toward their effect on business. *Date Technology Applications, 53,* 546–561.

[5] Donovan, R. and John, R. (1982). Store atmosphere: An environmental psychology approach, *Journal of Retailing, 58* (Spring), 34–57.

[6] Donovan, R.J., Rossiter, J.R., Marcoolyn, G. and Nesdale, A. (1994). Store atmosphere and purchasing behaviour, *Journal of Retailing, 70*(3), 284–293.

[7] Kotler, P. (1973). Atmosphere as a Marketing Tool. *Journal of Retailing, 49* (Winter), 48–64.

[8] Laroche, M., Saad, G., Cleveland, M. and Browne, E. (2000). Gender differences in information search strategies for A christmas gift. *Journal of Consumer Marketing, 17*(6), 500-524.

[9] Rhee, H. and Bell, D.R. (2002). The inter-store mobility of supermarket shoppers. *Journal of Retailing, 78*(2), 225–237.

[10] Schmitt, B. (2011). Experiential marketing: concepts, frameworks and consumer insights, *Foundations and Trends in Marketing, 5*(2), 55–112.

[11] Vanrompay, T.J., Tanja-Dijkstra, K., Verhoeven, J.W. and Vanes, A.F. (2012). On store design and consumer motivation: Spatial control and arousal in the retail context. *Environment and Behavior, 44*, 800–820.

Enhancement of Partially Burned Writing Through Hyperspectral Imaging (VSC-6000)

Harendra Kumar Bamburde[1] and M.P. Goutam[2]
[1]Government Institute of Forensic Science, Nagpur, Maharashtra
[2]Shri Vaishnav Institute of Forensic Science,
Shri Vaishnav Vidyapeeth Vishawavidyalaya, Indore, Madhya Pradesh
E-mail: [1]hkcb7fodex@gmail.com; [2]mpgoutam@gmail.com

ABSTRACT: Questioned documents are those documents whose authenticity is in dispute. Occasionally to conceal criminal activities documents are damaged or destroyed by fire. A document that has become black, darken, dirty and fragile due to burning or exposure to excessive heat is generally classified as charred document. The documents those intentionally destroyed and/or burnt accidentally are referred to the forensic laboratories for restoration and decipherment of writings on them. The burned or partially burnt documents are mainly concern with ransoms, forgery, fraud, and other white-collar offences. The burning of the documents is the most common phenomenon used by the criminals in order to destroy the evidences. In the present study Video Spectral Comparator (VSC) is used for the decipherment of writings on partially burned documents using the effect of floodlight and white spot and found that these are the most prominent lights for decipherment of writings on the partially burned documents.

Keywords: Charred Documents, Handwritings Enhancement, Hyperspectral Imaging, Partially Burnt Document, Video Spectral Comparator.

INTRODUCTION

Crime involving documents encompasses from fraud and anonymous letters to robbery, threatening, murder and suicide. During the investigations of white-collar crimes, the handwritings and signatures play significant role and are valuable kinds of evidences. Charred/partially burnt document are also obtained in cases of accidental fire and/or intentional fire, insurance and financial fraud and in cheating cases. Documents related to such cases are commonly referred to the forensic document examiners for the restoration and decipherment of writings. Due to effect of heat during burning, documents become fragile, lost their original shape, broke down into small fragments and the edges are also get deformed (Tidke *et al.*, 2019).

Therefore, examination of charred or partially burnt documents is a challenge to the document examiners. Various conventional and instrumental methods are used to examine documents such as photographic method (Ahluwalia, 2020), optical examination (Santacroce, 1999) and projectina Inspec-8 (Sharma *et al.*, 2020). Advances in document examination by video spectral comparator has also been described in detailed (Mokrzycki 1999). A new method was suggested for decipherment of charred documents (Taylor and Walls, 1941). VSC imaging found to be a useful tool for the examination of ink, hidden security features and alterations in documents. The enhancements of handwriting on selected charred document with VSC using floodlight and the white beam have been reported (Moorthy, 2016). The present study is focused on the examination of partially/charred documents under floodlight and spotlight by adjusting the wavelengths.

MATERIAL AND METHODOLOGY

Partially burned documents with the different colored inks on same type of papers were selected for the present study. Document examined under Visual Spectral Comparator VSC–6000 Foster & Freeman Co Ltd. England for decipherment of writing text. The 16 written documents with 16 different writing instruments were partially burnt over the flame in order to create a scenario of accidental or deliberate fire until the writings became invisible. These samples were marked here as D1 to D16 and were initially viewed under a hand magnifier for locating the unaffected or remaining writings. Then these documents examined using VSC 6000 selecting floodlight beam and white spot beam setting. Examined by Sidelight L, side light R, Floodlight, long-pass and UV light.

Table 1: Selection of Writing Materials Used in the Obliterated Handwriting

Writing Instrument							
Sl. No.	*Color*	*Trade Name*	*Nature*	*Sl. No.*	*Colour*	*Trade Name*	*Nature*
1.	Blue	Reynolds	Ball Ink	9.	Brown	Camlin	Sketch Ink
2.	Green	Montex	Gel	10.	Blue	Camlin	Gel Ink
3.	Brown	Cello	Sketch ink	11.	Brown	Camlin	Marker Ink
4.	Pink	Reynolds	Sketch Ink	12.	Green	Camlin	Gel Ink
5.	Black	Montex	Gel Ink	13.	Blue	Luxor	Gel Ink
6.	Blue	FlairPop	Ball Ink	14.	Red	Luxor	Gel Ink
7.	Blue	Reynolds	Gel Ink	15.	Black	Luxor	Sketch Ink
8.	brown	Flair Matrix	Ball ink	16.	Blue	Luxor	Gel Ink

Observations and Results

1a to 16a – photographs of partially burned documents
1b to 16b – photographs after visualization of writing

Sample-1 **Sample-2**

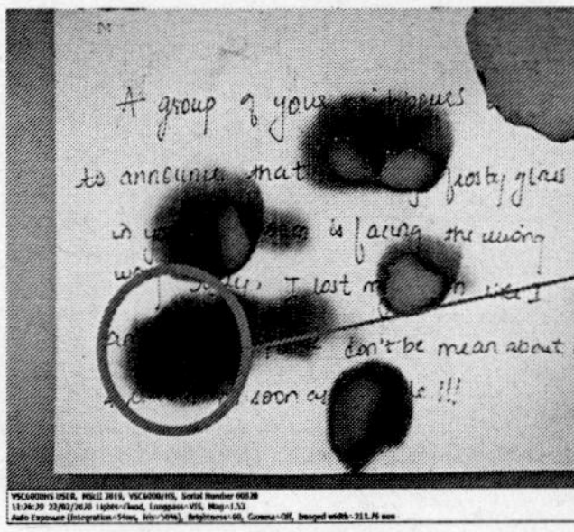

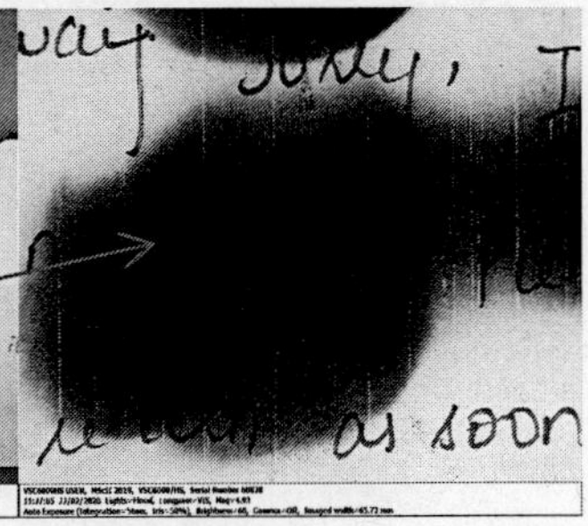

1A 1B 2A2B

Sample-3 **Sample-4**

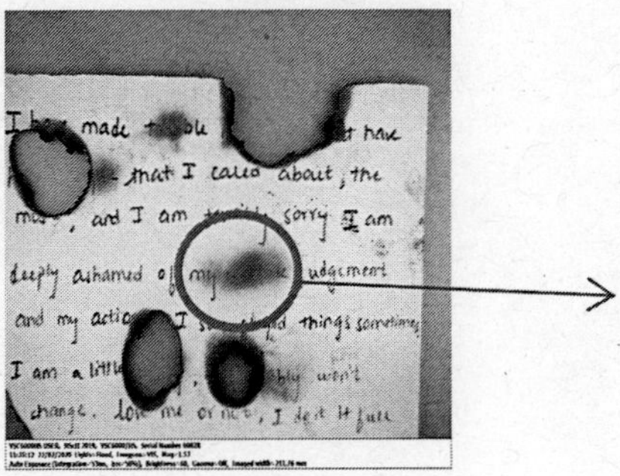

3A 3B 4A 4B

Sample-5 **Sample-6**

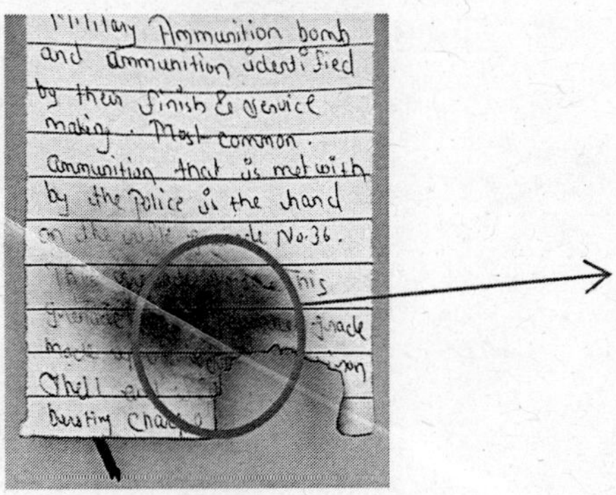

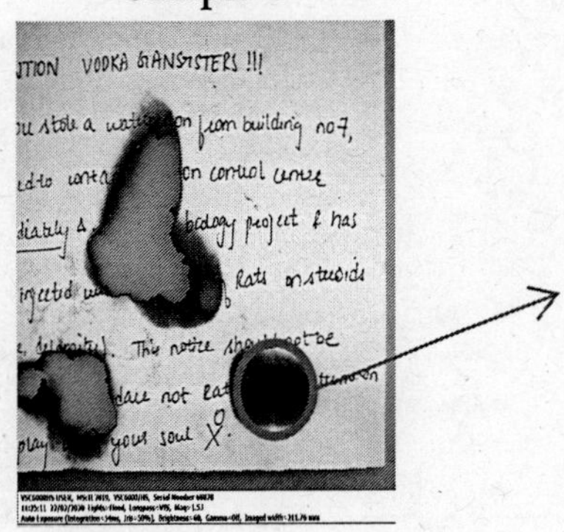

5A 5B6A 6B

Sample-7 **Sample-8**

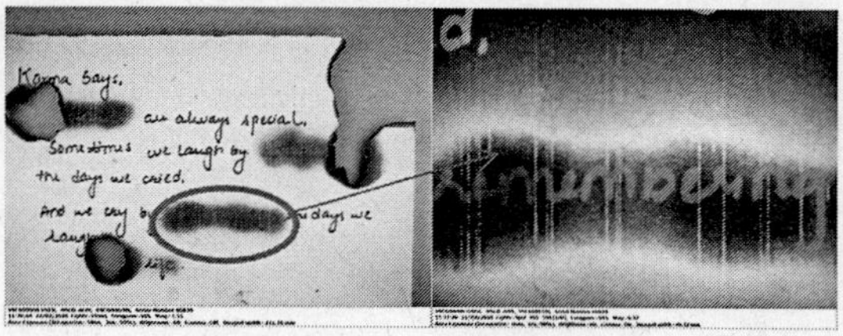

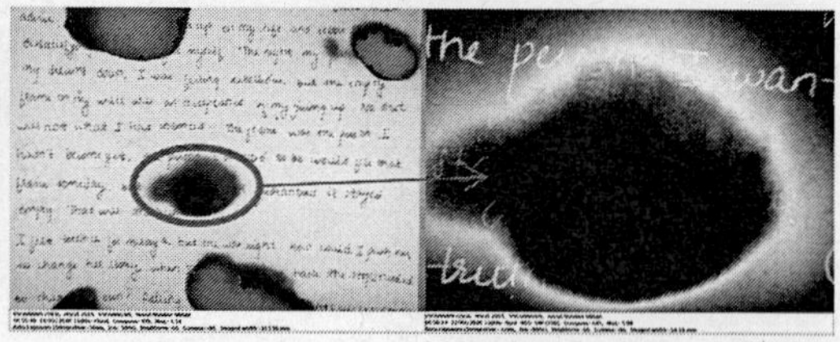

7A 7B8A 8B

Sample-9 **Sample-10**

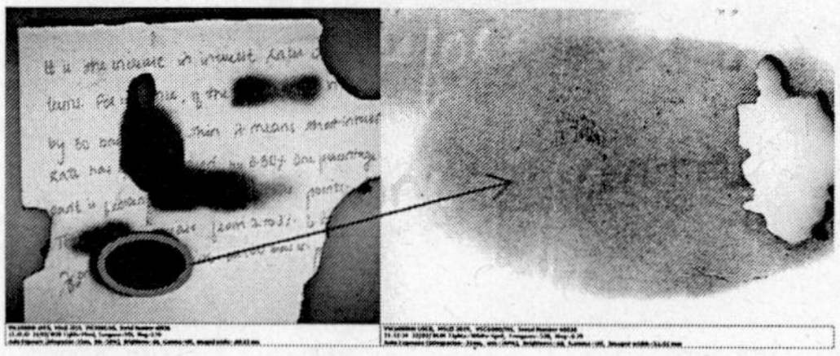

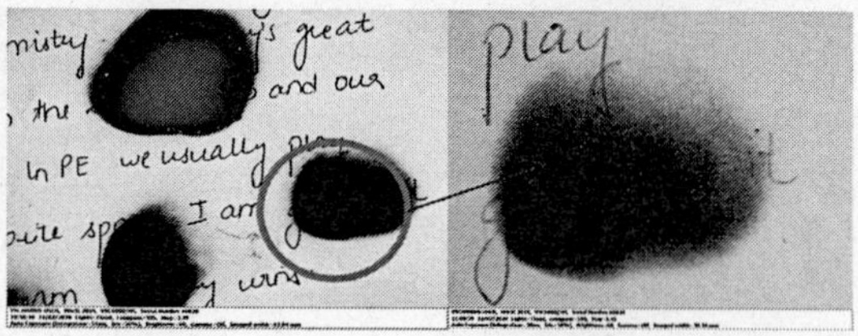

9A 9B10A 10B

Sample-11 **Sample-12**

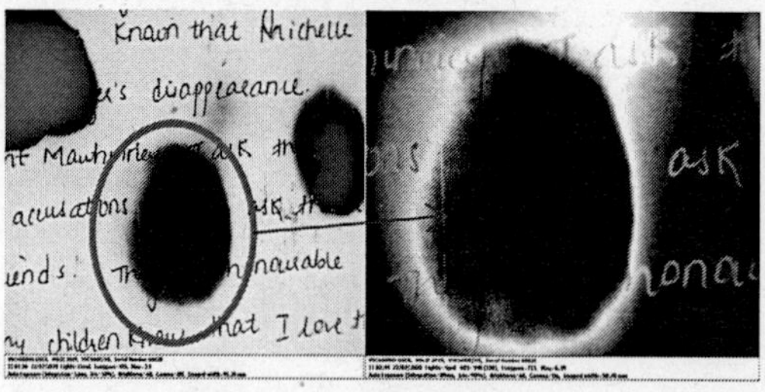

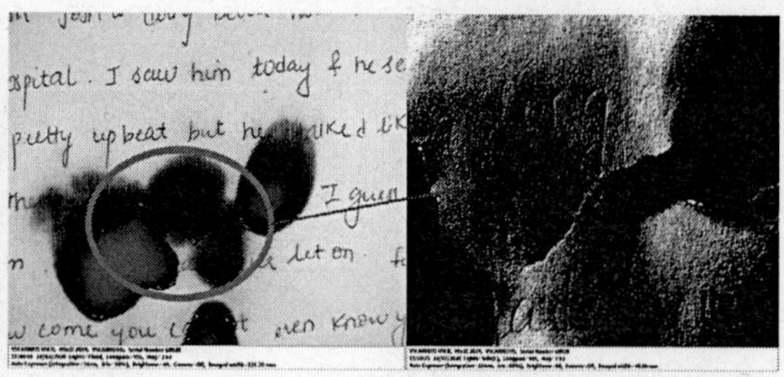

11A 11B12A 12B

Sample 13 Sample 14

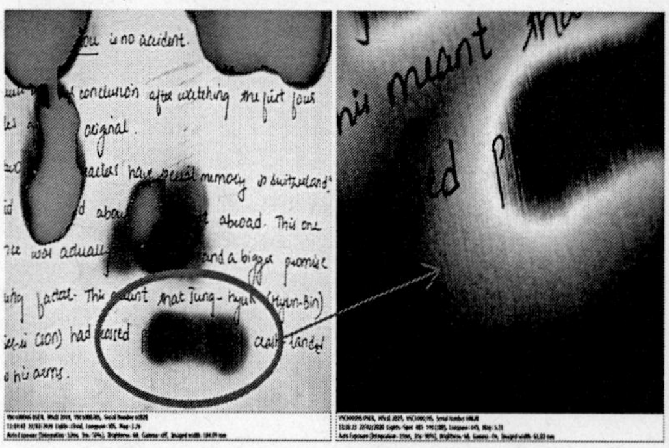

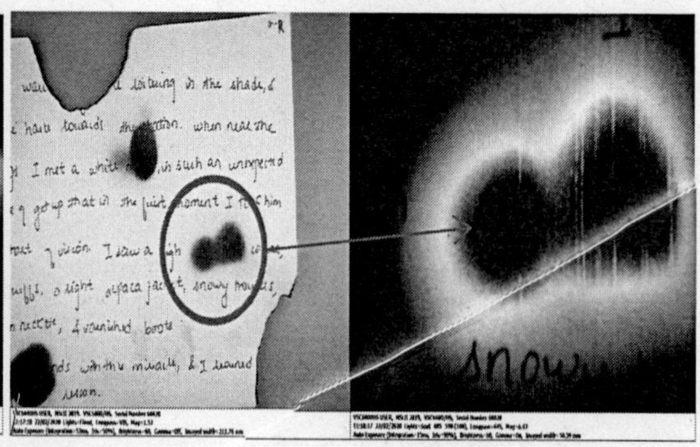

13A 13B14A 14B

Sample 15 **Sample 16**

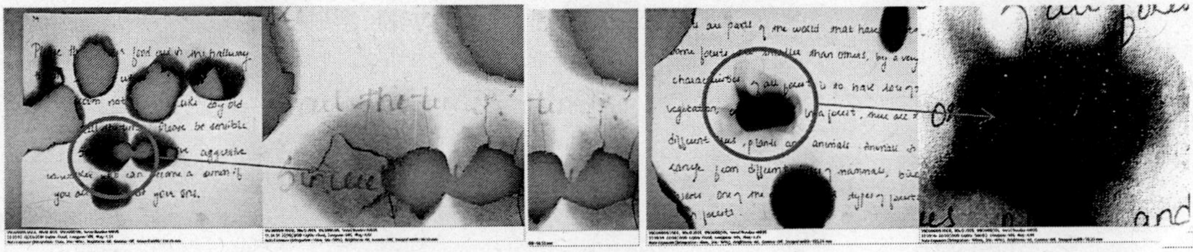

15A 15B16A 16B

Table 2: Instrumental Conditions for Sample 1 to 16 for Decipherment of Partially Burned Document

Sample No.	*Colour of Ink*	*Nature of Ink*	*Instrumental Condition*	*Sample No*	*Colour of Ink*	*Nature of Ink*	*Instrumental Condition*
1.	Blue	Ball Ink	Long pass visible	9.	Brown	Sketch Ink	White Spot 630 nm
2.	Green	Gel Ink	Flood light (VIS)	10.	Blue	Gel Ink	Flood light VIS
3.	Brown	Sketch ink	Spot light 645 nm	11.	Brown	Marker Ink	White Spot 540 nm
4.	Pink	Sketch Ink	Flood light VIS	12.	Green	Gel Ink	L Side light (VIS)
5.	Black	Gel Ink	Flood light VIS	13.	Blue	Gel Ink	Spot light 645 nm
6.	Blue	Ball Ink	Flood light VIS	14.	Red	Gel Ink	Spot light 645 nm
7.	Blue	Gel Ink	Spot light 645 nm	15.	Black	Sketch Ink	Flood light VIS
8.	brown	Ball ink	Spot light 645 nm	16.	Blue	Gel Ink	Flood light VIS

% of decipherment of VSC Light system

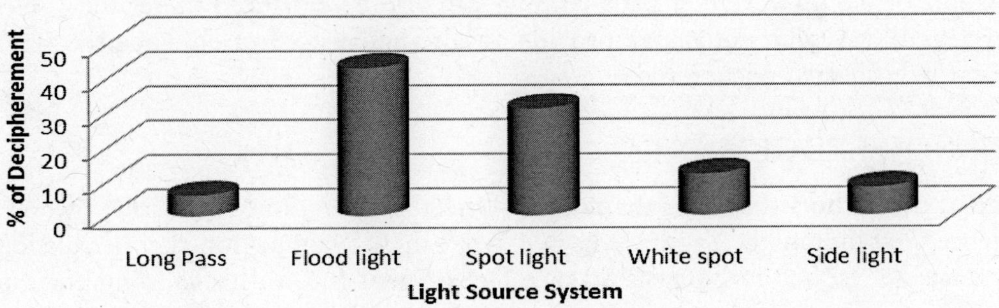

Table 3: Percentage of Distribution of VSC Light System for Decipherment of Partially Burned Writing

Nature of Light System	*VSC Long Pass Wavelength*	*Distribution Percentage*
Long Pass		6%
Flood light	VIS	43%
Spot light	645 nm	31%
White spot	540 nm	12%
Side light	VIS	8%

The decipherment of handwritings was observed on the partially burned documents using VSC-6000 under selected spot light and flood light with adjusted wavelengths (Figure D1-D16). The results showed that the visibility of indented impression of writing was comparatively more prominent in ballpoint pens writing under spot light. The ballpoint pen ink writings caused more prominent enhancement in compression to gel pen writing. Because pointed edge of ballpoint pen developed deep furrows on the papers. Better contrast and enhancement found by selecting wavelength 645nm and 780nm. The black and red marker writings were clearly visualized in spot light in comparison to the flood light. Document no. D11 and D16 showed minimal visibility of handwriting because these documents were heavily charred in comparison to remaining 14 documents. Using this method 88% of the examined documents gave promising results.

CONCLUSION

The decipherment of partially burned writing with different types and colored inks on the same type of papers is possible with this technique. Better enhancement could be observed under the white spot beam compared to the flood light beam. Pen pressure was found to be a helpful factor in the charred documents examination, irrespective of colors of the inks. Marker pens writings can also be enhanced under these selected wavelengths. Present study may provide an alternative tool to enhance the writings on partially charred documents.

ACKNOWLEDGEMENT

One of the authors (HCB) is thankful to Director, Government Institute of Forensic Science, Ravindranath Tagore Marg, Civil Lines, Nagpur for the permission to conduct the research in Forensic Science Department and for his constant encouragement.

REFERENCES

[1] Ahluwalia, A. (2020). Forensic examination of fire and water damaged documents. Retrieved on October 20, 2020 from https://legaldesire.com/forensic-examination-of-fire-and-water-damaged-documents

[2] Mokrzycki, G.M. (1999). Advances in document examination the video spectral Comparator. *Forensic. Science Communications*, 1, 1–6.

[3] Moorthy, T.N. (2016). Enhancement of handwritings on selected charred documents using video spectral comparator (VSC). *Arab Journal of Forensic Sciences & Forensic Medicine*, 1(4), 406–413.

[4] Santacroce, G. (1999). The forensic examination of fire and water-damaged documents. *International Journal of Forensic Document Examination*, *5*(1), 76–82.

[5] Sharma, B.K., Chand, D., Shukla, V.K., Thomas, A.A. and Jeridi, E. (2020). Decipherment of the written and printed matter on the charred document using UV And IR under different wavelengths. In *2020 International Conference on Computation, Automation and Knowledge Management (ICCAKM)*, 172-176, IEEE.

[6] Taylor, W.D. and Walls, H.J. (1941). A new method for decipherment of charred documents. *Nature International*, *147*, 417.

[7] Tidke, C.R. and Kushwaha, K.P.S. (2019). Decipherment of ball point pen writings on the charred/burnt paper. *International Journal of Forensic Science*, 2(1), 21–25.

Exploring the RASAS in Myriad Images of Krishna from Historical to Contemporary Art

Ruchi Agrawal[1] and Anu Ukande[2]

Shri Vaishnav Institute of Fine Arts,
Shri Vaishnav Vidyapeeth Vishwavidyalaya, Indore, Madhya Pradesh
E-mail: [1]ruchi.pankaj104@gmail.com; [2]anuukande1980@gmail.com

ABSTRACT: The focus of this paper is to study Krishna in arts with reference to the Indian aesthetic rasas. The entity and multifaceted personality of Krishna has influenced the course of religion, philosophy, art, culture and literature. The history of Vaishnavism in different parts of India has innumerable evidences preserved in museums across the globe. Stone carvings, terracotta, copper plate inscriptions having figures relating to the Krishna legend shows the popularity of this incarnation of Vishnu. Of all the Puranas, the Bhagavata has attained the greatest popularity because of its elaborate and lucid exposition specifically of Krishna's life and the artist has followed it in illustrating the Krishna legend.

Krishna is a God, incarnated in human form, who is lively and vibrant hero of Indian theology, that resonates in every heart. He has mostly been the all-time favourite hero of Indian scriptures, prose, poetry, painting, music, dance, drama, sculpture. Krishna's name has been mentioned in the Vedas. The earliest references of Krishna is in the Chandogya Upanishad (c. 8th or 7th century BCE). Next evidence is found in Megasthenes, the Macedonian ambassador at the court of Chandragupta Maurya (about 320BC) who wrote about India in his book.

The tradition of aesthetics has been defined in detail in Indian literature. According to the Natya Shastra by Bharat Muni- art needs to arouse emotions and should excite senses, thus creating rasas. There are plentiful emotion driven sequences in the tales of Krishna which can be adapted to the nava rasas. The most spirited exploration and elucidation of Krishna came during and post Bhakti movement. The country has abundance of native or primitive art forms which are the folk and the tribal arts.

Keywords: Aesthetic Rasas, Bhagavata, Natya Shastra, Puranas, Vaishnavism.

INTRODUCTION

Paintings have their origin in our ancient past. They depict the life and customs followed by the people of those times. Literary records on the art of painting show that from very early times paintings both secular as well as non-secular were considered as important form of artistic expression and were practised enormously. This need for expression is a very basic requirement for human and it has taken various forms since prehistoric times.

The art of painting is one such form with which you may have been come in contact with, in some way or the other. Indian painting is the result of the unification of various traditions and its development is an ongoing process. However, while adapting to new styles, Indian painting has maintained its indigenous character. Painting of this subcontinent in contemporary times is therefore, a reflection of the assimilation of a rich traditional and cultural inheritance with modern trends and ideas.

The art form of painting has flourished in India since very early times. The history of art and painting in India begins with the pre-historic rock painting at Bhimbetka caves, near Bhopal in M.P. Thousands of years ago, paintings and drawings had already appeared on the seals of Harappan civilization as well, followed by the Ajanta caves near Aurangabad, Badami caves in the south Deccan, and also at Malabar. These first artists were followed by the residents of Indus Valley Civilization who loved to decorate their terracotta potteries and earthen ware. Next were the mythological characters from the great epics which were drawn on the walls and floors of their homes and town.

The themes of Indian paintings historically revolved around the religious deities and kings. The works are mostly inspired by various scenes from Indian theology. These manuscripts and their illustrations lead to the fact that painting was supposed to be a part of curriculum and was taught in *gurukuls* and *ashrams.* The art of painting was considered a thing of glorious traditions. There are descriptions of painting in some of the Buddha and Jain literature and also in some dramas of that age, which throw light on the importance of painting in that age. In the epics like Ramayana and Mahabharata which are supposed to be of 600 to 500 B.C., there are references which clearly state that art was given importance.

The elements and principles of art on the six limbs of painting (*Shadangas)* has been described in the book by Vatsyayana which is supposed to have been written during 200–300 A.D. There are mentions in *Meghdoot* and *Raghuvansha* of Kalidas about paintings, art of decorating hands and feet of the *nayika,* the lovers keeping portraits of each other, or decorations done on the walls of house.

The Ajanta caves of second third century or the fourth fifth century Bagh murals indicated that perfection was attained only due to centuries of practice and a continuous perseverance. The tradition of painting could reach such heights of maturity because of the determination and encouraging response. In ancient India the tradition of painting was equivalent to that of literature, sculpture or architecture.

REFERENCES OF KRISHNA

The history of Vaishnavism in different parts of India has innumerable evidences preserved in museums across the globe. Stone carvings, terracotta, copper plate inscriptions having figures relating to the Krishna legend shows the popularity of this incarnation of Vishnu. The life of Krishna from childhood to later age has been a source of perennial inspiration to the poets and the artists. The entity and multifaceted personality of Krishna has influenced the course of religion, philosophy, art, culture and literature. The legend of Krishna has developed with manifold layers of stories over the centuries and stood the test of time. Krishna is a popular theme for artists, scholars and common man alike. It is for this reason that keeping Krishna at the nucleus, plenty of works have been done.

The origin and history of Krishna are complex. Legends associated with him pervade India's literature as well as its visual and performing arts. Krishna's name has been mentioned in the Vedas. A sage called Krishna is said to have composed *Rig Veda.* He is also called as *Angirasa* Krishna by the author of *Anukramani.* In the Chandogya Upanishad (8th or 7th century BCE) the earliest references of Krishna can be seen where he is known as Devakiputra-Krishna and also as the pupil of *Ghora Angirasa.* His references can be found next in the parts of the Mahabharata which may date from 400 B.C. The *Ashtadhyayi* by Panini probably from 350 B.C. also refer to Vasudeva and Arjuna.

Another evidence is found in Megasthenes, the Macedonian ambassador at the court of Chandragupta Maurya (about 320 B.C.) who states that Herakles is worshipped by the Sourasenoi (Surasena Kshatriyas) in whose land are two great cities, Methora (Mathura) and Kleisobora and through its flows the navigable river Joberes (Yamuna) (Bhattacharya, 1996).

Along with these literary references, there are inscriptions which show the marks of Krishna-cult in history. Ghosundi, near Nagari village in Rajasthan dated to the 2nd century BCE has inscriptions in Brahmi script which can be linked to Vaishnavism tradition. Another inscription is found at Besnagar on the Garuda Pillar, erected around 113 BCE which is written in Brahmi script and contains some of the earliest known writings of Vasudev- Krishna devotion. Studying the early growth of the Krishna- cult can be done through the scriptures like the *Harivansham*, the *Vishnu Purana*, the *Bhagavata-Gita*, and the *Bhagavata Purana.*

The *Bhagavata* is a strong basis of narration to inspire artists and devotees. Sculpture, painting, theatre, music and dance rely on these literary sources. Devotional poetries in many Indian languages were inspired by *Bhagavata Purana*. There was a marked change in the image of Krishna in the medieval period. The early life of Krishna spent in the midst of *Gopis* (cow-maidens) in the pleasant surroundings of Braj/Vrindavan developed a *Bhakti* movement with sentimental and religious emotions.

ANALYSING THE RASAS

In the book called *Natya Shastra* by Bharat *muni* optimum part was devoted to the art of drama, but in its broader implications its principles applied also to other visual arts. Art has been extensively discussed and the expression of ideas through colours has been mentioned. He defined such arts as *Kridaniyakam* (an act of the body – performing on stage, sculpting a stone piece, making a painting, or composing a poem, that recreated viewer's mind by exciting his senses, more particularly the eye and the ear (Jain, 2006).

Rasas can be spoken as the joy and pleasure experienced by the artist and the recipient. There are eight sentiments or the *Ashta rasas* as detailed in the *Natya Shastra*. They are *Shringara, Hasya, Raudra, Karuna, Bhibhatsa, Vira, Bhayanaka and Adbhuta*. Later ninth *rasa* was added, called the *Shanta Rasa*. Various art forms depict many emotions that stir the desired sentiments in the spectators. Krishna's story is full of highly emotive series.

Shringara: the rasa of love—Rukmini-Krishna, Radha-Krishna, *Raslila* etc. are very popular themes for this *rasa* and evoke *rati* or love. Every artist has taken refuge in Krishna stories for depicting *shringara* (Acharya, 2015). The Presiding deity is Lord Vishnu and is represented by the colour green.

Shringara rasa has been given the highest honour ever since the beginning of poetics. According to Bharata, anything which is sacred, pure, placid and worth seeing can be compared to *Shringar* (Prasad, 2016).

Hasya: Denotes comic or emotion of humour—The deity related to this *rasa* is Lord Ganesh and is represented by white colour—Krishna' childhood tales of stealing butter and sharing with *gopis* and monkeys, playing pranks on his friends are *lilas* where *hasya* is the prominent *rasa*.

Karuna: the emotions of pity, also denotes helplessness, humiliation, defeat, compassion and mercy—stories of Draupadi *vastra harana* and Sudama are those which stirs the sentiments of grief, remorse or *karuna rasa*. It is symbolized by the dove or grey colour. Lord *Yama* is the presiding deity.

Vira: The heroic sentiment—Narakasura *vadha*, killing Putna and other demons and Kansa in *Malla yuddha* etc. show Krishna as a fearless and courageous hero thus, evoking in the viewer the emotions of powerful heroism. The *rasa* is expressed using the saffron colour and the deity is lord Indra.

Raudra: The furious sentiment, one experiences anger when Krishna takes up the wheel of the cart to kill Bhishma at the Kurukshetra war, when Shishupala insults Krishna and then he is killed by Krishna, thus, the anger is seen. The presiding deity is Lord Shiva also known as *Rudra* and is indicated by red colour.

Bhayanaka: The terrible sentiment or the emotions of fear—Mother Yashoda is frightened when Krishna jumped into the waters of Yamuna to find Kalia *naag*, or when she sees the huge form of Putana or other demons etc. or when Radha goes to meet Krishna at no moon night are instances where the element of fear can be depicted. *Devi Kaal ratri* is the deity and is denoted by the black colour.

Bhibhatsa: The odious, disgust or emotions of aversion—Krishna's fellow *yadavas* giving in to all the depravity and fighting and killing each other (as cursed by Gandhari), the scene of Kurukshetra after Mahabharata are some rare instances that inspires the *bhava* of *bhibhatsa*. The presiding deity is Lord Shiva and is indicated by blue colour.

Adhabhutta: marvellous or the sentiments of dismay—Yashoda seeing the universe in little Krishna's mouth, when Krishna shows his *Virat-rupa* to Arjun at Kurukshetra, or when Krishna lifts the Govardhana mountain etc. creates the emotions of amazement. White is the colour for this *rasa* and Brahma is the presiding deity.

Shanta: *Rasa* of quiescent and peace—his yogic form inspires peace, Spiritual sublimation of a being for the lord or the ecstasy of the saints like Chaitanya *Mahaprabhu*, is a sort of divine sentiment. Shown with white colour and Lord Vishnu is the presiding deity.

These are few instances which reveals how legends of Krishna can be adapted to the *nava rasas*. There are bountiful emotion driven sequences in the tales of Krishna which find the dazzling expressions in fine arts.

EXPLORING KRISHNA IN VARIOUS ARTS

The self-abandonment of the *Gopies* for Krishna shows the highest spiritual devotion leading to the greatest divine experience. The compositions which were mainly responsible for popularising the legends of Krishna includes the *Geet Govind* by Jayadeva (12th century poet) and *Krishnakarnamrita* composed by Bilvamangala followed by numerous poets and composers of the *Bhakti* motion. To name a few Bhanudatta's *Rasmanjiri*, *Rasikpriya* of Keshav das, verses of Surdas in *Sursavali*, *Raagmala*, *Baramasa*, Bhartihari, Amaru, Vidhyapati, Chanidas, Kalidas etc., praise Lord Krishna with the imagery of his *Lilas*. These illustrations have been illustrated again and again. They spread the youthful exploits of Krishna among the common man throughout the length and breadth of India. His influence over the art form is almost unmatchable.

Using illustrations as part of story—telling is an ancient technique practised in India. Scrolls, murals and sculpted panels on the walls of temples have been used to narrate the legends. Several regional and folk traditions also depict the events of Krishna's life as a major part of their tradition. Krishna's influence over the folk dance and most of the classical dance forms of India is exceptional. One can't imagine dance without Krishna. Be it the themes or styles or stories or emotions, Krishna is omnipresent. (Acharya, 2015).

The country has abundance of native or primitive art forms of painting which are the folk and the tribal arts. To name a few, *Madhubani* art of Bihar, *Pattchitra* from Orissa, *Picchwai* and Sanjhi art of Nathdwara, Tanjore of Tamilnadu, Kerala murals, Phad and Kavad of Rajasthan, Kalighat paintings of Bengal and so on depicts the legendary Krishna and his divine plays or 'lilas.' Artist like Jamini Roy of Bengal, throughout his career tried to capture the essence of simplicity of the folk people and to give Indian arts its own identity. The series on Krishna leela is one of his magnum opuses. He is considered one of the most iconic figures of modern Indian art of the mid-20th century.

Many other artists from modern times have also painted Krishna from time to time. Apart from tales and legends of his life and deeds, saints, poets, devotees and artists alike have had their own understanding of Krishna and thus, a variety of expressions can be found for this evergreen hero of Indian art. Krishna paintings came to be admired not merely for their religious sentiments but also as objects of aesthetic beauty.

CONCLUSION

The role played by religion, tradition and culture is determining in the evolution of folk art and is the assimilating force behind the aesthetic creativeness. The themes get visual expression in a painting by fundamental values of culture and the devotional minds. They wrote verses and poems in which Radha's adventures with Krishna and their romance were described devotedly and aesthetically which gave the artist a wider imagery to illustrate and narrate. The most spirited exploration and elucidation of Krishna came during and post *Bhakti* Movement. The motion related to *Vaishnav Bhakti* initiated the inclusion of the myriad images of Krishna themes in different art forms which were being practised then and still continues with the tradition.

Rasa is the basis of art and the main aim of any art is to evoke *rasa* in the mind of the receiver or the viewer. The concept of *rasa* is the heart of Indian artistic expression. *Rasa*, or the juice or extract, like the word "essence" has both a concrete and abstract significance. The absorption of tradition and the historical past is helpful for the present and it brings with it the experience to shape up the future. Portrayal of cultural and traditional vibrancy through conventional arts have been practised. Krishna has been one of the most cherished themes of arts, who has been illustrated from ancient times as well narrated in folk and tribal arts of contemporary period. Narrations may be of many forms like written words, music, drama, dance and visual arts.

REFERENCES

[1] Acharya, M. (2015). A reflection of Krishna's kaleidoscopic presence in dance. Journal of Humanities and Social Science, 52–54.

[2] Bhattacharya, S.K. (1996). Krishna-cult in Indian Art. New Delhi: M.D. Publications Pvt. Ltd., New Delhi.

[3] Jain, P.C. (2006). Indian Miniature Painting: Manifestation of a Creative Mind. Brijbasi Art Press, New Delhi.

[4] Prasad, R. (2016). Śringāra Bhakti of Rādha in Gitagovinda: A Nāyika Perspective. International Journal of Recent Advances in Organizational Behaviour and Decision Sciences, 2,(2).

Hempcrete: An Alternate Construction Material

Vinta Sarath Chandra Reddy[1], **Jaya Prasanth Golagani**[2], **Vajrapu Harika**[3] **and M. Bandan Kumar**[4]

GITAM School of Architecture, GITAM (Deemed to be University), Gandhi Nagar, Rushikonda, Visakhapatnam, Andhra Pradesh

E-mail: [1]121925501019@gitam.in; [2]121925501009@gitam.in; [3]121925501017@gitam.in; [4]bmishra@gitam.edu

ABSTRACT: The extensive use of conventional materials (Red clay brick, A.A.C. blocks, fly ash bricks, etc.,) in construction has led to an increase in carbon footprints, extensive use of energy, pollution, and many other negative impacts to the environment. Due to this fact, there is a call for change in the way materials are used for construction. Green materials that constitute less carbon footprint, low embodied energy with rapid renewability could be the solution to the adverse effects created by the construction industry on environment and its resources. Use of vegetal concretes as an alternative building material could be one of the effective methods that addresses the issues regarding embodied energy, carbon footprint, material availability etc. Vegetal translates plant based that can be by-products of agro industries like straw bale, hemp, rice rusk, etc. Hempcrete, is an example of vegetal concrete formed from a mix of hemp hurds, lime, sand, and pozzolans (Sandrine, 2017). Hemp hurd is the stalk part of the hemp plant. The other parts of this plant are used in medicine and textile. The stalk part of the plant is left unused. Its exceptional features and composition gives it the ability to be termite resistant, mould-free, fire resistant, water resistant, and carbon negative. The paper provides an in-depth comparative analysis of Hemp Crete to that of Red clay bricks, Autoclaved aerated concrete (AAC) blocks with the help of its physical, mechanical properties and workability. It further looks its potential to replace the conventional methods of material usage in construction.

Keywords: Alternate Material, AAC, Carbon Negative, Hempcrete, Red Clay.

INTRODUCTION

In an era of rapid urbanization and global climatic disruption, attention is increasingly focused on methods for reducing energy consumption and carbon emissions in the building industry. It is estimated that the production and ongoing operation of buildings is responsible for over 40% of all energy consumption in industrialized countries. In such times, there is a need for environmentally conscious building design that creates a healthy indoor environment while supporting a healthy outdoor environment. These types of buildings, in its design, construction and operation can reduce the negative impacts on the environment while addressing the energy conservation crisis. To reduce energy consumption in buildings some of the avenues that are being explored are phase change materials (PMCs), passive house techniques, and other similar measures. The integration of solid organic PMCs such as hempcrete can result in the development of a building material with improved thermo-physical properties for the construction of sustainable and comfortable buildings.

Hempcrete constitutes of hemp hurds and a lime-based binder. Hemp is a collective name for the high-growing varieties of the cannabis Sativa plant (THC $\leq$0.3%) used for industrial purposes such as textiles, medicine, food, plastics, paper etc. It was found that every kilogram of hemp hurds absorbs about 1.6 to 1.8 kg of carbon dioxide. A recent study shows that hemp was used in the lime and clay plaster of the Ellora caves that are more than 1500 years of age. (Jami, 2018)

Hemp hurd is one of the most widely used and studied plant particles for the manufacture of building materials, and hemp concrete is one of the most widely studied bio-based concretes.

Fig. 1: Hemp Blocks close up view (left), Hemp Blocks (right)

HEMPCRETE AND ITS COMPOSITION

Hemp plant's stem is cut into small sizes of 5 to 25 mm pieces. These Hemp pieces get mixed with a binder agent like lime or cement and water to form Hempcrete. Various hempcrete mixture compositions and techniques are used for its applications on walls, floors, and roofs (Demir, 2020).

- **Hemp Hurd:** Hemp Crete composites use the woody core of the plant stalk known as hurd (Hirst, 2010). Hemp is grown as a break crop and harvested after 3–4 months. Once collected and bailed, the hemp is introduced into a processing plant which separates the hurd from the fiber and removes any dust, dirt and other particulates. The main markets for hemp fiber are currently within the automotive, paper and the textile industries.
- **Binder:** The binder helps to hold the particles of the hemp hurd. Within the mix after setting, forms very porous structure which helps in providing good sound absorption and very slight deforming ability. Earlier, it was assumed that only cement can be used as a binder, but in recent research it is observed thatusage of lime and pozzolans as binders can help in improving the performance of hempcrete (Demir, 2020).Once mixed within the composite, lime (Ca) mixed with water reacts to carbon dioxide (CO_2) in the atmosphere around and goes under calcination process forming calcium carbonate ($CaCO_3$). This absorption of CO_2 partially offsets the CO_2 released during production of the binder.
- **Water:** Potable water is essential in activating the reactive elements within the binders. Using lime as binder in ratio with hemp hurds and water produces higher hygrothermal tolerance when compared to other conventional material and binder mixes which are used in wall applications.

The most important part of the material is the binder. A lime-based binder is the chosen variety of binders because of its abundance and low emissions during the process of manufacturing. Nevertheless, the lime binders are more compatible with hemp hurds than cement since they absorb large quantities of water and interfere with the hydraulic activity, preventing the setting of the inner parts of the hemp-cement composite. Therefore, hemp concrete research and commercial applications around the world rely on either natural hydraulic lime (NHL) or commercial binders.

Table 1: General Properties of Hempcrete

General Specification	*Rating*
Compressive Strength: 0.5–3.5 MPa	(low for structural components)
Thermal Conductivity: 0.05–0.20 W/mK	(generally low)
Thermal Capacity: 1000–1560 J/kgK	(high)
CO_2 Sequestration: 108 kg/m^3	(high)
Acoustical Absorption Factor: 0.5–0.9	(quite high)
Moisture Diffusion Coefficient: ~1.10^{-9} m^2/s	(very good)
Water vapour Diffusion Resistance Factor: ~4.85	(high)
Water Absorption Coefficient: 0.0736–0.15 kg/m^2/s	(high)

Table 2: Binder Type, Hurd Ratio, Water Ratio, Curing Conditions, Physical and Mechanical Results (Demir, 2020)

Binder Type	*Hurd Ratio*	*Water Ratio*	*Curing Conditions*	*Physical and Mechanical Results*
Magnesium Phosphate Cement	0.08 0.12 0.16 0.2	1	1d, 7d, 28d 20 ± 2 C 50–55% RH	Compressive strength obtained 0.714 MPa and thermal conductivity obtained 0.103 $Wm^{-1}K^{-1}$ were measured at the 20% hempcrete sample. It is reported that Young's modulus decreases as the hemp ratio increases. It has been determined that long curing time has a positive effect on Young's modulus. The values of maximum strain slightly increased as the hemp content increased.
70% natural lime 30% hydraulic lime and pozzolans	0.4 0.5 0.67	0.52 0.63	90 days 20°C 50% RH	In samples produced with both types of binders, the thermal conductivity decreased by 8% to 30% as the hemp ratio increased. Thermal conductivity in samples produced with a lime-based binder was obtained by 20% more than samples produced with a natural prompt cement-based binder. The thermal conductivity decreases of about 9%–16% after drying.
Starch	8 10	5.55	40d 50d 20°C	S/B = 10. The compressive strength is 0.57 MPa for S/B = 8 and 0.60 MPa for S/B = 10. The Young's modulus is 2.47 MPa for S/B = 8 and 2.33 MPa for S/B = 10. The thermal conductivity at the dry state varies in the range of 0.06–0.07 $Wm^{-1}K^{-1}$. When the S/B ratio increases, the mechanical characteristics slightly decreases due to the increase of the porosity and the decrease of the load transfer.

Properties

Hemp and lime concrete exhibits interesting mechanical, thermal, hygroscopic and acoustical properties. In the experimental studies conducted, the density of hempcrete was obtained between 300 and 600 kgm^{-3} depending on the mixing proportions. The observed porosity rate of hempcrete is 65%, thermal conductivity of 0.07 to 0.2 $Wm^{-1}K^{-1}$ at 23°C, 50% relative humidity (RH) (Demir, 2020). The obtained acoustic absorption coefficient ranged from 0.5 to 0.9.

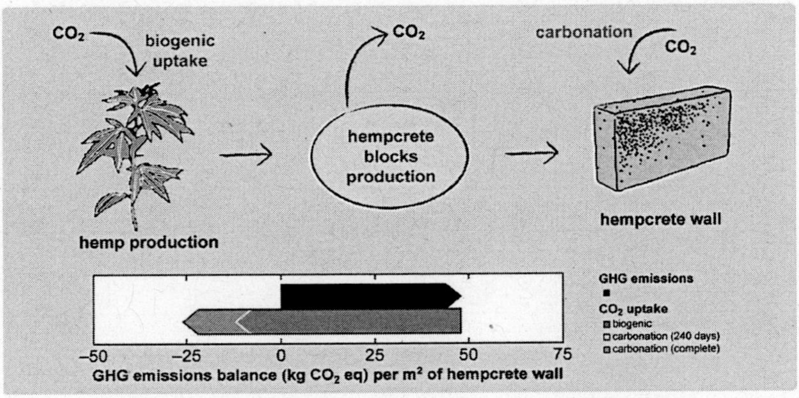

Fig. 2: Carbon Emission, Segregation of Hempcrete with Net Emissions Balance Exhibiting Carbon Negativity

In its current form, LHC is too weak to be used as a load-bearing material. It has been observed in studies carried out by various authors that LHC undergoes a considerable amount of compaction upon application of loads, after which an increase in load-bearing capacity takes place before failure. The density of the binding material (lime) affects the mechanical strength and the thermal conductivity of hemp concrete. Hemp concrete when manufactured using the projection process has hardness values that vary between 2·20 and 4·51 MPa.

It is observed that the increase in the densities of the samples is directly proportional to the increase in compressive strength. One of the parameters that affect the compressive strength of LHC is the binder-to-hemp ratio (B/H ratio). A lower B/H ratio (i.e., higher hemp hurd content) results in an increase in the compressive strength.

High compressive yield strength of 4·74 MPa for one of their mixes, for which the green density (920 kg/m^3) was relatively higher, the hemp content (500 kg/m^3, 0·54 B/S ratio) was higher.

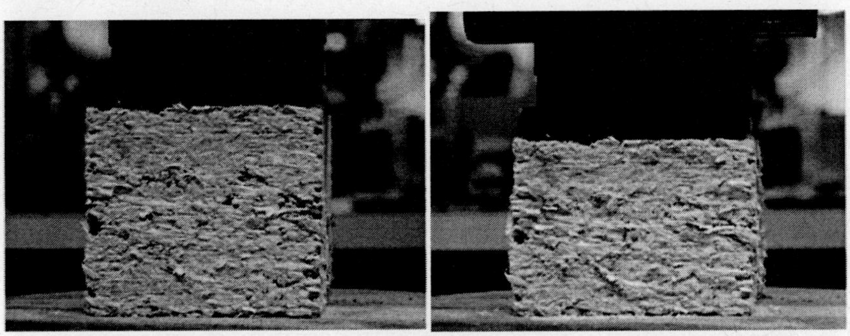

Fig. 3: Illustration of Compaction of Material under Compression: (Left) Before and (Right) After Compression Test

Table 3: Mechanical Properties of LHC as Found in Literature Published by Various Authors

Author	*Density: kg/m³*	*Hardness: MPa*	*Compressive Strength: MPa*	*Young's Modulus: MPa*
(Elfordy *et al.*, 2008)	417	2.20	–	–
	475	2.78	–	–
	496	4.86	–	–
	551	4.51	–	–
(Nguyen *et al.*, 2010)	850		–	131
	670		–	113
(Arnaud, 2011)	460		0.18	5
(Kioy *et al.*, 2013)	610		1.88	43
	830		1.98	52
(Cerezo *et al.*, 2005)	356		0.3	14
	391		0.35	44
	504		0.7	15
(Tornet *et al.*, 2016)	–		1.36	43
	–		1.63	51
	–		2.13	70
	–		4.74	147
	–		3.95	122

THERMAL CONDUCTIVITY OF HEMPCRETE

The thermal conductivity of lime hempcrete varies between 0·06 and 0·27 for various mixes depending on the application of the mix. The porous nature of hemp hurds and the porosity of LHC contribute to the decrease in thermal conductivity. It has been observed that LHC mixes that do not undergo compaction register a very low value of thermal conductivity. Pre-compressed or compacted batches of LHC have a considerably smaller volume of pores while rendering a greater compressive strength. This contributes to an increase in thermal conductivity. The values registered are not large enough to be considered undesirable, as they are lower than that of the thermal conductivity of conventional concrete (0·8 W/(m K)). Layer stratification of hemp hurds takes place normal to the direction of the applied compressive load, resulting in a discontinuity of binder layers.

Table 4: Thermal Conductivity of Various Combinations

Mix	*RH*	*Thermal Conductivity (W/m K)*	*Thermal Diffusivity (mm^2/s)*	*Specific Heat Capacity (KJ/kg K)*
A	15	0.105 ± 0.004	0.274 ± 0.022	0.385 ± 0.017
A	65	0.116 ± 0.004	0.249 ± 0.023	0.469 ± 0.031
B	15	0.094 ± 0.003	0.282 ± 0.018	0.333 ± 0.021
B	65	0.100 ± 0.003	0.300 ± 0.020	0.300 ± 0.020

The values of thermal conductivity registered by LHC mixes (Strandberg, 2008) are slightly inconsistent as the relative humidity changes with respect to the area. These higher thermal conductivity values reported could be attributed to a greater binder-to-hemp mass ratio. Another revelation regarding the same is the probable requirement of greater workability for the projection process, which might have in turn warranted a greater B/H ratio. In one of the study, it has been asserted that the thermal conductivity of LHC varies more with the density than with the moisture content. They were able to establish that the thermal conductivity for a high density is higher than twice the value for a low density with the same formulation. Although the effect of moisture content on the thermal conductivity of the LHC mix is small, it must be considered for the overall hygrothermal design of the building.

Hygric Properties of LHC (Lime Hempcrete)

LHC has a high moisture diffusion coefficient; its water vapor permeability is approximately $2{\cdot}3 \times 10^{-11}$ kg/(Pa m s) and is nearly constant for a low or mid relative humidity (RH). LHC has a moisture buffer value (MBV) of greater than 2 g/(m^2 %RH). It is observed that LHC has the ability to regulate the indoor %RH even under varying outdoor %RH values as a result of its excellent moisture buffer capacity. It is observed that an MBV greater than 2 g/(m^2 %RH) is considered to be excellent. A study conducted at Lund University, Sweden, reported an MBV of 0·37 ± 0·04 g/(m^2 %RH) for concrete.

Acoustical Properties of Hempcrete

The acoustical properties of hempcrete are relatively good due to its low density and high porosity factor. By experimenting with the ratio of hemp hurds, binder and water in hempcrete the acoustic absorption can be increased while reverberation can be controlled. The hemp hurds act as sound absorbent and the binder acts as a reflector. The hurd-binder-water ratio is an important factor in defining the acoustical absorption extent. The techniques of installation also play a major role to obtain maximum acoustical absorption and minimum reverberation. Hempcrete with lime as binder has the highest sound absorption rates compared to the other available binders.

Density and Durability

Hempcrete density depends on the quality and quantity of material, binder, and water used, hemp hurd size, porosity, and compression ratio (Demir, 2020).Hempcrete wall density differs with respect to its application methods. Density between 400 kg/m^3 and 500 kg/m^3 can be achieved in cast-in-situ method, density between 200 kg/m^3 to 250 kg/m^3 can be achieved in spray method. Hempcrete (with lime as binder) changes to limestone as the lime reacts with the CO_2 in the atmosphere around ultimately giving strength to the structure and micro bonds within the structure. (Demir, 2020)

APPLICATIONS OF HEMPCRETE

Hempcrete walls are breathable, allows for a self-regulation of the humidity within the building often reducing the need for mechanical ventilation. In all cases, it provides sufficient insulation for the building and no additional material is normally required. Different mixtures of Hemp hurds and binders produce Hempcrete materials with different functions. Hempcrete mixtures can be used as infill walls in framed structures. Higher density hempcrete mixtures are used to produce roof or floor insulation materials and lower density mixtures are used for producing insulating indoor and outdoor plasters. Prefabricated panels can also be produced with the same mixture of Hemp and lime.

Hemp Blocks

Hempcrete blocks are manufactured at industrial level using appropriate methods and equipment. They can be very easily installed, by applying mortar between the blocks. Precast Hempcrete blocks help in rapid construction as the blocks don't need to be dried and are more preferred than Cast Hemp concrete walls.

Other innovations include Physical interlocking of blocks without mortar. The five major hempcrete block advantages are:

- Thermal regulation.
- Humidity regulation.
- Acoustic insulation.
- Protection and fire resistance.
- Health and environmental qualities.

Furthermore, since a vegetal component is included in the mixture, the blocks must be protected from water and rising damp. To avoid rotting of hurds, External walls should be protected by the rain gale with sand and lime plasters.

Fig. 4: Details of Non-Load-Bearing Walls Made of Hempcrete Blocks: (a) Wall Erection; (b) Side View; (c) Front View

Cate-in-Situ Hempcrete Walls

In Caste in-situ Hempcrete walls, the hemp concrete mixture is poured into the formwork and tamped using a tamping rod to ensure that there are no voids and

(a) (b)

(c) (d) (e)

Fig. 5: Figures a-e; Mixing and Construction Method Followed in Cast-in Situ Process

proper compaction is attained. Owing to the low density of the hemp hurds, self-compaction, or compaction due to gravity does not take place and external compacting stresses need to be applied. After every 300 mm of filling into the formwork, the hemp concrete walls are tampered gently using a trowel. The Spraying/Projection method is also an in-situ casting method.

Spraying and Projection Method

Spraying and Projection method usually saves time during the task. Using a pipe pressure, hemp lime mix is sprayed evenly on to the plywood sheets that are fixed at the required position. The spray applied concrete attaches to the plywood sheets that are used. Spraying and projection method works on the principle of pipe pressure. The pressure is generated when the hemp and binder slurry mixes at the nozzle of the sprayer and the concrete finally attaches to the plywood surface.

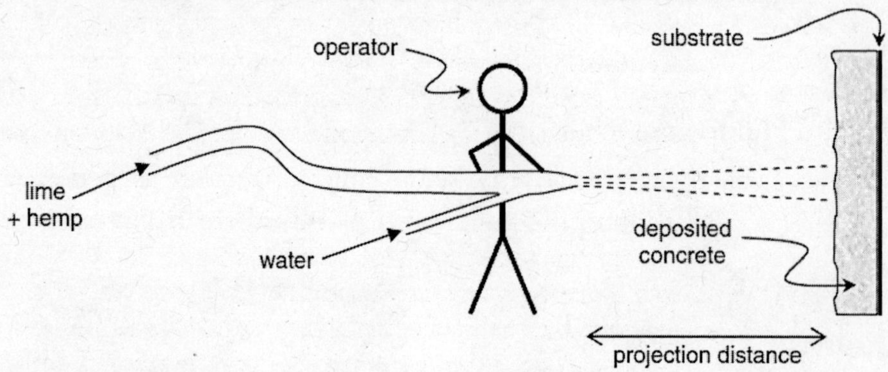

Fig. 6: Principle of Projection Process

Fig. 7: Device for Spraying Hempcrete

COMPARATIVE ANALYSIS

The following table below enlists the properties and workability of various materials through research information collected from various authors.

Table 5A: Various Materials with Properties and Workability Details from Various Authors

S. No.	*Properties*	*Hempcrete*	*Burnt Brick*	*ACC Blocks*
01.	Dry Density	270–340 kg/m^3	1900 kg/m^3	550–650 kg/m^3
02.	Thermal Conductivity	0.006–0.524 W/mK	0.81–0.98 W/mK	0.24 W/mK
03.	U-value at 300mm	0.21 W/m^2	1.3 W/m^2	0.79 W/m^2
04.	Compressive Strength	0.1–0.2 N/mm^2	14 N/mm^2	2.0–7.0 N/mm^2
05.	Energy savings	Low thermal conductivity – 45%	High Thermal Conductivity-No saving	Low Thermal Conductivity – 30%
06.	Cost of Construction	High	Economical	Low
07.	Workability	Rapid	Slow	Rapid
08.	Pest Control	Pest Proof	Pest Prone	Pest Proof
09.	Embodied Energy	Low	High	Low
10.	Carbon footprint	Negative Carbon	2.5 kg of CO_2	2.13 kg of CO_2
11.	Recyclable	Fully Recyclable	Not Recyclable	Partially Recyclable
12.	Fire Rating	3 hr/300 mm	1 hr/300 mm	4 hr/150 mm
13.	R-value	4.96 m^2 K/W	0.274 m^2 K/W	0.7 m^2 K/W
14.	Strength by Aging	Gains Strength	Wear and Tear in due time	Gains Strength
15.	Water Absorption	13% by volume	20% by volume	12%–15% by volume
16.	Range of Application	Non-Load bearing	Load Bearing	Non-Load bearing
17.	Joints Mortar	Chemical and Natural Binders	Chemical Binders	Chemical Binders

Table 5B: Various Materials with Properties and Workability Details from Various Authors

S. No.	*Properties*	*Fly Ash Brick*	*Porotherm Block*	*CLC Blocks*
01.	Dry Density	1650 kg/m^3	750–790 kg/m^3	750–800 kg/m^3
02.	Thermal Conductivity	0.639 W/mK	0.22 W/mK	0.132–0.151 W/mK
03.	U-value at 300 mm	1.92 W/m^2	1.0 W/m^2	0.67 W/m^2
04.	Compressive Strength	100 N/mm^2	3.5 N/mm^2	2.0–7.0 N/mm^2
05.	Energy savings	High Thermal Conductivity – No saving	Low Thermal Conductivity – 25%	Low Thermal Conductivity – 40%
06.	Cost of Construction	Expensive	Low	Low
07.	Workability	Slow	Rapid	Rapid
08.	Pest Control	Pest Proof	Pest Prone	Pest Proof
09.	Embodied Energy	High	High	Low
10.	Carbon footprint			2.0 kg of CO_2
11.	Recyclable	Partially Recyclable	Recyclable at high cost	Partially Recyclable
12.	Fire Rating	2 hr/50 mm	4 hr/400 mm	5 hr/50 mm
13.	R-value	0.52 m^2 K/W	1.0 m^2 K/W	1.49 m^2 K/W
14.	Strength by Aging	Gains Strength		Gains Strength
15.	Water Absorption	14.3%–17.5% by volume	15% by volume	12%–15% by volume
16.	Range of Application	Load bearing	Non-Load bearing	Non-Load bearing
17.	Joints Mortar	Chemical Binders	Chemical Binders	Chemical Binders

In the above Tables *5A, 5B* the comparison between 6 materials has been conducted based on the derived properties and workability where hempcrete properties were much more near to the conventional materials with the fact that it is carbon negative, pest proof, fully recyclable, least embodied energy among the materials compared.

The thermal conductivity of the hempcrete block is very low compared to other conventional material which is very advantageous in case of Indian climate.

Fig. 8: Images from Left to Right- Hempcrete Block: Burnt Brick: ACC Block: Fly-ash Brick: Porotherm Block: CLC Block

CONCLUSION

Hempcrete being a vegetal concrete mixture reduces the carbon footprint and has a high absorption capacity of CO_2 compared to any other conventional walling material. Hemp Crete sequesters 109.5 Kilograms of CO_2 for every cubic meter. By substitution of mineral aggregates with plant aggregates, the 40% energy spent on construction could drastically reduce. Comparing various walling materials and properties, the advantage of hempcrete over other conventional material was quite evident.

The volume of insulating materials used to reduce the energy bills are Hemp Crete being a vegetal concrete mixture reduces the carbon footprint and has a high absorption capacity of CO_2 compared to any other conventional walling material could overcome the Indian scenario in construction. Hempcrete Block has high porosity and doesn't shrink when exposed to extreme climatic conditions. In terms of porosity, it performs efficiently when compared to AAC blocks or any other conventional walling materials which develops cracks due to insufficient hydration.

Prime advantages of porosity characteristics in hemp Crete are, Lighter in weight and reduces load on the structural elements, reduces the time and cost of labor, superior fire resistance and transporting hassle free. Hempcrete walls are more efficient when compared to convention walling materials, as they don't require a vapor barrier, rain screen systems, or any advanced systems to prevent moisture accumulating in the walls. Vapor permeable hemp Crete blocks regulate indoor humidity.

Indian Construction and Building sector consumes about 31% of the gross energy production, as per Ministry of statistics and Program Implementation. Adapting sustainable envelope materials can reduce the consumption of energy by 30%. Most of the volume in construction is taken by walling materials. Burnt red bricks which are vastly used as a conventional material have high embodied energy and carbon footprint. These can be replaced by Energy efficient hempcrete blocks.

In India Hempcrete was disregarded due to paucity in awareness about the material and its energy saving characteristics. The current scenario can be overcome by conducting constant researches on long-term performance of the material. Government of India taking initiative of adapting Hempcrete in the low-cost housing projects for economic weaker section. Such initiatives can bring awareness in communities to adapt sustainable materials. Subsidies on such materials by government could help to bring awareness and replace conventional materials.

REFERENCES

[1] Arnaud, L. and Gourlay, E. (2012). Experimental study of parameters influencing mechanical properties of hemp concretes. *Construction and building materials*, *28*(1), 50–56.

[2] Cérézo, V. (2005). Propriétés mécaniques, thermiques et acoustiques d'un matériau à base de particules végétales: approche expérimentale et modélisation théorique. *Institut National des Sciences Appliquées, Lyon*.

[3] Daly, P., Ronchetti, P. and Woolley, T. (2012). Hemp Lime Bio-composite as a Building Material Irish Construction. *Environmental Protection Agency, Ireland*.

[4] Demir, İ. and Doğan, C. (2020). Physical and Mechanical Properties of Hempcrete. *The Open Waste Management Journal*, *13*(1).

[5] Elfordy, S., Lucas, F., Tancret, F., Scudeller, Y. and Goudet, L. (2008). Mechanical and thermal properties of lime and hemp concrete ("hempcrete") manufactured by a projection process. *Construction and Building Materials*, *22*(10), 2116–2123.

[6] Hirst, E., Walker, P., Paine, K. and Yates, T. (2010, June). Characterisation of low density hemp-lime composite building materials under compression loading. In *Second international conference on sustainable construction materials and technologies* (pp. 28–30).

[7] Jami, T., Karade, S.R. and Singh, L.P. (2018, March). Hemp concrete—A traditional and novel green building material. In *Proceedings of the International Conference on Advances in Construction Materials and Structures (ACMS-2018) IIT Roorkee, Roorkee, Uttarakhand, India* (pp. 7–8).

[8] Marceau, S. and Delannoy, G. (2017). Durability of Bio-based concretes. In *Bio-aggregates Based Building Materials* (pp. 167–187). Springer, Dordrecht.

[9] Nguyen, T.T., Picandet, V., Carre, P., Lecompte, T., Amziane, S. and Baley, C. (2010). Effect of compaction on mechanical and thermal properties of hemp concrete. *European Journal of Environmental and Civil Engineering*, *14*(5), 545–560.

[10] Strandberg, P. (2008). Hemp concretes: mechanical properties using both shives and fibres. Sveriges Lantbruksuniversitet. https://pub.epsilon.slu.se/1913

[11] Tronet, P., Lecompte, T., Picandet, V. and Baley, C. (2016). Study of lime hemp concrete (LHC)–Mix design, casting process and mechanical behaviour. *Cement and Concrete Composites*, *67*, 60–72.

Motherhood as a Social Construct in Doris Lessing's The Fifth Child

Pamila Neema[1] and Anurag Joshi[2]

Shri Vaishnav Institute of Social Sciences, Humanities and Arts,
Shri Vaishnav Vidyapeeth Vishwavidyalaya, Indore, Madhya Pradesh
E-mail: [1]pamilaneema2972@gmail.com; [2]janurag5@gmail.com

ABSTRACT: This paper studies the concept of Mothering and motherhood as depicted in Doris Lessing's novel The Fifth Child which was published in 1988. The novel explores the facets of idealistic role of a mother named Harriet who enjoys the dream of being a mother of many children but when she experiences conflict in mothering, her perception changes and she becomes indifferent to her idealistic role as a mother. Harriet leads her life as a staunch follower of her husband and socially conformed patterns. Everything goes normal until her fifth child Ben is born. He is a different child both physically and mentally. Harriet feels different for this child and David and other children start rebelling. The paper exhibits the perception of patriarchal society towards a dedicated wife and mother. It also questions the motherhood as a social construct of parenting which leads to mother guilt and mother blame.

Keywords: Mother Blame, Mother Guilt, Mothering, Patriarchal Society, Social Construct.

INTRODUCTION

Mothering a child is a celebrated individual experience of motherhood. Harriet, the protagonist of the novel *The Fifth Child* is an idealistic woman. She is a traditional woman who follows social norms set for a married woman by the society. The novel is set in 1960s England. Harriet is fully devoted and committed to her household responsibilities. She keeps her parents' relationship as the ideal for her own life. Although she has had a job but she feels that a happy household and motherhood is the true essence of one's life. In a party David and Harriet meet and they quickly get attracted towards each other and share their dreams mutually as they both are conformists. They decide to have at least six children.

Harriet is a suitable traditional woman who surrenders herself to families' desires and specially David's large family dreams. She is committed to David's aspirations that does not mind to have many children. She is modest and the right wife of David Lovett and mother of four children Luke, Helen, Jane and Paul. Harriett and David are the dreamers of an extended family and want a large family and a large house. David and Harriet buy a house at countryside in London. David's father pays off the installments and despite having financial problems, they lead a happy life. Harriet surrenders to a continuous motherhood and related responsibilities.

She unknowingly engages herself to the long driven family ties as women in love do not understand the power relationship. Patriarchy is used more generally now-"to refer to male domination, to the power relationships by which men dominate women, and to characterize a system whereby women are kept subordinate in a number of ways" (Bhasin 2006:3).

Harriet's fifth pregnancy brings a different experience to her. She has nightmares at nights with pain which is exceptional to the previous experiences of her pregnancy days. Unlike the previous births of her four children, this child is ugly and deformed. He was born with big muscular body, heavy shouldered hunched look and green yellow eyes. He does not look like his siblings. David and Harriet see him as a 'throwback', 'goblin', 'troll' and 'dwarf' and is presented in the novel as an unwanted and unpleasant child.

Ben being different, disturbs the conventional family set-up, as he seems unfit to the social conformity of his parents. Ben's parents are by-product of outer society and they desire that Ben's identity should also be acceptable in that society. Harriet is unable to have an emotional connect as Ben is physically deformed child. In the absence of parental liking, it is difficult to be liked by the outside world. Here a sense of otherness crops in. Harriet insists to change Ben and David believes that Ben should get socialized to follow family norms.

Harriet and David go through sleepless nights due to Ben. As Ben was growing, he was getting stronger. When she feeds him, he bites her nipples until they turn black; he bites Harriet's thumb badly until "her bone bend" (FC 87). Ben attacks the pets of neighborhood. A visitor's cat dies followed by a neighbor's dog. Harriet says "If he could kill a dog, then why not a child?"(FC 122)

Harriet comes to the conclusion that Ben should be institutionalized, when he injures his brother's arm badly. Harriet then decides to send Ben to an institute where deformed and disabled children are admitted. She is conscious of difficulties through which Ben will have to go. The strenuous living in the institution may even lead to his death. When she visits the institution, in 'the nightmare ward', she could not withstand to see Ben in that atmosphere and decides to take him home knowing that it will not be an easy step to take him to the place where no one is ready to accept him.

Harriet's taking Ben back to home shows the emotional distress of motherhood. An ideal mother cares and protects her children and looks forward for the best possible solutions for her children's problems. She initiates all the actions to protect the child from bad habits and bad company. Harriet knows that she will be alone in her sufferings of being Ben's mother if she tries to accept Ben.

The relationship between Ben and parents influenced his siblings emotional state. All the four siblings remained individualistic when they were teenagers as no emotional bonding between them had developed. Other children could not tolerate the state of affairs and moved from home by deciding to live with their grandparents except Paul who was sent to psychoanalyst for help. Harriet spends her entire time with Ben which resulted in widening the emotional gap with her other children. When Ben was of five years, Luke and Helen announced they wanted to go to boarding-school. They were thirteen and eleven. They preferred to be away from the family and Ben. This was quite contrary to what Harriet and David believed in. Accordingly, the family bond between the members was weakening and the couple's desire for an extended and happy family remained just a dream.

Some feminists believe that Motherhood is the ultimate acceptance of patriarchal oppression. Such as, Adrienne Rich in her milestone work-*Of Women Born* describes motherhood as an experience and an institution which distinguishes motherhood and mothering as different concepts. She expresses that the motherhood signifies restrictions of patriarchal institution and mothering is related to a divine individual experience. This individual experience of mothering is considered to be a source of power. (OWB10) which she terms as empowered mothering.

In *The Fifth Child* doctors decline in helping Harriet to find out what is wrong with Ben since they cannot figure out his disability. When she consults Dr Brett and Dr Gilly they explicitly blame Harriet and ignore Ben's nature. "[Dr. Brett] said, [i]t is not abnormal to take a dislike to a child. I see it all the time. Unfortunately" (FC 67). Harriet also consults Dr Gilly who answers: "I'm going to come straight to the point, Mrs Lovatt. The problem is not with Ben, but with you. You don't like him very much" (FC124). The doctors in the novel antagonize Harriet. This blame has its roots in Harriet's own lack of self knowledge. She does not know if she likes Ben or hates him as he is the cause of all her problems both as a mother and wife. The blame in itself attributes a sense of power which she is not able to realize.

The novel depicts the power of patriarchy through David's dream. *The Fifth Child* begins with a dream of a large Victorian house which would be filled with many children. David is an ambitious architect who is conservative and chooses the right woman to become the part of his dream. Harriet unknowingly surrenders to the patriarchal forces of a perfect family. She does not know about the unpleasant life waiting on the way to their dream. According to David, Harriet is the perfect woman for fulfilling his traditional household dream. But, after Ben being not normal, David blames Harriet for not living up to the expectations of being the traditional ideal wife.

Squires said that "Blame is more like holding an opinion than expressing it. Blame can be implicitly directed in a way that is not obvious." (Squires, 56). For example, Harriet feels blamed by her family, not explicitly but rather they do it through gestures. At several moments in the novel, she feels blamed because of David and other family members: "She [Harriet] knew when they had seen him [Ben], because of the way they looked at her afterwards. As if I were a criminal! She raged to herself" (Lessing, 74).

Harriet experiences sensations of guilt and blame. She is under the impression that she has opposed the "rules" of family life and the requirements of motherhood, and is thus feeling guilt. One more reason of Harriet's guilt is that she procures sensations of guilt for not having enough time for all four children, and for the fact that David is exhausted, being the one and only contributor of the family, when Harriet is competent to work as well. So, guilt and self-blame are present both in conventional and modern motherhood.

This very idea presents motherhood as a dual institution. On the one hand, motherhood fulfills and completes a woman's life whereas, on the other hand it takes away women's ultimate freedom. *The Fifth Child* shows the patriarchal construct of the conservative society and tries to idealize the concept of motherhood which is shattered with the birth of *The Fifth Child,* Ben. The birth of four children in the 6 years of Lovett couple signifies an ideal family following patriarchal values. Everything with Lovetts was according to the social order in patriarchal construction.

CONCLUSION

The novel *The Fifth Child* is presented as a dilemma story initially but closely it portrays the patriarchal forces, social relations and the institution of motherhood. Harriet engages herself in building up David's home by giving birth to Lovett's four children and when Harriet needs the utmost support of her husband and her family, she is dejected and blamed as she does not fit in the ideal mother picture of the society. Feminist critics opine that subsequent gender roles have caste women in a second position in societal structure. To blame the mother for mistakes and wrongdoings is a normal phenomenon. She is held responsible for molding the child in such a way so that he grows into a healthy citizen who functions normally within the set norms of the society. Motherhood is a part of parenthood. It is a collaborative responsibility which society narrows down to gender role. Lessing's writing about mothers' socially constructed role in *The Fifth Child* demands and looks forward for a big change in the society.

REFERENCES

[1] Bhasin, K. (2006). What is patriarchy? Women unlimited, New Delhi.

[2] Bassin, D. and Kaplan, M.M. (Eds.). (1996). *Representations of motherhood.* Yale University Press.

[3] Dictionary, O.E. (2000). Oxford English Dictionary Online, 2nd.

[4] Neyer, G. and Bernardi, L. (2011). Feminist perspectives on motherhood and reproduction. *Historical Social Research/Historische Sozialforschung,* 162–176.

[5] Lessing, Doris. *The Fifth Child.* London: Harper Perennial, 2007.

[6] Raefipour, N. (2012). Ben, a Stranger in the Dark Society of Mirrors. *Epiphany, 5*(1).

[7] Sundberg, B. (2011). Patriarchy and Masculinity in Doris Lessing's The Fifth Child and in Ben in The World.

[8] Squires, J.E.R. *Blame.* "The Philosophical Quarterly." 18.70 (1968): 54–60.

[9] Thurer, S. (1994). *The myths of motherhood: How culture reinvents the good mother.* Houghton Mifflin Harcourt.

Positive Ageing: An Opportunity to Face New Challenges

Santosh Dhar[1] **and Upinder Dhar**[2]
Shri Vaishnav Vidyapeeth Vishwavidyalaya, Indore, Madhya Pradesh
E-mail: [1]deanresearch@svvv.edu.in; [2]vc@svvv.edu.in

ABSTRACT: Ageing has been inevitably associated with passivity, decline in physical health and disengagement. The loss of authority, status, and prospects become upsetting blocks to the sense of future well-being for ageing people. Uncertainty about freedom, growing dependence on others, unable to tap opportunities of service and hence no new views for living are the deep challenges for creating gratifying futures. Old face the world with dread post-career. It is here that positive resolutions can serve as a springboard to a new life-under-design. Answers of potentials and possibilities can redirect energies toward optimistic planning. Positive ageing calls for individuals to draw upon not only psychological factors and individual traits but also social and community resources to live and function optimally in old age. Resources such as paid or unpaid work, health care, education, extended family ties, and religion can offer tremendous support as individuals enter into old age. Positive ageing suggests that older persons actively manage these resources. In doing so, they initiate at will and start intervention. The concept of positive ageing emphasizes fitness, lifelong activity, good health, and high self-esteem.

Older people can make choices that will preserve and enhance their well-being. In particular, taking measures to maintain good physical health, seeking personal or intellectual growth experiences, and developing a reliable network of social relationships. This can be helpful in maintaining well-being in old age. In addition, it is important to focus on the positive aspects of growing old. Feeling pride in one's past and present accomplishments, the enjoyment of one's circle of family and friends, and the possibility for new life experiences coupled with enhanced perspectives are the aspects to be embraced in old age. Positive-ageing framework defies previous notion that ageing is inexorably associated with detachment, inactiveness and waning. The negative effects of ageing can be reduced through various coping strategies with modifications of earlier adaptive strategies. This chapter will discuss different perspectives on ageing, as well as strategies and practical suggestions for challenging or resisting maladaptive or destructive mechanisms. It will offer a paradigmatic shift in the concept of ageing with a glimpse into the ways in which ageing can he experienced positively.

Keywords: Good Health, Old Age, Passivity, Positive Ageing, Self-Esteem.

INTRODUCTION

Ageing is part of the normal human development which belongs to the life span of everyone. Healthy Ageing is defined by the World report on ageing and health as "the process of developing and maintaining the functional ability that enables well-being in older age." Healthy Ageing enables people to be and do what they value throughout their lives by creating the conducive environment and appropriates opportunities. Healthy ageing does not require a person to be free of disease as many older adults have one or more health conditions that do not limit their living in general. Being able to live in an environment that supports and maintains an individual's innate capacity and functional capability is key to Healthy Ageing. Components of well-being refer to personal and social functioning, and they express what a person values doing or being. Well-being contains more than just one person. Environment includes the home, community and broader society, and all the elements within them such as the built environment, people and their relationships, attitudes and values, health and social policies, the systems that support them and the services that they offer.

When people celebrate their 60th birthday, they begin to confront a challenge that is both unfamiliar and daunting. This is the uneasy state of being regarded as old. It happens with everybody. Regardless of an individual's contribution to the workplace, to families, or any other cultural domain, one begins to feel the threat. In part, the threat is crystallized in the pervasive anxiety that accompanies noticeable changes in one's body: greying or disappearing hair, increasing wrinkles, poorer eyesight and less acute hearing, expanding girth, slower reflexes, and diminished stamina. All are signals that capacity to maintain participation in the active and productive world of adulthood is on decline. These are also signals of impending mortality.

Restrained relationship with others further adds to this plight. In the workplace younger colleagues and employers seem eager for an announcement of retirement. People offer their seat on public transit, help with the luggage or grocery bags, and address with an extra tone of formality which makes one feel that he/she has grown old. Sometimes there is an air of impatience if one does not move swiftly or confidently enough, walking or driving. To seemingly subdue these fears, the advertising industry suggests that products and services are available that can help one to control or hide these defects: Iiposuction, plastic surgery, Botox, hair dyes, cosmetics, exercise equipment, yoga, health clubs, pills and psychotherapy. Yet, the very pressure to yield to these age-defying efforts, are also reminders of slow decaying.

An individual tries to defy his age but continuous questioning of competence and activity from others who want to show concern like *Are you still working such long hours... still skiing... still scuba diving...still having tremendous stamina,* and so on further compel an individual to think that one is withering. Such questions suggest that whatever one is doing is becoming exceptional, as decline and withdrawal are "normal." With retirement, the barrages of questions intensify: Where will you live? What will you do? Where will you go? Once one is no longer committed to a workplace, the options for living seem obscure, and there are no viable criteria remaining for choice. And, encrusted under these stressful questions are those painful uncertainties one regales in private: I have become forgetful, less attractive, mentally slower, and physically less capable, less sexually appealing, and so on.

In a survey, it has been found that pessimism appears to grow as people move out of their 30s into middle age before falling late in life. Those 70 and older were least likely to express worry about age bringing poor health, a move into a nursing home or memory loss. They also were least likely to fear that old age could prompt them to be disrespected or become a burden on their families. People in their 60s and beyond had the lowest fear of losing their independence. Research has also pointed to greater satisfaction, happiness and optimism among older people. People often find in their later years a growing appreciation for facets of life they may have focused on less when they were younger, including spirituality and personal relationships. Fulfillment from those things can help bolster overall happiness, even in the face of potential physical decline.

The basis of these irksome questions is primarily the ageing process itself. Decline seems natural and obvious. But is this what timely happens? To be sure, there are changes, but why they are counted as deterioration? The word "decline" is an evaluative judgment that is not given in the change itself. There is nothing about greying or thinning hair that is intrinsically worse or better than a full head of dark hair. To see these as decline is arbitrary. To one it may be decline but for others it may be maturity .Whether people shoe size changes with age is not obvious, primarily because attention is never directed to this possibility. In effect, ageing is not so much in the body of an individual as it is in the way one thinks. According to Gergen & Gergen (2004), life is largely in terms of the meaning an individual assigns to the world, and this meaning is social in its origin. Thus, ageing is not so much a state of nature as it is a state of social meaning.

The questions and doubts that often plague lives of older are not due to the ageing process in itself, but due to existing cultural meaning. To ask this question to oneself is to accede to the assumption that ageing is decline. As one enquires into the problems of age, he/she essentially constructs a world in which the problems are central. These become the dominant realities that burden every-day existence. In effect, the questions one asks are self-created. While bodily changes may be inevitable, cultural meanings are subject to change. Thus, there are social processes now at work that can provide grounds for resistance to the traditional construction of age as decline. These processes can help in overcoming a bias that is deeply upsetting the quality of life. In fact, it is a matter of life or death. Gerontologists have demonstrated that those who are optimistic about their lives live longer. Those who viewed their entry into the latter years most negatively, subsequently die earlier than those who were more positive in their orientation (Danner *et al.*, 2001; Mamta *et al.*, 2000).

New scenario of ageing is underway. Life expectancy research gives an encouraging picture. The life has become easier, less dangerous, and more peaceful than those of the ancestors, who often struggled with deprivations, such as poor nutrition, inadequate health care, and dangerous occupations. 100 years ago, the lucky man who lived to be 55 had a life expectancy of 72; today that 55 year old's life expectancy is almost ten years longer, and a 60 year old's is 82. And, for every additional year one lives, the average life-span increases. Simultaneously, because of the greater vigor of today's elderly population, gerontologists have shifted their disagreements as well. The new classification distinguishes between the "young old" as opposed to the "old old" (people in their eighties and beyond). Social clock is the time in life when one is expected to engage in certain activities and events. In the 1950s, in social clock there was a social template that suggested that after one's education was completed, marriage soon followed. Gender roles were quite rigid as well. The wife might or might not be employed for a couple of years to help build a nest-egg, and then stop to nurture a family. Hubby got a promotion, and they moved to a bigger house. Her questions to herself "Am I declining?" contributed to the reality of decline.

The significant question, then, is how to shift to a more positive register of questioning. Organizational change agents work on the power of positive questions in Appreciative Inquiry (AI). Drawing from organizational development Barrett and Fry (2005) in Appreciative Inquiry concluded that questions determine whether capacity to grow and develop diminishes, or increases over a period of time. Thus, among AI practitioners, problem talk is avoided because problem talk in itself becomes a problem. It is often a series of blame, doubts and a sense of bleak future. Such talk is replaced with a focus on strengths, sources of energy and value hence desirable ends. To achieve this end, participants ask individually to tell each other personal stories, such as, "What is the most significant and invigorating experience you have had in the past? On the basis of their accounts, the positive core of the person is revealed. Other groups also relish approaches that maximize the potential for change using a positive questioning mode.

Adams (2004) placed emphasis on questions that stress openness and curiosity as a basis for creating dialogues with others that promote change. Rejected are questions such as "Who is responsible for this mess?" which are primarily useful in judging and blaming others. In their place questions are set in motion that suggests a desire for new perspectives and ideas. An individual can ask, for example, "How can we find something of worth in the crunch we find ourselves in?" Rather than being drawn into a process of being judgmental and mutual blame, people can work together to improve common outcomes.

Vogt *et al.,* (2003) emphasized that questions with positive possibilities can open up tremendous opportunities for varied groups. Dominant questions can be those that generate curiosity, evoke questions, touch issues of deeper significance, bring to the surface underlying assumptions, invite creativity and generate energy to stimulate reflective conversation. Questions related to action can mobilize the capacity to create a positive mind set and Human systems naturally evolve toward the questions that they ask. Today, as organizational consultants work more intensely with individuals as coaches for various professional developmental tasks, it is equally important to bring positive and powerful questions to bear in these encounters.

It is often the case that executives and professionals who have given their lives to their careers are filled with dread at the empty space that might follow their exit from organizational life. The loss of power, prestige and prospects for deep challenges are daunting barriers to their sense of future well-being. It is here that positive questions can serve as a springboard to a new life-under-design. Questions that emphasize freedom, new opportunities for control, creativity and service and new vistas for living are helpful in the creation of fulfilling futures. Instead of facing the world post-career with dread, questions of potentials and possibilities can redirect energies toward optimistic planning. The appreciative theorizing developed in organizational change practices apply no less to the world of daily life.

POSITIVE THINKING AND SELF-ESTEEM

Replacing negative self-talk with positive self-talk, identifying triggers for negative thinking and responding to them in new ways, envisioning positive scenarios and enjoying small pleasures are all ways to create a positive thinking habit. The definition of positive thinking, the way psychologists, researchers and medical professionals define it, is simply self-talk that is realistic and self-affirming. Research shows that optimism and positive thinking lead to decreased stress, greater resistance to catching the common cold, easier breathing for people with certain lung diseases and reduced risk of coronary artery disease. Positive thinking needs positive attitude towards life. This can tickle positive thoughts. It takes as much effort to think about the negative as it is for the positive. Concentrating on the positive leads to positive results. Associating with colleagues with a positive attitude also reinforces positive thinking. When something goes not in the desired direction—a positive thinking person concentrates on solutions instead of the problem.

Some colleagues have a natural tendency to point fingers when things do not go right? They tend to whine and complain instead of starting to work on a solution immediately? Positive thinkers live up to the challenge of the problem and commit themselves to seeking a solution to the problem. They do not dwell in unproductive activities. Positive thinking involves "I can", "I will", "I am able", "I am ready". It also involves taking the initiative to seek answers and solutions. They are proactive in learning about the information needed to complete the assignment at hand. A positive thinker concentrates on the assignment and is not distracted by negative thoughts. Positive thinking is referred to as hope, optimism, happiness, confidence and positive illusions. Individuals with high levels of positivity exhibit confidence and approach challenges with enthusiasm and persistence (Carver & Scheier, 2003). Positivity has motivational value for right mindset.

Positive thinking is exhibited and valued in our aphorisms and music, churches and businesses, politics, media and child development practices. Increasingly, church pastors espouse a new positive theology that leads to success, wealth and good health (Ehrenreich, 2009). Social and medical scientists have given experimental evidences that dispositional optimism has a positive general outlook in life matters and contributes to physical and psychological wellbeing. For example, optimistic cancer patients face lower mortality risk (Schulz *et al.*, 1996). Optimists experience faster recovery after coronary artery bypass surgery than pessimists (Scheier *et al.*, 1989). Optimists adjust more smoothly to major life transitions (Aspinwall & Taylor, 1992) or failure to achieve a desired pregnancy (Litt *et al.*, 1992). Scheier and Carver (1993) found optimistic patients reported more positive results including better coping, health habits and even less physical symptoms.

Peterson *et al.,* (1998) reported that individuals with an optimistic outlook as children survived negative outlook individuals by approximately two years. Puri and Robinson (2007) considered that moderate levels of positive thinking can help individuals but excessive high levels are not good. Individuals with low levels of optimism tend to lack motivation as they assume that their efforts are not going to bear any results. People tend to have a propensity to focus on negative information which reinforces their view that ruin awaits them. For these reasons, they often withdraw. Moderate optimists tend to set moderately high, yet realistic, goals and put forth the necessary effort to reach their goals. These individuals recognize a balance of positive and negative cues within their environment, noting both the potential benefits and risks associated with each decision alternative. This is more balanced approach that tends to make them above-average performers. Extremely optimistic individuals, in contrast, tend to set unrealistic high goals and often could be over-confident that they will attain their goals and they also overestimate the likelihood of their success (Baron & Shane, 2005). Excessive optimism is cited as a primary cause for the high failure rate of new business ventures.

In a longitudinal study of men and women ranging in age from 25 to 104, researchers surveyed a total of more than 3,600 adults living in the United States. The researchers assessed self-esteem by asking respondents to rate their level of agreement with statements such as, "I take a positive attitude toward myself," which indicates high self-esteem; and "At times I think I am no good at all!" and "All in all, I am inclined to feel that I am a failure," both of which signify low self-esteem. Respondents were also asked about their ethnicity, education, income, work status, relationship satisfaction, marital status, health, social support, and if they had undergone stressful life events. Self-esteem was minimum among young adults, but increased throughout adulthood, peaking at age 60, before it started to decline. On an average, adult women had lower self-esteem than adult men, but self-esteem levels coincided as men and women reached their 80s and 90s.

Blacks and whites had similar self-esteem levels throughout young adulthood and middle age. In old age, average self-esteem among blacks dropped much more sharply than whites. This was the result even after controlling the differences in income and health. Education, income, health, and employment status had effect on self-esteem, especially as people aged. People who have higher incomes and better health in later life are able to maintain their self-esteem as they age. Attitude typically starts declining around the time of retirement. A study has found that self-esteem enhances steadily as people age but starts declining around the time of retirement. Higher self-esteem is likely to be associated with wealth and health.

The independence in wealth and health gives a good feeling as one is able to contribute to the family and society, which in turn boosts the person's self-esteem. People of all ages in gratifying and complementary relationships are likely to have higher self-esteem. However, some researchers have suggested that people in happy relationships experienced the similar drop in self-esteem during old age as people in unhappy relationships, despite maintaining higher self-esteem in their early lives. Thus, being in a happy relationship does not safeguard a person against the dip in self-esteem that typically occurs in old age. There are number of theories as to why self-esteem is elevated in middle age and then declines after retirement. Midlife is a time of highly stable work, family, and romantic relationships. People mostly occupy senior positions of power and status, which trigger self-esteem. In contrast, older adults experience a change in roles such as loneliness, retirement and obsolete work skills besides deteriorating health.

Given the increasing evidence that optimism and longevity go together, there is good reason to rethink the ways in which individuals commonly evaluate themselves as they age. Rather than asking about what is failing or declining, what they have lost, or what they might have been, they can ask questions that focus on what they appreciate in life, who they might enrich with their gifts, what sources of joy can be found in the days ahead, what they are grateful for, how they might savor the moment they are a part of, and what they have gained by their experiences in the past?

In a workshop elderly people were asked to address the declines in physical abilities; chronic illnesses; retirement; lower sexual drive and interest; fewer economic opportunities; less income; changing physical appearance; children growing up and leaving home; dementia; loss of partner, family members or friends through death; and personal death. In each case, the groups were asked if they can locate any positive outcomes of these events; are there ways in which these conditions may be beneficial to well-being? It was surprising to find that diverse creative and emotionally stirring possibilities emerged from the groups. For example, the loss of physical abilities, they pointed out, can give rise to more frequent moments of tranquility, to a greater sense of personal skill as one finds ways to compensate for the deficit, and to the development of new and engaging hobbies or interests to replace the old.

In effect, when asking the right question, people can locate means of transforming otherwise negative outcomes to acceptable, nourishing, and even joyful alterative (Hedke & Winslade, 2004). The most important wisdom for growing old well may lie in the art of posing positive questions. People can change the way they age by staying active, to the fullest extent possible, within all areas of life: physical, spiritual, emotional, intellectual, professional, environmental and social. Ageing within these dimensions of wellness keeps us involved, alert and enjoy a productive life. The concept of active ageing is summed up in the phrase "engaged in life." Individuals can participate in life as fully as possible, regardless of socio economic status or health conditions, within the wellness dimensions.

Researchers at Yale University studied a group of more than 4,000 adults aged 60 and above and found those who held positive beliefs about ageing had a 44 per cent lower risk of developing dementia than those who held negative beliefs suggesting that positive age beliefs may act as a "protective factor" against dementia, supporting the case for a public health campaign against ageism. Age beliefs are malleable as some researchers have shown. In a study Dr. Levy and her colleagues at Yale School of

Public Health recruited 4,765 "dementia free" American adults with an average age of 72.The first step was to assess the participants' attitudes towards ageing, before assessing them every two years on a range of cognitive skills to determine whether they had developed dementia. They were interested in knowing whether the age beliefs they had taken in from their surrounding culture influenced their risk of developing dementia. Participants' beliefs about ageing were assessed using an "Attitude toward Ageing" scale, in which they were asked about the degree to which they agreed or disagreed with statements such as, "The older I get, the more useless I feel". If somebody strongly agreed with that statement, for example, they would be given a score that indicates they have a more negative belief about ageing. But if they disagreed, then they would receive a score that indicates a positive view of ageing."

To assess the potential effects on people genetically predisposed to dementia, 26 per cent of people included in the sample were carriers of the APOE-e4 gene variant, one of the strongest risk factors for dementia affecting about one-quarter of the US population (and one-fifth of Australia's).The researchers found that participants holding positive beliefs about ageing had a 43.6 per cent lower risk of developing dementia over the course of four years compared to those holding negative beliefs. Among those with the APOE-e4 gene variant, the difference was even more pronounced: those holding positive beliefs had a 49.8 per cent lower risk of developing dementia compared to their high-risk counterparts holding negative beliefs. It was found that positive age beliefs can reduce the risk of one of the most established genetic risk factors of dementia. The results considered other factors that could influence the findings, including age, education, sex, race, cardiovascular disease, diabetes and baseline cognitive performance.

Creativity in the Elderly: Many people make major creative contributions well into their so-called retirement years. Born on 7th May 1861, Indian polymath – a poet, musician and artist - and Nobel Laureate, *Rabindranath Tagore* reshaped Bengali literature and music, as well as Indian art with contextual modernism in the late 19th and early 20th centuries. Author of Gitanjali and its "profoundly sensitive, fresh and beautiful verse", he became in 1913 the first non-European to win the Nobal Prize in Literature. Tagore's interest expanded to science in his last years as listed in a 1937 collection of essays. He wove the process of science, the narratives of scientists, into stories till his death in 1941, aged eighty.

Sir Mokshagundam Vishweshvaraya, born on 15th September 1861, was an Indian engineer, scholar, statesman, and 19th Diwan of Mysore. He received India's highest honour, the Bharat Ratna, in 1955. 15th September is celebrated as Engineers Day in India in his memory. He is regarded as the chief engineer responsible for the construction of the Krishna Raja Sagar Dam in the North-West suburb of Mysore city. He gave his valuable technical advice for the construction of Mokama Bridge over Ganga in Bihar when he was over 90 years old. He was on the Board of Directors of Tata Steel from 1927–1955, that is, when he was more than 66 years old—he started his tenure on this board till he was 94. He died on 12th April 1962 at the age of 100 years.

Sarvepalli Radhakrishnan, born on 5th September 1988, was an Indian philosopher and statesman who was the first Vice President of India (1952–1962) and the second President of India from 1962–1967. He died on 17th April 1975 (aged 86). He received Bharat Ratna in 1954. He was one of India's most distinguished twentieth-century scholars of comparative religion and philosophy. *C.V. Raman*, born on 7th November 1888, was an Indian physicist and Nobel laureate who retired from the Indian Institute of Science in 1948 and established the Raman Research Institute in Bangalore a year later. He served as its director and remained active there until his death in 1970, in Bangalore, at the age of 82. *Johann Wolfgang Goethe,* a German scholar, was born on 28th August 1749. He died on 22nd March 1832 at the age of 82. He completed *Faust* at the age of around 80 years.

Anna Mary Robertson Moses (September 7, 1860 – December 13, 1961), known by her nick name *Grandma Moses,* was an American folk artist. She began panting in earnest at the age of 78 and is often cited as an example of an individual who successfully began a career in the arts at an advanced age. Sophocles completed *Oedipus Rex* at 70 and Electra at around 90. Born in 497/496 BC, Sophocles died in 406/405 BC at the age of 90–92 years. *Pablo Casals,* 29th December 1876 – 22nd October 1973, was giving *cello* concerts at 88. He was cellist, composer and conductor from Spain. *Mahatama Gandhi* led India's opposition to British occupation in his late seventies. He was born on 2nd October 1969 and died on 30th January 1948. These examples suggest that the years past 65 can be a time of real consolidation—a time when the ideas and skills developed over most of a lifetime can be brought together to produce major new achievements. Most people will not achieve at the level of these examples at any age (Morgan *et al.*, 1986).

The retiree travel industry is growing, especially as baby boomers leave the workforce; witness the cruise and travel companies that specialize in tours for "active older adults." Working part-time or as a consultant is another option embraced by more and more retirees after they leave full-time employment. Even after about 10 years of retirement, they are probably reevaluating their use of time. Part of it may be a desire to move on to something else. Perhaps it is a reduced physical energy level or the onset of a disabling condition such as vision loss, arthritis, or hip replacement. They may want to devote more time to physical and mental fitness. An additional factor may be that the things that mattered or were on the wish list; working to stay in the game or traveling to faraway places lose their importance. Shopping and acquiring material goods is less and less appealing.

Literature indicates that financial literacy can help individuals to plan for better retirement life (Brown & Graf, 2013). Framing a retirement plan is a complex and challenging process and individuals who lack knowledge in interest and inflation rates are at a higher risk of overestimating their retirement income (Nyamute & Maina, 2011). There is a positive association between financial literacy and retirement confidence as individuals who are financially literate are able to have better retirement plans (Kim *et al.*, 2005). Financial literacy can encourage individuals to practice healthy financial management (Zaimah *et al.*, 2013). In fact, financial literacy facilitates individuals to learn importance of financial management and promotes regular implementation of financial management in routine, thereby making them more optimistic about their retirement. This is because as people plan for their retirement, they will most probably perceive themselves as being well-prepared and feel more confident about their ability to be self-sufficient.

In sum, old people are still on the go. They may continue to have adventures they wanted to take but their priorities shift toward a more inward reflection on what is most important to them in the years that remain. They may well be at the midpoint of the retirement smile, having spent more money right after retirement on travel and entertainment and now finding that the simpler things like taking walks in the country and spending time with friends and family are more satisfying. Insights into where a client is in life can provide clues about how they see the years ahead. The conversation also can bridge to the financial implications. Perhaps the changes in use of time may result in wishing to donate more to charity, giving more money to children and grandchildren now rather than waiting until death, taking the grand cruise, or hosting a big family destination reunion.

HEALTH AND LONGEVITY

Some people as they grow older begin to think more about their shortened time horizon. That may manifest it in wanting to live life to the fullest, making the most of every living moment. It also may cause olds to consider their legacy to a greater degree than before; not only from a financial standpoint but also from the perspective of how they want to be remembered by children, grandchildren, and those whose lives they have touched over the years. And they probably have begun thinking about their final wishes and how they want to be cared for in very old age. Legacy and mortality may not be issues that rise to the top in the life of old, but they loom in the background as people at that age wonder what's next for them. Will they or their spouse be able to have a satisfying life into the eighties and nineties, and if so, how can they contribute to their families and communities and make a difference? Wills, estate plans, living wills, and powers of attorney should be up to date. This is a good age to review these documents and final wishes with the client, while they are healthy and active. It is also a time to make plans if a client should become incapacitated.

A discussion of legacy may also provide an opportunity to meet the adult children or trusted friends who will be involved in financial and care decisions. This will be helpful should anything happen to a client and also will establish a relationship between advisor and the family. Age 75 is an appropriate time for this type of review, as death seems a ways off but still not too far in the future. People who have reached age 75 are at the midpoint of their retirement; most of them are active and enjoying life. They have had 10 years to find out what their new retirement life stage is like, make changes along the way, and begin to plan for their older ages. Just-in-time planning and our youth culture mentality can get in the way of thinking seriously about the future, but we might look at age 75 as a benchmark for financial planners. At that age, retirees are still young enough to fully engage but old enough to understand deep down the significance of the waning years ahead. It is a perfect time for advisors to raise some of the value-based subjects, often hidden from sight, that are on the minds of their clients and, at the same time, prepare them for the journey that lies ahead.

Life satisfaction is a vital driving force in life and an essential factor of an individual's personality. It is a synthetic and multi-layered indicator of the quality of life or personal well-being (Starc & Zabukovec, 2013). Ramovš & Lipar (2013) stated that satisfaction with one's own life is a person's well-being as a result of experiencing one's own life as coherent enough with one's own needs and wishes. A satisfied person has a positive attitude towards his own life. It is all about an individual's assessment of life, which includes his/her past as well as the life that is still in front of him. Life satisfaction depends on experiencing oneself, fulfilling one's goals, ability to cope with daily activities, interpersonal relationships, harmony with others, one's mood, medical condition etc. Life satisfaction is of great importance particularly in the old age. Self-image and self-esteem are two important elements of the quality of life. Self-image is a set of concepts and images that people have about them, it is about an individual's experience of oneself. It is a dynamic structure, composed of several dimensions that can alter concurrently with an individual's maturation and ageing (Zaletel, 2011).

A person can have several self-images simultaneously, such as social self-image, academic self-image, physical and emotional self-image because it is formed in various areas (Babsek, 2009). A significant influence on the development of one's self-image has been reported that of childhood experiences, successes, failures, and the environment. An individual having a bad self-image is critical towards himself/herself, feels insecure and does not trust his/her abilities. Kristančič (2005) stated that self-image requires specific efforts to accept one. According to Musek (2005), self-esteem reflects a critical judgment about one's values. It is a mix of how other people perceive us and of how we perceive their judgments. It reflects that discrepancy between the actual and the ideal image of oneself (Escolar & Guzman, 2014).

The more successful and reputed a person is in his environment, the greater is his self-esteem. Higher self-esteem helps him to cope with life's challenges, whereby the sense of anxiety decreases, and general well-being increases this capacity. Men and women have different perspectives on self-esteem. In men, it is a correlate of physical appearance, whereas in women it is a correlate social behavior (Halit, 2014). It has also been established that individuals with higher self-esteem achieve better health and well-being than those with lower self-esteem. The decline in self-esteem can give rise to a number of health problems, such as depression, anxiety, apathy, and a sense of loneliness. High self-esteem individual accepts oneself as he/she is, respects self, and feels worthy of respect. It plays a crucial role in the mental well-being of a person.

Research has shown that spiritual capabilities increase with ageing, whereas physical and mental abilities decline. Spirituality is a promising human ability, which subscribes to healthy ageing The spiritual domain is an integral part, inseparable and inalienable from a human being which helps to establish the purpose of one's life. Greed, rivalry, exploitation of other people and nature, distrust, fear and hatred would spread fast in the society in the absence of spiritually awakened people. Spiritual domain of a person is included in the holistic concept of the treatment of a human being. A human being has a wide range of bio-psycho-social and spiritual needs. A person as a whole includes the body, the mind, emotions and spirituality, which should be in equilibrium (Tjale & Bruce, 2007).

Disequilibrium leads to health problems. According to Koenig *et al.,* (1999), there is a positive impact of religious involvement on health status. McFadden and Levin (1996) summarized the positive association on the pretext that religious commitment affects health behavior e.g., smoking, alcohol consumption; religious participation affect social support; religious worship and prayer may produce positive emotional experiences; religious beliefs may be consistent with positive health beliefs; religious beliefs may lead to optimism and a positive mental attitude and a combination of these elements may produce the positive association.

Self-esteem, self-image and spirituality index are important for life satisfaction in the old age. Questions like • What is working? • What gives life to the relationship? • How far one is successful because of the way he/she relate? Stimulate these ideas into action in one's personal life. When the extended family meets for dinner, family often begins the meal by having each person, young and old, say something about what they appreciate about the day. It is amazing how this ritual animates dialogue replete with mutual caring, enthusiasm and novelty. It has been found that certain activities and relationships are important to one another and each person has a special spark to contribute to the dynamism of the whole.

Puri and Robinson (2007) in a survey from the Federal Reserve Board's Survey of Consumer Finance (SCF), a triennial assessment of U.S. families 'financial and demographic information collected demographic and health related information. The researchers combined these data to determine participants' statistical life expectancies. Then they compared the statistical and self-reported life expectancies and categorized anyone who expected to live longer than the data predicted as an optimist. The researchers labeled the top 5 percent as—extreme optimists, those who thought they will live an average of 20 years longer than was statistically likely. It was found that optimists 1) worked longer hours; 2) saved more money; and 3) were more likely to pay their credit card balances on time.

On the other hand, extreme optimists 1) worked significantly fewer hours; 2) saved less money; 3) were less likely to pay off their credit card balances on a regular basis; and, interestingly, 4) were more likely to smoke. The differences between optimists and extreme optimists were remarkable, and suggested that over-optimism, like overconfidence, may in fact lead to behaviors that are unwise. High levels of optimism might cause individuals to become overly confident which could lead to difficulties coping with reality. In an extreme case, these extreme levels of positive thinking could even result in delusional thoughts. Positive people believe that the future will be bright and looking on the bright side leads to good health, prosperity, and success (Ehrenreich, 2009).

Older workers are often perceived as generally less effective with less adaptability in their current roles (Iweins *et al.*, 2012). Such stereotypes are not totally without foundation as Kooij *et al.*, (2008) concluded from an extensive literature review that achievement motivation and the desire to learn new things decrease with age. Studies have shown positive perceptions of older adults with respect to characteristics such as perceived warmth, interpersonal skills, maturity, experience, loyalty, reliability, and willingness to help (Chen and Wang, 2012). A concept apparently related to willingness to help is the generativity motive. Generativity has been described as exhibited by a person who "teaches, leads, and promotes the next generation while generating life products and outcomes that benefit the social system and promote its continuity from one generation to the next.

According to Erikson's Psychosocial Development Theory, in midlife and beyond, the individual's concern for sustaining and guiding the present and succeeding generations becomes a powerful motivator (Erikson, 1950; 1964). The generativity increases with age (Zacher *et al.*, 2011; Villar, 2012). Thus, the tasks such as teaching and mentoring seem likely to motivate older workers (Kooij *et al.*, 2008). Mentoring younger people seem to be an ideal manner in which to satisfy the generativity motive while, at the same time, contributing to the society.

Pundt *et al.,* (2015) suggested that post-retirement older people differentiated between perceived life and work satisfaction. The motives of achievement, appreciation, autonomy, contact, and generativity directly affected life satisfaction and indirectly affected work satisfaction. Occupational characteristics assessing achievement, appreciation, autonomy, contact, and generativity has direct effects on work satisfaction but not on life satisfaction except for occupational autonomy. Age is positively associated with motivation for generativity-related, but not growth-related tasks. Personal and job resources are positively and differentially related to task-specific motivation. Supporting older workers' motivation in light of the demand for longer individual work lives is becoming an important agenda.

People are healthier and live longer after the traditional retirement age. Living longer cultivates a varying set of needs and traditional retirement becomes obsolete. People's shifting aspirations, desire for purpose and want for ongoing application of their talents changes their outlook towards life. When individuals pass 50, they generally shift their gaze into being productive in areas that have meaning to them and start to think about how they will be remembered. They start looking at fulfillment as a primary objective over pay. With a generative urge, ageing people are willing to contribute with powerful inventory of talent, knowledge and human skills. Reason being twofold. The first is as a status symbol, displaying themselves as high-performing and valued members of society to keep their worth to prospective employees up while also being involved in something they feel worthwhile about. These altruistic efforts are often looked on with envy, even more than net worth. The second is a way for them to place themselves in an unfamiliar environment where they can build and expand upon their own skill sets, in particular, leadership skills—a form of anticipatory careering to develop the skills they need for career progression. Older people with their experience and ability bring emotional stability, complex problem solving skills, nuanced thinking, high emotional intelligence and institutional know-how, not the typical skills a youthful cohort tends to carry.

There is ample evidence that social engagement has positive effects on health and longevity. Social isolation is as strong a risk factor for early mortality as cigarette smoking. The 55-to-64-year-olds just about to join the ranks of the elderly are far less socially engaged now than their predecessors were at the same age 20 years ago. And this pattern emerged across virtually all traditional measures of social engagement now elders are less likely to participate in community or religious organizations than were their counterparts 20 years ago. They are less likely to be married. They talk with their neighbors less frequently. It doesn't stop with participation in communities and neighborhoods these people report fewer meaningful interactions with their spouses and partners than did previous generations, and they report weaker ties to family and friends.

Old women are working longer, which offers its own kind of social connection. Another possibility is that they are interacting in nontraditional ways, using social media and participating in global communities, though this is unlikely to fully explain the phenomenon, given that many old people remain digitally averse. But it is also possible that patterns of social disengagement reflect the price that these people will pay for having rejected family values and traditions many years ago. These behavioral changes may lead to their health issues as they withdraw from meaningful engagement. But if they stay engaged as they age, they may spark a second social revolution. Instead, boomers could become an army of millions of gray-haired people, better educated than any previous generation, armed with unprecedented financial resources and decades of experience, ready to solve the practical problems of life. This revolution could finally help the nation become a better place for young people.

Yuan *et al.,* (2018) found that older adults who are engaged in social activities and community events stay fit in their mental, physical, and emotional health. Personal and collaborative agency in a community context, with health as an outcome is coproduced by an individual and other engaged community members. Irrespective of living arrangements, engaged in a diverse range of coproduction activities, including physical, socializing, service, discussion, and interest-based activities reinforce positive attitude towards life.

The central focus of selective optimization with compensation model is on the management of the dynamics between gains and losses, i.e., a general process of adaptation, consisting of three interacting elements. First, there is the element of selection, which refers to an increasing restriction of one's life to fewer domains of functioning because of an age-related loss in the range of adaptive potential. The second element, optimization, reflects the view that people engage in behaviors to enrich and augment their general reserves and to maximize their chosen life courses (and associated forms of behavior) with regard to quantity and quality. The third element, compensation, results also (like selection) from restrictions in the range of adaptive potential. It becomes operative when specific behavioral capacities are lost or are reduced below a standard required for adequate functioning.

The lifelong process of selective optimization with compensation allows people to age successfully, i.e., to engage in life tasks that are important to them despite a reduction in energy. For instance, the famous pianist Rubinstein remarked in a television interview that he conquers the weaknesses of ageing (adaptation) in his piano playing in the following manner: First, he reduces his repertoire and plays a smaller number of pieces (selection); second, he practices these more often (optimization); and third, he slows down his speed of playing prior to fast movements, thereby producing a contrast that enhances the impression of speed in the fast movements (compensation).

Genetic ageing factors are out of a person's control, for example, sex and heredity. There are, however, non-genetic factors that are within an individual's control. Non-genetic factors are lifestyle choices, for example, diet, physical activity, gender roles, and mental activity (Aitken & Rudolph, 2012). Genetics are beyond control but non-genetics can be controlled by one's lifestyle. Mentally, it is important to have a strong support system in older age due to numerous transitions each older adult experiences between retirement and late adulthood. Weak support system may lead to depression. Social factors play a role in ageing, similar to biological and psychological factors. Social factors that impact ageing include family ties, friendship, and integration into society. The lack of social ties can also negatively impact how an individual ages and experiences a good old age. Social support and social networks have been strong influences on a higher quality of life for older adults.

To conclude, the social support appears to lower the risk of mortality in older adults (Haber, 2013). For individuals who place high significance on physical and mental health, old age is an opportunity to face new challenges and focus on the positive aspects of their lives. They concentrate on life reflection and emphasize that they should enjoy the time they have left with (Aitken & Rudolph, 2012). Successful ageing is a focus on positive ageing, productive ageing, or ageing well instead of gauging age on a success scale.

REFERENCES

[1] Aitken, M. and Rudolph, M. (2012). Biological and Social Theories of Ageing. In R. Padilla, S. Byers-Connon and H. Lohman (Eds.), Occupational Therapy With Elders: Strategies For The COTA .Maryland Heights: Elsevier/Mosby.

[2] Adams, M. (2004). Change your questions, change your life. San Francisco: Berrett-Koehler.

[3] Aggar, C., Ronaldson, S. and Cameron, ID. (2011). Self-esteem in careers of frail older people: Resentment predicts anxiety and depression. *Ageing & Mental Health*, 15*(6)*, 671–678.

[4] Barrett, F.J. and Fry, R.E. (2005). Appreciative inquiry: A positive approach to building cooperative capacity.

[5] Brown, M. and Graf, R. (2013). Financial literacy and retirement planning in Switzerland. Available from: *http://scholarcommons.usf.edu/cgi/viewcontent.cgi?article=1133&context=numeracy*

[6] Chagrin Falls, O.H., Taos Institute Publications. Cooperrider, D. and Avital, M. (Eds.) (2004). Advances in appreciative inquiry: Constructive discourse and human organization. New York: Elsevier.

[7] Chen, H.J. and Wang, Y.H. (2012). "Age Stereotypes of Older Primary Teachers in Taiwan", *Educational Gerontology,* 38(5), 362–371.

[8] Danner, D.D., Snowdon, D.A. and Friesen, W.V. (2001). Positive emotions in early life and longevity: Findings from the nun study. *Journal of Personality and Social Psychology*, 80, 804–813.

[9] Dychwald, K. (1999). Age Power: How the 21st century will be ruled by the new old. New York: Penguin.

[10] Erikson, E.H., Insight and Responsibility, Norton, New York, 1964.

[11] Escolar, C.R.L. and de Guzman, A.B. (2014). Effects of third age learning programs on the life satisfaction, self-esteem, and depression level among a select group of community dwelling Filipino elderly. *Educational Gerontology 40*(2), 77–90.

[12] Gergen, K.J. and Gergen, M. (2004). Social constructionism: Entering the dialogue. Chagrin Falls, OH: Taos Institute Publications.

[13] Hagestad, G.O. (1991). The Ageing Society as a Context For Family Life. In N.A.S. Jecker (Ed.). Ageing and Ethics: Philosophical Problems in Gerontology. Clifton, NJ: Humana Press.

[14] Halit, A.H. (2014). Self Esteem and its relation to depression among the elderly. *International Journal of Business and Social Science, 5*(3), 266–273.

[15] Haber, D. (2013). Health promotion and ageing: Practical applications for health professionals. New York: Springer.

[16] Hedke, L. and Winslade, J. (2004). Remembering lives: Conversations with the dying and the bereaved. Amityville, NY: Bay wood Publishing.

[17] Koenig, H.G., Hays, J.C., Larson, David B., George, Linda K., Cohen, H.J, McCullogh, M.E., Meador, K.G. and Blazer, D.G. (1999). Does religious attendance prolong survival? *Journal of Gerontology: Medical Sciences, 54*A, M370–M376.

[18] Kooij, D., de Lange, A., Jansen, P. and Dikkers, J. (2008). Older Workers' Motivation to Continue to Work: Five Meanings of Age. *Journal of Managerial Psychology*, 23(4), 364–394.

[19] Mamta, T., Colligan, R., Malinchoc, M. and Offord, K. (2000). Mayo Clinic Proceedings, 140–143.

[20] McFadden, S.H. and Levin, J.S. (1996).Religion, emotions and health. In C. Maggi & S.H. McFadden (Eds.), Handbook of Emotion, Adult Development, and Ageing. San Diego: Academic Press.

[21] Morris, C.R. (1996). The AARP: American's most powerful lobby and the clash of generations. New York: Random House.

[22] Neugarten, B. (1980). When age does not matter, Newsweek, August 11, 1980. 73.

[23] Nyamute, W. and Maina, J.K.M. (2011). Effect of financial literacy on personal financial management practices: a case study of employees of finance and banking institutions', Available from: http://erepository.uonbi. ac.ke/bitstream /handle/11295/9897/aibuma2011-submission224%20-%20EFFECT%20OF%20FINANCIAL%20LITERACY%20ON%20 PERSONAL%20FINANCIAL%20M ANAGEMENT%20PRACTICES.pdf?sequence=1

[24] Positive thinking about ageing may lower dementia risk, study finds *ABC Premium News*, Feb 08, 2018.

[25] Pundt, Leena Maren; Wöhrmann, Anne Marit; Deller, Jürgen; Shultz, Kenneth, S. (2015). Differential predictors of post-retirement life and work satisfaction. *Journal of Managerial Psychology*, 30(2), 216–231.

[26] Ramovš, J. and Ramovš, M. (2013). Duhovne potrebe in zmožnosti v luči staranja in sožitja. In: Ramovš, J. (Ed.) Staranje v Sloveniji. Ljubljana: Inštitut Antona Trstenjaka za gerontologijo in medgeneracijsko sožitje, 443–474.

[27] Starc, M. and Zabukovec, M. (2013). Zadovoljstvo s svojim življenjem v luči življenjskih sprememb. Kakovostna starost, 16(1), 19.

[28] Stavros, J.M. and Torres, C.B. (2005). Dynamic relationships, Unleashing the power of appreciative inquiry in daily living. Chagrin Falls, OH: Taos Institute Publications.

[29] Stamov-Roßnagel, Christian; Biemann, Torsten (2012). Ageing and work motivation: a task-level perspective. *Journal of Managerial Psychology*, 27(5), 459–478.

[30] Tjale, A.A. and Bruce, B. (2007). A concept analysis of holistic nursing care in Pediatrics Nursing. Curationis, 30(4), 45–52.

[31] Vogt, E.E., Brown, J and Isaacs, D. (2003). The art of powerful questions: Catalyzing insight, innovation, and action. Positive Ageing Newsletter. Waltham, MA: Pegasus Communications.

[32] Villar, F. (2012). Successful Ageing and Development: The Contribution of Generativity in Older Age. *Ageing and Society*, *32*(7), 1087–1105.

[33] Watkins, J. and Mohr, B. (2001). Appreciative Inquiry: Change at the speed of imagination. San Francisco, CA: Jossey Bass Pfeiffer.

[34] Whitney, D. and Trosten-Bloom, A. (2003). The Power of Appreciative Inquiry: Apraetieal Guide to Positive Change. San Francisco, CA: Berrett-Koehler.

[35] Yuan, C.W., Hanrahan, B.V., Rosson, M.B. and Carroll, J.M. (2018). Coming of Old Age: Understanding Older Adults' Engagement and Needs in Coproduction Activities for Healthy Ageing. *Behaviour & Information Technology, 37*(3), 232–246.

[36] Zacher, H., Rosing, K., Henning, T. and Frese, M. (2011). "Establishing the Next Generation at Work: Leader Generativity as a Moderator of the Relationships between Leader Age, Leader-Member Exchange, and Leadership Success. *Psychology and Ageing, 26(*1), 241–252.

[37] Zaimah, R., Sarmila, M.S., Lyndon, N., Azima, A.M., Selvadurai, S., Suhana, S. and Er, A.C. (2013). Financial behaviours of female teachers in Malaysia. *Asian Social Science, 9*(8), 34–41.

Quality Education for Sustainable Development: An Exploratory Study

Prakash Choudhary[1] and Upinder Dhar[2]
[1]Prestige Public School, Indore, Madhya Pradesh
[2]Shri Vaishnav Vidyapeeth Vishwavidyalaya, Indore, Madhya Pradesh
E-mail: [1]pchoudhary06@yahoo.co.in; [2]vc@svvv.edu.in

ABSTRACT: Quality Education has been widely recognized as an important contributor towards sustainable development. Lack of quality leads to the state of dis-satisfaction. The researchers have identified various parameters responsible for quality education. Number of studies have been conducted to seek the answer to the questions like, how does school leadership style influence the quality of education? To what extent the role is played by physical infrastructure, facilities, parents/ guardians and safe & healthy environment? The present paper is aimed to understand the importance of various parameters responsible for the quality education for sustainable development.

Keywords: Higher Performance, Minimum Level of Learning, Participatory Framework, Parents, Teachers.

INTRODUCTION

The 21st Century global economy can thrive in an environment that focuses on creativity, imagination, critical thinking and problem solving skills. Empirical analysis reveals a strong positive relationship between education and economic growth. India has a large population of 30.5 crore, in the school going age of 6–18 years, which is around 25% of the total population (Census, 2011). India has the potential to use this demographic dividend to its advantage if the children could be imparted education that prepares them to face the real world with confidence (Khuntia, 2016). The importance of education is best driven by the Chinese proverb that says:

"If you want to think one year ahead, plant rice; If you want to think 10 years ahead, plant trees; But if you want to think 100 years ahead, give education to people."

The question is: How successful are we in delivering quality education to our students? Quality education means that majority of the students, if not all, are able to meet the expectations of the "Minimum Level of Learning". It means stimulating creative thinking, developing problem-solving and life skills while laying emphasis on application of knowledge (Chabungbam, 2017). Whenever quality in education is discussed, a reflection on what is understood by the term quality becomes necessary. Many thinkers have defined this term and, thus, number of definitions are available in the literature. The quality of knowledge in a society depends upon the quality of education it provides. Quality makes education socially and individually relevant, but if the quality of education is not assured then the education, which is advocated as a solution to social problems, may itself become a problem. Quality education thus is required to enable persons, societies and nations to acquire the skills and competencies required for living meaningfully in a competitive global world.

The key concern for education, in any formal educational system, has been its quality. Every stakeholder, direct or indirect, is concerned about its quality. Parents, irrespective of their socio-economic status, want to educate their children with best quality education, which would add better value to their ward's life. Unfortunately, in India, where government runs 90 percent primary schools, most of them located in rural areas; they lack the average criteria for quality education. There is no single definition for 'quality of education' which has universal acceptance. In education, perception of quality is around students (Mukhopadhyay, 2001). The performance of the students like examination results, learning achievements, ability to apply learned knowledge in practical life, exhibit the quality of education. For some, "Quality of education" means value addition in education; excellence in education (Peters and Waterman, 1982); for others, fitness of education outcomes and experience for use (Juran and Gryna, 1988).

The quality teachers are capable of helping their students to learn. They have mastery of both their subject and pedagogy (Darling-Hammond, 1997). Researchers in Guinea and India have reported that teachers are very poorly trained in evaluation techniques and the continuous evaluation procedures recommended by official programs are not practiced (Carron & Chau, 1996). Indeed, many teachers and educational systems continue to depend almost exclusively on traditional paper-and-pencil tests of factual knowledge which promote rote memorization rather than higher order thinking (Colby, 2000). Kioupi & Voulvoulis (2019) developed a participatory framework that allows education practitioners and stakeholders together with communities of learners to decide on common visions for sustainability. Although the SDGs are a global framework, localising them in terms of educational outcomes helps the realisation of both community vision and of global priorities.

Continuous professional development and training of employees, life-long learning, and family-friendly measures; including better access to childcare, more flexible working schemes and employer incentives could support job prospects (including women and disabled persons) to return to work and to improve their wellbeing (Camilleri & Camilleri, 2020). One of the best things that any government can do to stimulate progress is to provide the best minds to help the nation tackle future challenges. Since the whole world is geared towards the attainment of the global Sustainable Development Goals (SDGs), it is pertinent to set the key performance indicators for assessing progress in line with the overall vision of the development agenda. Amongst the 17 sustainable development goals (SDGs), quality education has been addressed as SDG-4 because it is the 4th goal of the SDGs (Nazar *et al.*, 2018)

OBJECTIVE

To identify the most important parameters that influence the quality of school education.

METHOD

The Study: The study is exploratory in nature and aimed to identify the most important parameters that influence the quality of school education.

The Sample: The final sample of 62 principals, 143 teachers and 681 parents was chosen randomly. The respondents were from Indore, Dewas, Balaghat and Jabalpur districts of Madhya Pradesh.

The Tools

1. *For Data Collection*: On the basis of informal discussion and review of literature, an inventory of parameters for Quality School Education was designed. The inventory included the parameters like Infrastructure, Teachers, Teaching Approach, Contents, Methods of Assessment, Caliber of Students, Income of Parents, Education of Parents, Involvement of Parents and School Environment. At first stage, 100 copies of the inventory were distributed to the principals and out of these 78 were received back, 16 were found incomplete or invalid, thus removed. Finally, 62 copies of the filled up inventory were taken into account for further analysis. At second stage, 280 copies of the inventory were distributed to the teachers and out of these 200 were received back, 57 were found incomplete or invalid, thus removed. Finally, 143 copies of the filled up inventory were taken into account for further analysis. At third stage, 1200 copies of the inventory were distributed to the parents and out of these 860 were received back, 179 were found incomplete or invalid, thus removed. Finally, 681 copies of the filled up inventory were taken into account for further analysis.
2. *For Data Analysis*: The data was analysed by administering Ranking Technique and Spearman's Rank correlation.

NULL HYPOTHESES

H_{01} : There is no significant difference in the perception of principals and teachers with respect to the parameters that influence the quality of education in schools.

H_{02} : There is no significant difference in the perception of parents and teachers with respect to the parameters that influence the quality of education in schools.

H_{03} : There is no significant difference in the perception of principals and parents with respect to the parameters that influence the quality of education in schools.

RESULTS AND DISCUSSION

Respondents were instructed to assign the rank to all the parameters given in the inventory. The outcome of such ranks was then converted into scores with the following formula:

$$\text{Percent position} = \frac{100(R_{ij} - 0.5)}{N_j}$$

where

R_{ij} = Rank given for the ith variable by j^{th} respondent.
N_j = Number of variables ranked by j^{th} respondent.

The parameter having highest mean value is considered to be the most important parameter. Following table shows the corresponding scores of percent positions.

Percent Position

Rank	*Percentage*	*Score*
1	5	82
2	15	70
3	25	63
4	35	58
5	45	52
6	55	48
7	65	42
8	75	36
9	85	29
10	95	18

Tables 1 to 6 show the rankings of parameters by principals, teachers and parents respectively. From these tables, it can be derived that 1st rank is given to *Teachers* by principals, teachers and parents for influencing the quality of education in schools. The schools can attract meritorious students, if they have quality teachers. Teachers play an important role in ensuring learning among students. Students are always benefitted by quality teachers. Beamish and Morey (2013) in their study revealed that parents wanted teachers to be the role models who were dedicated, qualified, interested and involved with kids.

Table 1: Frequency of Ranks given by Principals

	Parameters/Ranks	*1st*	*2nd*	*3rd*	*4th*	*5th*	*6th*	*7th*	*8th*	*9th*	*10th*	*Total*
1.	Infrastructure	1	0	6	2	7	11	6	11	13	5	62
2.	Teachers	25	18	7	8	2	1	1	0	0	0	62
3.	Teaching Approach	12	22	12	8	1	4	2	0	1	0	62
4.	Contents	4	5	11	17	12	5	3	3	2	0	62
5.	Methods of Assessment	0	5	6	8	17	11	6	5	2	2	62
6.	Calibre of Students	1	3	7	6	10	11	13	7	4	0	62
7.	Income of Parents	0	0	1	1	1	1	1	5	5	47	62
8.	Education of Parents	0	0	1	2	2	5	10	9	26	7	62
9.	Involvement of Parents	2	1	3	3	8	7	11	18	8	1	62
10.	School Environment	16	8	8	7	2	6	10	4	1	0	62

Principals, teachers and parents have given second rank to *Teaching Approach*. Teaching approach is very important. Good teachers know very well that best teaching approach is one by which the last student of the class is able to understand. As curriculum should be child-centered and relevant, so should be the instructional methods. The limited perspective of teaching as presentation of knowledge no longer suits the current understanding of how and what students should learn. Instead, instructions should channelize students to build on prior knowledge to develop attitudes, beliefs and cognitive skills; as well as expand their knowledge base. In today's scenario, student centric approach is preferred as it gives opportunity to every student and teacher for feedback.

Principals, teachers and parents ranked *School Environment* at 3rd place. School environment is very important, because school is second home for child where he spends almost 1/3rd of his/her time. Hsu and Yuan-Fang (2013) in their study demonstrated that there is a high positive correlation between school environment and parents' choice as a junior high school. Children learn from environment, healthier

Table 2: Ranks given by Principals on the basis of Henry Garrett's Ranking Table

	Parameters	*1st *82*	*2nd *70*	*3rd *63*	*4th *58*	*5th *52*	*6th *48*	*7th *42*	*8th *36*	*9th *29*	*10th *18*	*Total*	*Average Score*	*Rank*
1.	Infrastructure	82	0	378	116	364	528	252	396	377	90	2583	41.66	8
2.	Teachers	2050	1260	441	464	104	48	42	0	0	0	4409	71.11	1
3.	Teaching Approach	984	1540	756	464	52	192	84	0	29	0	4101	66.15	2
4.	Contents	328	350	693	986	624	240	126	108	58	0	3513	56.66	4
5.	Methods of Assessment	0	350	378	464	884	528	252	180	58	36	3130	50.48	5
6.	Calibre of Students	82	210	441	348	520	528	546	252	116	0	3043	49.08	6
7.	Income of Parents	0	0	63	58	52	48	42	180	145	846	1434	23.13	10
8.	Education of Parents	0	0	63	116	104	240	420	324	754	126	2147	34.63	9
9.	Involvement of Parents	164	70	189	174	416	336	462	648	232	18	2709	43.69	7
10.	School Environment	1312	560	504	406	104	288	420	144	29	0	3767	60.76	3

Table 3: Frequency of Ranks given by Teachers

	Parameters/Ranks	*1st*	*2nd*	*3rd*	*4th*	*5th*	*6th*	*7th*	*8th*	*9th*	*10th*	*Total*
1.	Infrastructure	6	11	14	9	9	17	8	13	27	29	143
2.	Teachers	78	30	13	9	5	2	4	2	0	0	143
3.	Teaching Approach	13	57	29	17	9	8	4	3	3	0	143
4.	Contents	4	9	21	24	28	26	11	9	4	7	143
5.	Methods of Assessment	1	8	17	28	30	21	15	15	6	2	143
6.	Calibre of Students	5	2	8	14	24	23	30	17	15	5	143
7.	Income of Parents	0	5	1	2	1	11	9	14	31	69	143
8.	Education of Parents	2	4	6	14	9	7	18	34	37	12	143
9.	Involvement of Parents	0	4	9	10	18	14	34	24	15	15	143
10.	School Environment	34	13	25	16	10	14	10	12	5	4	143

Table 4: Ranks given by Teachers on the Basis of Henry Garrett's Ranking Table

	Parameters	*1st *82*	*2nd *70*	*3rd *63*	*4th *58*	*5th *52*	*6th *48*	*7th *42*	*8th *36*	*9th *29*	*10th *18*	*Total*	*Average Score*	*Rank*
1.	Infrastructure	492	770	882	522	468	816	336	468	783	522	6059	42.37	7
2.	Teachers	6396	2100	819	522	260	96	168	72	0	0	10433	72.96	1
3.	Teaching Approach	1066	3990	1827	986	468	384	168	108	87	0	9084	63.52	2
4.	Contents	328	630	1323	1392	1456	1248	462	324	116	126	7405	51.78	4
5.	Methods of Assessment	82	560	1071	1624	1560	1008	630	540	174	36	7285	50.94	5
6.	Calibre of Students	410	140	504	812	1248	1104	1260	612	435	90	6615	46.26	6
7.	Income of Parents	0	350	63	116	52	528	378	504	899	1242	4132	28.90	10
8.	Education of Parents	164	280	378	812	468	336	756	1224	1073	216	5707	39.91	9
9.	Involvement of Parents	0	280	567	580	936	672	1428	864	435	270	6032	42.18	8
10.	School Environment	2788	910	1575	928	520	672	420	432	145	72	8462	59.17	3

Table 5: Frequency of Ranks given by Parents

	Parameters/Ranks	*1st*	*2nd*	*3rd*	*4th*	*5th*	*6th*	*7th*	*8th*	*9th*	*10th*	*Total*
1.	Infrastructure	40	74	79	62	90	61	82	71	70	52	681
2.	Teachers	266	122	95	43	34	36	18	31	14	22	681
3.	Teaching Approach	130	197	101	70	51	41	37	23	18	13	681
4.	Contents	35	43	85	97	91	96	80	64	55	35	681
5.	Methods of Assessment	20	48	110	122	96	87	74	51	40	33	681
6.	Calibre of Students	18	28	59	85	113	102	101	91	49	35	681
7.	Income of Parents	18	29	13	31	21	50	53	75	112	279	681
8.	Education of Parents	35	32	33	39	46	55	84	113	175	69	681
9.	Involvement of Parents	24	33	38	51	69	92	96	106	94	78	681
10.	School Environment	95	75	68	81	70	61	56	56	54	65	681

Table 6: Ranks given by Parents on the Basis of Henry Garrett's Ranking Table

	Parameters	*1st *82*	*2nd *70*	*3rd *63*	*4th *58*	*5th *52*	*6th *48*	*7th *42*	*8th *36*	*9th *29*	*10th *18*	*Total*	*Average Score*	*Rank*
1.	Infrastructure	3280	5180	4977	3596	4680	2928	3444	2556	2030	936	33607	49.35	6
2.	Teachers	21812	8540	5985	2494	1768	1728	756	1116	406	396	45001	66.08	1
3.	Teaching Approach	10660	13790	6363	4060	2652	1968	1554	828	522	234	42631	62.60	2
4.	Contents	2870	3010	5355	5626	4732	4608	3360	2304	1595	630	34090	50.06	5
5.	Methods of Assessment	1640	3360	6930	7076	4992	4176	3108	1836	1160	594	34872	51.21	4
6.	Caliber of Students	1476	1960	3717	4930	5876	4896	4242	3276	1421	630	32424	47.61	7
7.	Income of Parents	1476	2030	819	1798	1092	2400	2226	2700	3248	5022	22811	33.50	10
8.	Education of Parents	2870	2240	2079	2262	2392	2640	3528	4068	5075	1242	28396	41.70	9
9.	Involvement of Parents	1968	2310	2394	2958	3588	4416	4032	3816	2726	1404	29612	43.48	8
10.	School Environment	7790	5250	4284	4698	3640	2928	2352	2016	1566	1170	35694	52.41	3

the environment, happier the children will be. Schools and teachers must try to create conducive environment so that learning takes place in real sense. Learners in supportive environments have high levels of self-efficacy and self-motivation.

Principals and teachers ranked *Content* as 4th while parents ranked it 5th. Quality content refers to the intended and taught curriculum of schools. National goals for education and outcome statements that transform those goals into measurable objectives should provide the starting point for the development and implementation of curriculum. It should also have scope for individual differences, closely coordinate and selectively integrate subject matter and focus on results or standards and targets for student learning (Glatthorn & Jailall, 2000).

Method of Assessment is ranked 4th by parents while 5th by teachers and principals. Assessment is important because on its basis, all the decisions about the children's future are taken. Assessment should be tailored to a specific purpose and should be reliable, valid and fair for that purpose. Assessments designed for one purpose are not necessarily valid if used for other purposes. Assessment should be age appropriate (Morrison, 2010).

Caliber of Students' is ranked 6th by principals and teachers whereas 7th by parents. It's important that child should have caliber for the stream he chooses in terms of aptitude because by the end of the session child has to appear in examination. Teachers and schools can only facilitate child. The quality of children's lives before beginning formal education influence the kind of learners they become. Many ingredients go into making a quality learner including health, early childhood experiences and support of the family.

Infrastructure is ranked 6th by parents, 7th by teachers and 8th by principals. School infrastructure is a key base for effective teaching and learning in schools. Buildings, classrooms, laboratories and library - are crucial elements of infrastructure in schools. There is strong evidence that high-quality infrastructure facilitates better instructions, improves student outcomes, and reduces dropout rates, among other benefits (Teixeira, 2017). According to David K. Cohen and Monica P. Bhatt, the major obstacle in education system is lack of proper educational infrastructure (Choudhary, 2017).

Involvement of Parents is ranked 7th by principals, whereas teachers & parents raked it 8th. Parents' involvement in children's learning is positively related to the achievements. The more active forms of parents' involvement produce greater achievement benefits. It strengthens the bond between parent and school. Henderson and Berla (1994) reported that students, with parents who are involved in their school, have fewer behavioural problems and exhibit better academic performance. Parents' involvement supports students' learning, behavior and attitude regardless of other parameters such as income, education level, and occupation of parents. This contention is supported by the fact *Education of Parents* and *Income of Parents* have been ranked 9th & 10th by principals, teachers and parents respectively.

The Spearman's Rank correlation between principals, teachers and parents were found as under:

Principals and Teachers	:	0.988
Teachers and Parents	:	0.976
Principal and Parents	:	0.952

Further, perception of principals, teachers and parents is significantly correlated. In other words, all the three stakeholders agree with the rankings given to various parameters, which influence the quality of education in schools. All the three null hypotheses stand rejected.

CONCLUSION AND RECOMMENDATIONS

There are various parameters inside and outside the school which contribute to the quality education. The present study was focused only on some of the parameters that influence the quality education. The key role of the educators is to teach their students effectively so that students are able to demonstrate higher performance in their studies. To achieve this objective, it is necessary to understand the role of various parameters in the academic achievement of students.

It was found that, **teachers, teaching approach and school environment** are primary parameters of quality education, followed by content, method of assessment, caliber of students, infrastructure and involvement of parents. Surprisingly, education of parents and income of parents are given least importance i.e., 9th and 10th ranks. In other words, involvement of parents precedes their education and income.

It is recommended that schools should give priority to the appointment of quality teachers, who are well qualified with relevant background. The teaching approach is equally important to accommodate the students of varied learning styles effectively. Further, schools need to ensure conducive environment for quality education.

REFERENCES

[1] Beamish, P. and Morey, P. (2013). School choice: What parents choose. *TEACH Journal of Christian Education*, *7*(1), 7.

[2] Camilleri, M.A. and Camilleri, A.C. (2020). The sustainable development goal on quality education. In *The Future of the UN Sustainable Development Goals*, 261–277, Springer, Cham.

[3] Carron, G. and Chau, T.N. (1996). *The Quality of Primary Schools in Different Development Contexts*. Paris: UNESCO.

[4] Chabungbam, D. (2017). *Parents, Teachers and Quality Education, E-PAO. http://e-pao.net/epPageExtractor.asp?src=education.Parents_Teachers_and_Quality_Education.html.*

[5] Choudhary, P. (2017). *Level of Education and Socio Economic Status As Determinants of Criteria for The Selection of A School. Doctoral Thesis*. Shri Vaishnav Vidyapeeth Vishwavidyalaya, Indore, India.

[6] Colby, J. (2000). *Learning outcomes in international context*. Paper presented at the Annual Meeting of the Comparative and International Education Society, San Antonio, Texas.

[7] Darling-Hammond, L. (1997). *Doing What Matters Most: Investing in Quality Teaching*. New York: National Commission on Teaching and America's Future.

[8] Glatthorn, A. and Jailall, J. (2000). *Curriculum for the new millennium*. In Brandt, R. (Ed.), Education in a New Era: ASCD Yearbook 2000. Alexandria, Virginia: Association for Supervision and Curriculum Development.

[9] Henderson, Anne T. and Berla, Nancy (1994). *A New Generation of Evidence: The Family is Critical to Student Achievement*. Columbia, MD: National Committee for Citizens in Education.

[10] *Henry Garrett Ranking*: Chapter 3 Research Methodology. *https://www.scribd.com/doc/141092918/Garrett-Ranking*

[11] Hsu and Yuan-fang (2013). An analysis of Factors Affecting Parents' Choice of a Junior High School: Centre for Promoting Ideas, USA. *International Journal of Business, Humanities and Technology, 3*.

[12] Juran, J.M and Gryna F.M. Jr. (Eds.), (1988). *Juran's Quality Control Handbook*. New York: McGraw Hill.

[13] Khuntia, S.C. (2016). *Press Information Bureau, Government of India, Special Service and Features, Improving the Quality of School Education, 1*.

[14] Kioupi, Vasiliki and Voulvoulis, Nikolaos (2019). *Education for Sustainable Development: A Systemic Framework for Connecting the SDGs to Educational Outcomes*. MDPI, Centre for Environmental Policy, Imperial College, London. *Sustainability,* 11 (21), 6104. *www.mdpi.com/journal/sustainability*

[15] Morrison, G.S. (2010). *Why is Assessment Important?* New Jersey: Pearson Allyn Bacon Prentice Hall.

[16] Mukhopadhyay, M. (2001). *Total Quality Management in Education*. New Delhi: NIEPA Publication Unit. http://pib.nic.in/newsite/printrelease.aspx?relid=149293

[17] Nazar, R., Chaudhry, I.S., Ali, S. and Faheem, M. (2018). Role of Quality Education for Sustainable Development Goals (SDGS). *PEOPLE: International Journal of Social Sciences, 4*(2), 486–501.https://grdspublishing.org/index.php/people/article/view/1451

[18] Peters, T.J. and Waterman R.H. Jr. (1982). *In Search of Excellence*. New York: Harper and Row.

[19] Teixeira, J. (2017). *Why Education Infrastructure*. Romania: The World Bank.

Role of Biomimetic Materials in Achieving Sustainability

Manali Basu[1], Moturu Surya Ratna Srinivas[2], Vandanapu Vahini Spandana[3] and J. Rupa[4]

GITAM School of Architecture, GITAM (Deemed to be University), Gandhi Nagar, Rushikonda, Visakhapatnam, Andhra Pradesh

E-mail: [1]121925501012@gitam.in; [2]121925501013@gitam.in; [3]121925501018@gitam.in; [4]rjawal@gitam.edu;

ABSTRACT: The plant and the animal kingdom have an intrinsic property through which they have the ability of self-healing themselves to survive against any injuries or defects. Self-healing biomimetic materials are those that have been inspired by this self-repairing property of Nature and they tend to incorporate natural elements in the material itself that ultimately leads to more sustainable and even regenerative buildings. In this paper, the different types of self-healing biomimetic materials such as self-healing concrete, self-healing bricks and self-healing lime mortar and the roles played by them in overcoming the issues related to cracks in the buildings have been focused upon. Such self-healing biomimetic materials are generally incorporated with bacteria having spores which activate on coming in contact with water and help in repairing the cracks. This paper also focuses on the different types of cracks that appear in concrete and masonry works over the years due to the continuous usage and wear and tear of the buildings which can even lead to the collapse of the structures in the worst-case scenarios.

The paper focusses on how these cracks can be self-repaired by the application of such self-healing biomimetic materials instead of the conventional materials and how efficient these materials are as compared to the conventional building materials. For the research purpose the Architecture building at the GITAM (Deemed to be University) Campus, Visakhapatnam has been considered and study has been done to identify what type of cracks have developed in the building and how they could have been self-repaired if such self-healing biomimetic materials had been used instead of the conventional ones. Further, by using these self-healing biomimetic materials how sustainability can be achieved has also been discussed in this paper.

Keywords: Cracks, Self-Healing Biomimetic Materials, Self-Healing Concrete, Self-Healing Bricks, Self-Healing Mortar.

INTRODUCTION

Over the years, concrete has been one of the most produced and commonly used building materials in the construction industry ever since it was invented almost 2000 years ago during the construction of the Colosseum by the Romans. Its production has increased down the ages and it is the most consumed material after water. Though it is durable, traditional concrete tends to develop cracks when subjected to tension which is why it is often reinforced with steel to withstand the tensile forces. The cracks developed leads to the corrosion of the steel reinforcements and can further lead to the collapse of the structures in the worst case scenarios. Continuous usage and wear and tear of the buildings also lead to the formation of cracks in the concrete and masonry works due to which the structures often need to undergo maintenance and repair and a huge amount of money is spent every year in doing so.

The self-healing biomimetic materials have been invented by taking inspiration from the intrinsic self-healing properties of the plant and animal kingdom. Some examples of such self-healing biomimetic materials include self-healing concrete, self-healing or living bricks and self-healing lime mortar. The healing agents in the biomimetic materials are bacteria having spores. They could remain in a dormant state for about 200 years, but they can be re-activated upon further cracking. This leads to increased sustainability as well as reduction in the maintenance and repair costs when compared with the conventional materials.

The aim of the present study is to understand the different types of cracks that develop in concrete and masonry works. The study has been performed in an existing building which is in the Warm and Humid climatic zone of India. The scope of the study is to analyze and review the benefits of using self-healing materials over the conventional ones.

SELF-HEALING BIOMIMETIC MATERIALS

Biomimetic materials are those that have been inspired by the self-repairing property of Nature. They tend to incorporate natural elements in the material itself. This helps in the creation of more sustainable and even regenerative buildings. Such materials possess the ability to self-sense, self-diagnose any defects or damages and self-heal themselves and include materials such as self-healing concrete, self-healing or living bricks and self-healing lime mortar.

Self-healing Concrete

The concept of self-healing concrete was first developed by Carolyn Dry, a Professor of Architecture at the University of Illinois at Urbana-Champaign in the early 1990s. After that, a microbiologist named Hendrik Jonkers at the Delft University of Technology in Netherlands came up with the idea of repairing the cracks developed in concrete at its very first stage to protect the steel reinforcement from getting corroded by using self-healing concrete. The concept behind this concrete was based on the natural body processes where the bone fractures heal through mineralization of the osteoblast cells in order to reform the bones. Jonkers used bacteria as the healing agent and mixed it with ordinary concrete. Concrete is an extremely alkaline material as cement and water when mixed together has a pH value of up to 13. Most organisms die in an environment with a pH value of 10 or above. Finding a bacteria that could survive in such an environment was a difficult task for him.

Strains of bacteria genus Bacillus were found suitable as they can survive in extreme alkaline environments by producing spores which are comparable to plant seeds and have extremely thick cell walls enabling them to remain intact for up to 200 years. The bacteria needs a food source to produce the repair material (limestone). It was provided by infusing the bacteria with calcium lactate in capsules made from biodegradable plastic. The two self-healing agents that include the bacterial spores and the calcium lactate- based nutrients are incorporated in the concrete generally within two separate expanded clay pellets having a width of 2–4 mm. This ensures that the agents will not be activated during the cement mixing process and activate only when the cracks open up the pellets and the water that seeps in through the cracks brings the calcium lactate in contact with the bacteria (Jonkers, 2011).

When water starts to seep in through the cracks, the spores of the bacteria germinate and multiply on encountering water and nutrients. After being activated, the bacteria start to feed on the calcium lactate and calcium is combined with carbonate ions to form insoluble calcite (limestone) which solidifies on the surface of the cracks thereby sealing the cracks and healing the concrete. This process takes about three weeks to heal the concrete.

Self-healing or Living Bricks

Wil Srubar, Assistant Professor at the University of Colorado Boulder and his research team developed a strategy for using bacteria to develop building materials that live, multiply and heal their own cracks. The research team started experimenting with cyanobacteria which belongs to the genus Synechococcus and under the right conditions absorb carbon dioxide to help them grow and make calcium carbonate which is the main ingredient in limestone. The manufacturing process starts by incorporating colonies of cyanobacteria into a solution of sand and gelatin and with the right tweaks, the calcium carbonate churned out by the microbes mineralize the gelatin which binds the sand together. The researchers also discovered the fact that the bacteria could make their material reproduce like a tree grows out of the seeds sown. If one half of the bricks is chopped into half then each half has the capability of growing into a new brick (Strain, 2020).

Self-healing Lime Mortar

Up to a certain extent, lime mortars have the capacity of self-healing which might also contribute to its durability. The process of self-healing in lime mortar may be compared with carbonate diagenesis in sedimentary basins although major differences exist between the two processes. The mortars in which the self-healing property has been noticed include air lime, hydraulic lime and pozzolanic lime-based mortars.

Generally, mortars with only cement as a binder do not have self-healing properties so it is necessary that a considerable amount of free lime is present in order to make the process of self-healing occur. The self-healing process in lime mortar occurs when (rain) water allows the dissolution of calcium bearing compounds, transport them from a zone rich in binder to the voids and cracks developed in the mortar and the small cracks may be filled up with re-crystallized calcium compounds in a natural and spontaneous self-healing process (Lubelli et al., 2011).

CAUSES AND TYPES OF CRACKS IN CONCRETE

Traditional concrete tends to develop cracks when subjected to tension which is why it is often reinforced with steel to withstand the tensile forces. The cracks developed leads to the corrosion of the steel reinforcements and can further lead to the collapse of the structures in the worst-case scenarios. Continuous usage and wear and tear of the buildings also lead to the formation of cracks in the concrete. The different causes of cracks in concrete are as follows:

Before hardening: The causes of cracks before hardening include constructional movement, settlement shrinkage, setting shrinkage

After hardening: The causes of cracks after hardening include physical, chemical, thermal, stress concentrations, structural design, accidents, different types of cracks such as flexure cracks, torsional cracks, etc. develop in the reinforced concrete beams, cracks like splitting cracks, corrosion cracks, etc. develop in the concrete columns and cracks like shrinkage cracks, settlement cracks, etc. develop in the concrete slabs and floors respectively. Cracks in concrete may also be classified according to the common sight of the cracks such as horizontal, vertical, and diagonal etc. and according to their widths such as fine, medium and wide cracks respectively (Figure 1, Figure 2).

CAUSES AND TYPES OF CRACKS IN BRICK WALLS

Cracks develop on the brick walls due to continuous usage and wear and tear over time. While such cracks do not always indicate serious structural damage but can make the buildings prone to water damages. The causes in brick walls are as follows soil subsidence, climate and seasonal changes, corrosion and deterioration of building materials, construction works around the buildings, reactive soils and trees close to the buildings. The types of cracks in brick walls may be classified based on the location of the cracks such as interior and exterior wall cracks, based on direction such as horizontal and vertical brick cracks and based on the depth such as structural and cosmetic cracks respectively.

Types of cracks in brick mortar joints and break down of masonry

The types of cracks seen in brick mortar joints include vertical or horizontal cracks. Bond breaks are the cracks that develop parallel to the lines of the mortar joints. During decomposition of joints, the cracks running perpendicular to the joints connect with the parallel cracks and pieces of mortar joints at these intersections start falling out. As mortar joints erode, the damage spreads to the bricks, stones and blocks (Bloom, 2020).

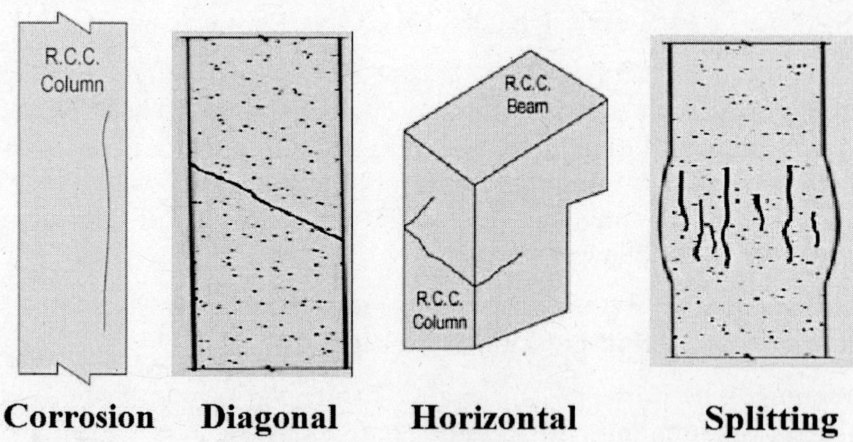

Fig. 1: Image showing the four types of cracks in concrete columns.
(4 types of cracks in concrete columns and their causes retrieved from https://theconstructor.org/concrete/types-cracks-concrete-columns/26433/)

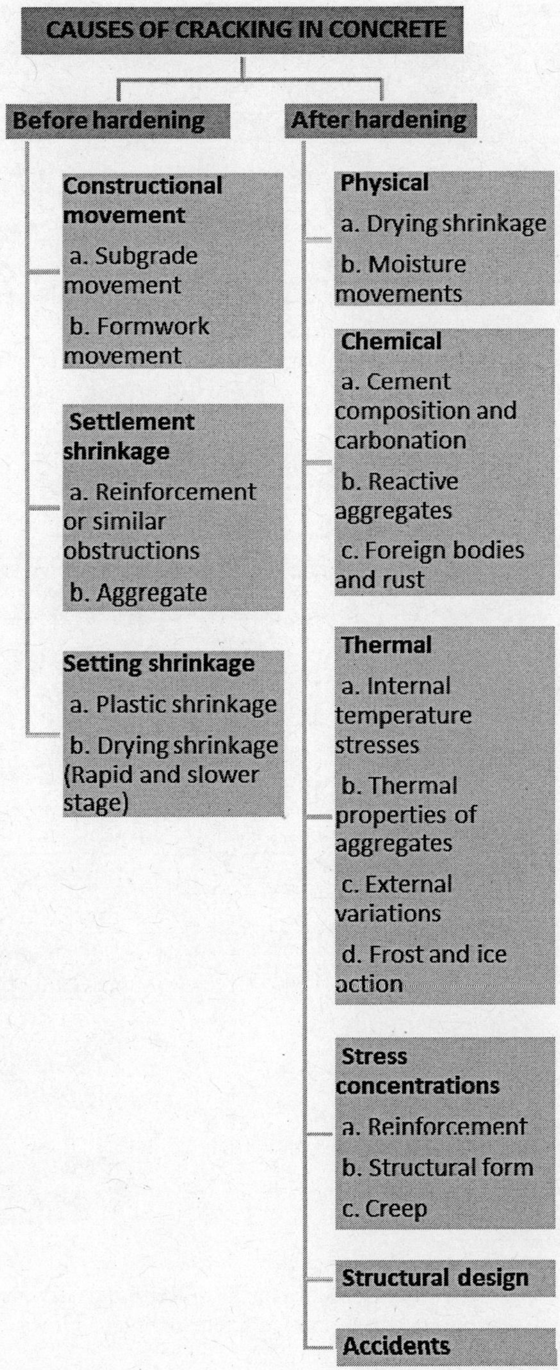

Fig. 2: Flowchart Showing the Different Causes of Cracking in Concrete Before and After Hardening

Fig. 3: Image Showing Cracks in Brick Walls (Cracks in brick walls: Why brick walls crack and how to repair cracked bricks retrieved from https://rb.gy/rjdmfu)

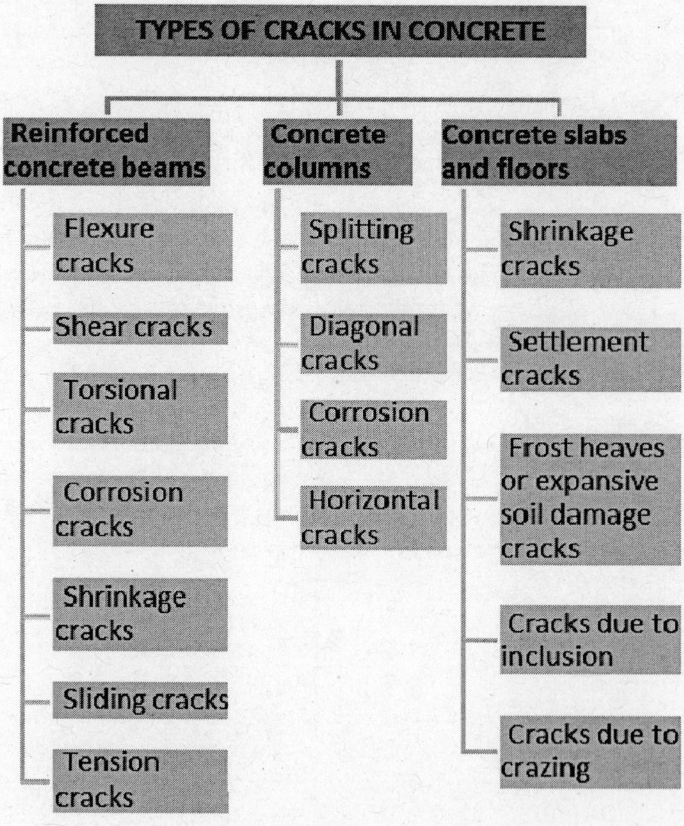

Fig. 4: Flowchart Showing Types of Cracks in Reinforced Concrete Beams, Concrete Columns and Concrete Slabs and Floors

Types of cracks that can be self-repaired by using self-healing concrete and self-healing lime mortar.

Among the different types of cracks discussed above, the types of cracks that can be self-repaired by using self-healing concrete include the cracks which are up to 0.5 mm in width. The other types of cracks that can be healed include the expansion cracks, shrinkage cracks, cracks due to thermal movement and cracks due to crazing. Self-healing lime mortar can heal cracks up to the width of 1 mm but it works best for cracks up to 0.5 mm width.

METHODOLOGY

For the research purpose, the city of Visakhapatnam which lies in the Warm and Humid Climatic Zone of India was selected and the Architecture Building at the GITAM (Deemed to be University) Campus, Visakhapatnam which is known as the GITAM School of Architecture was considered. Photographs of the cracks that have developed in the chosen building were collected and then discussions were done with the Structural Engineers in order to analyze and identify the type of cracks that have developed in the building. The next step after the identification of the cracks was to provide suggestions about the appropriate type of self-healing biomimetic materials that could have been used instead of the conventional materials so that the cracks could have been self-repaired.

Visakhapatnam and its Climatic Conditions

Visakhapatnam is a port city in the Eastern Coast of Andhra Pradesh and is popularly known as Vizag. It is the largest metropolis in the state of Andhra Pradesh and the seventh largest in India. Visakhapatnam is vulnerable to natural disasters such as storm surge, cyclones and erosion. The two tropical cyclones namely Hudhud (October 13, 2014) and Phylin (October 11, 2013) that formed at the Bay of Bengal had devastating impacts on the coastal region of Visakhapatnam. Visakhapatnam has been affected by 60 tropical cyclones from the year 1971 to 2014.

The latitude and longitude of Visakhapatnam are 17.72°North and 83.23°East respectively and it lies in the Warm and Humid Climatic Zone of India. In Visakhapatnam, the highest average temperature of 31.2°C is recorded in the month of May and the lowest average temperature of 23.5°C is recorded in the month of January. The highest average monthly relative humidity of 85% is recorded in the month of September and the lowest average monthly relative humidity of 68% is recorded in the month of March. (Climate data retrieved from Climate Consultant). The highest average rainfall of 259 mm (10.2 inch) is recorded in the month of October and the lowest average rainfall of 6 mm (0.2 inch) is recorded in the month of December.

GITAM School of Architecture, Visakhapatnam

GITAM School of Architecture is an integral part of the 10 schools functioning under the GITAM (Deemed to be University), Visakhapatnam. It was established in the year 2007. This building was studied and photographs of the cracks that have developed were taken. The types of cracks that were observed in the building include:

- Brick joint crack.
- Masonry and RCC beam joint crack.
- Masonry and RCC column joint crack.
- Masonry crack including Brick crack and Mortar joint crack.

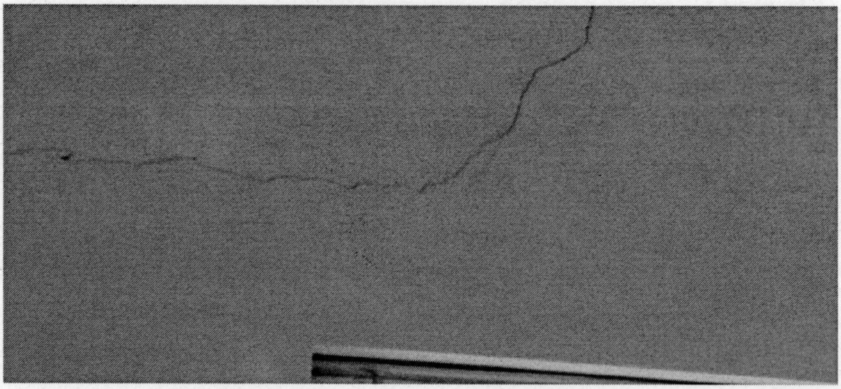

Fig. 5: Image Showing Brick Joint Crack, Possible Brick Crack, Masonry and RCC Beam Joint Crack

(*Image Courtesy:* Department Faculty)

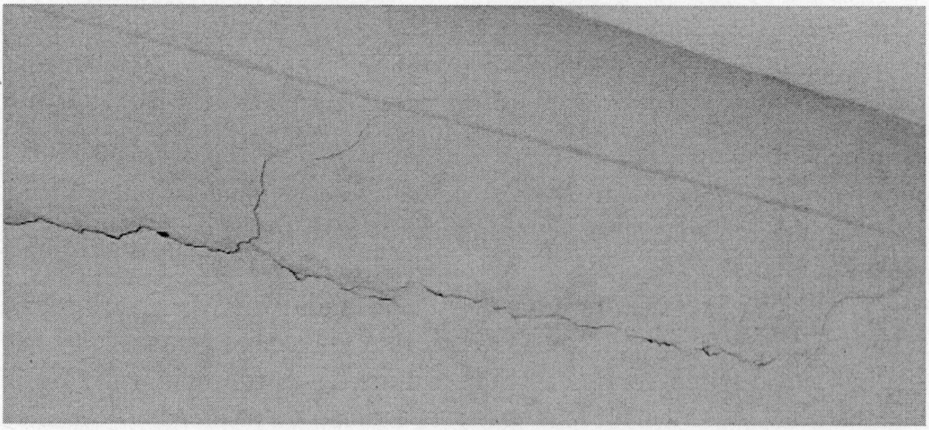

Fig. 6: Image showing Masonry crack (Brick crack and Mortar joint crack)

(*Image Courtesy:* Department Faculty)

Fig. 7: Image Showing Masonry and RCC Column Joint Crack
(Image Courtesy: Department Faculty)

Fig. 8: Image Showing Masonry and RCC Column/Beam Joint Crack
(Image Courtesy: Department Faculty)

ANALYSIS AND DISCUSSION

Cracks shown in Figures 5, 7 and 8 have developed due to the difference in the expansion of two different materials at the joints. Crack shown in Figure 15 has developed due to structural fault in the brick masonry. All the cracks (shown in Figures 5 to 8) that have developed in the concrete and the bricks are within the width of 0.5 mm. So, they are well within the self-healing capacity of the biomimetic materials. Cracks that have developed in the mortar joints are up to 1 mm wide. Hence, they are also within the self-healing capacity of self-healing lime mortar. Therefore, the cracks shown in Figures 5 and 6 could have been self-repaired if self-healing lime mortar and self-healing or living bricks were used instead of the conventional materials. Cracks shown in Figures 7 and 8 could have been self-repaired if self-healing lime mortar was used. Cracks that have developed in the slabs (images not provided in the paper) could have been self-repaired by the use self-healing concrete.

The spores of the bacteria used in the self-healing concrete germinate only when water seeps in through the cracks. Cyanobacteria which is present in the self-healing or living bricks need humid conditions to survive. Researchers kept the bricks at 50% relative humidity to test how long the microorganisms in the bricks could survive. On the other hand, the highest and the lowest relative humidity levels recorded in Visakhapatnam are 85% and 68% respectively which are much higher as compared to the relative humidity levels assumed during the research process. Under a range of humidity conditions, the living bricks have about the same strength as that of the mortar used today. One can step on the bricks and they would not break (Strain, 2020). In case of self-healing lime mortar, one of the important factors necessary for the self-healing process to occur is the presence of high moisture content in the walls as sufficient water should be present for the dissolution and transport of the low soluble calcium compounds towards the cracks. Visakhapatnam being in the Warm and Humid climatic zone of India has high humidity levels which is advantageous for the self-repairing processes of the materials to take place. So, the use of self-healing biomimetic materials in the Warm and Humid climatic zone instead of the conventional ones can be an appropriate solution to overcome the issues related to the cracks in the buildings.

Sustainable Aspects of the Self-healing Biomimetic Materials

When compared with the conventional materials, the self-healing materials have been found to be more efficient and environmentally friendly. They also help in reducing the maintenance and repair costs by self-healing the cracks. Further, they help in extending the lifespan of the buildings thereby contributing to social, economic and environmental sustainability. Every year a lot of money is spent in the maintenance and repair of the cracks that develop in concrete and the masonry works which are not economically sustainable at all. Self-healing concrete has a significantly higher production cost, almost twice that of conventional concrete as it is difficult to prepare the bacteria and the capsules and the calcium lactate which acts as the food source is also expensive (Table 1). Although self-healing concrete is initially very expensive, it possess the ability to extend the lifespan of the building (Figure 9) and reduce the overall cost of the building by reducing the maintenance and repair costs.

Table 1: Cost Comparison for 1 cum of Concrete Work in M20 of Conventional Versus Self-healing Concrete

S.No.	Things Required	Quantity	Cost/Unit	Concrete (M20)	SH-Concrete (M20)
1.	Cement Bag	8	400/-	3200/-	3200/-
2.	Self Healing Agent	5	500/-	---------	2500/-
3.	Grit & Sand	---------	1500/-	1500/-	1500/-
	Total			4700/-	7200/-

(Self-healing concrete by Shubham Arora retrieved from https://www.slideshare.net/ShubhamArora73/self-healing-concrete-82681922)

Buildings need to be demolished often due to the cracks that develop in the structure which results in the production of huge number of wastes. Also, concrete is not easily recyclable and cannot be reused efficiently since it does not retain its parent strength. Cement which is one of the key components of concrete releases a high percent of the world's carbon emissions during its production which in turn contributes to global warming. By using self-healing concrete, concrete manufacture can be reduced thereby leading to the reduction in cement production which would ultimately decrease the carbon emissions. Self-healing concrete consists of spores containing the bacteria which take up volume and thereby leads to a reduction in the production of cement which further reduces carbon emissions into the atmosphere. Moreover, the precipitation of biogenic calcium carbonate by the bacteria in the Self-healing concrete is one of the most environmentally friendly materials for use in the engineering applications and it does not disrupt the local ecosystem as the material is produced by the living organisms.

Since, traditional concrete is difficult to recycle and cracks often lead to damages of the buildings, a large amount of the waste generated during the demolition or rebuilding the structures forms a large volume of the landfills thereby damaging the local ecosystems adversely by displacing the local flora and fauna. So, using self-healing concrete will help in reducing these issues to a great extent by reducing the production of cement and the amount of the demolition wastes. Cyanobacteria which are used in the self-healing or living bricks absorb carbon dioxide in the process of churning out calcium carbonate whereas, the traditional process of making cement usually releases carbon dioxide in the environment and according to some estimates, cement is responsible for producing about 7% of carbon emissions worldwide. So, by using self-healing or living bricks the amount of carbon dioxide emissions can be reduced as it helps in removing carbon dioxide from the air instead of releasing it into the environment.

The use of self-healing concrete also focuses on futurity. By using self-healing concrete long lasting buildings can be created (Figure 9) as well as the maintenance and repair costs can be reduced which will ensure that the future generations would have a secure and sustainable built environment to live in. This also meets the concept of social sustainability. The use of self-healing concrete would also be very beneficial in India due to its diverse climate that varies from place to place and specially in the Warm and Humid regions where the high humidity levels would be helpful for the self-repairing processes of the self-healing biomimetic materials.

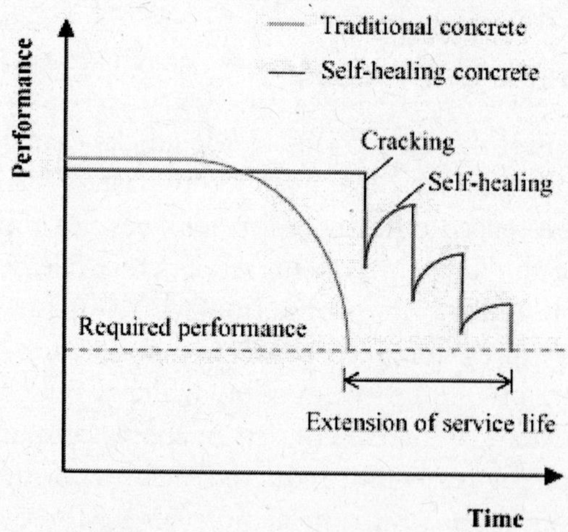

Fig. 9: Image Showing the Extension of Service Life Achieved Using Self-healing Concrete over Traditional Concrete

(*Self-healing in cementitious materials:* Materials, methods and service conditions retrieved from https://www.sciencedirect.com/science/article/abs/pii/S0264127515309515)

CONCLUSION

The use of self-healing biomimetic materials not only help in achieving economic and environmental sustainability, but it also ensures a safe and secure built environment for the future generations to enjoy and live in. Moreover, the requirement of high humidity levels for the bacteria in these materials to carry out the processes of self-repairing shows that they can be the best possible solutions for overcoming the issues related to cracks that appear in the buildings located in the Warm and Humid climatic zones. Such materials also increase the lifespan of the buildings and reduce the maintenance and repair costs as well as the amount of the demolition wastes. Though there are certain disadvantages of using these materials such as they are more expensive than the conventional ones and require skilled labor still, they prove to be more efficient than the conventional materials and can be used to increase the sustainability of the built environment and also for creating long-lasting structures.

REFERENCES

[1] Beal, D. (2020). Types and causes of cracks and cracking. Retrieved on October 19, 2020 from https://www.grangequarry.co.uk/wp-content/uploads/2018/05/Classification-Of-Concrete-Cracks.pdf

[2] Bloom, D. (2020). How mortar breaks down. *Stonehenge Masonry Company*. Retrieved on October 19, 2020 from http://stonehengemasonry.ca/how-mortar-breaks-down

[3] Building materials come alive with help from bacteria. Retrieved on October 19, 2020 from https://www.sciencedaily.com/releases/2020/01/200115120602.htm

[4] Causes and types of cracks in masonry buildings and their repair methods. Cracks in Brick Walls: Why Brick Walls Crack and How to Repair Cracked Bricks. Retrieved on October 19, 2020 from https://fantastichandyman.com.au/blog/brick-wall-cracks-guide

[5] How to Evaluate Cracks in Poured Concrete Slabs. Retrieved on October 20, 2020 from https://inspectapedia.com/structure/Concrete_Floor_Cracks.php

[6] Jonkers, H. (2011). Self-healing concrete. *Ingenia, marzo, 46*, 39–43.

[7] Living bricks that can reproduce could help create self-healing green buildings – By Matthew Griffin Futurist. Retrieved on October 19, 2020 from https://www.fanaticalfuturist.com/2020/01/living-bricks-that-can-reproduce-could-help-create-self-healing-green-buildings

[8] Lubelli, B., Nijland, T.G. and Van Hees, R.P.J. (2011). Self-healing of lime based mortars: microscopy observations on case studies. *Heron, 56 (1/2).*

Studies on Mind-Altering Plants of Forensic Interest

M.P. Goutam[1], Shubhra Goutam[2] and Poonam Yadav[3]

[1,3]Shri Vaishnav Institute of Forensic Science,
Shri Vaishnav Vidyapeeth Vishwavidyalaya, Indore, Madhya Pradesh
[2]State Forensic Science Laboratory, Raipur, Chhattisgarh
E-mail: [1]mpgoutam@gmail.com; [2]shubhragoutam@gmail.com;
[3]yadavpoonam077@gmail.com

ABSTRACT: Humanity has a perpetual and strong relationship with medicinal plants. The use of plant metabolites has helped in the treatment of diseases in performing religious ceremonies and as a beautifying agent. The knowledge of poisonous/narcotic plants perhaps is as old as the human race. The importance of the study of these plants cannot be overrated. On the one hand, many plants in regulated doses constitute potent and effective remedies for amelioration of disease, on the other, some of them are a serious menace to life and physiological activity of man and animals. There are some plants, which amazingly, affect the brains and mental states of the humans who ingest them; therefore, plant-originated psychoactive plants are designated as "Botanical Weapons".

Nowadays mind altering hallucinogenic or narcotic plants have become prominent for the detrimental societal impacts. Therefore, there is a need to get the complete knowledge of these plants. Present review highlights the Chemical, Toxicological and Medico legal aspects of such mind-altering plants. As some plants are used for different kinds of criminal activities e.g. homicide and suicide, as stupefying poisons prior to robbery, kidnapping and rape and as abortifacients. Various plants and herbs are also used as a love-philtres and as aphrodisiac.

Keywords: Cannabis, Cocaine, Dhatura, Magic Mushrooms, Mescal Buttons.

INTRODUCTION

The plants and their products are the greatest gift of the nature on the service of mankind. The use of the plants to prevent and cure diseases goes for back in the history of man. The plants have been used for defense, protection and nourishment by human beings with the down of. (de Sa, and Elisabetsky, 2012), The primitive man in his quest for food must have come across plants containing poisonous substances and by accident and by experience must soon have learnt to avoid them as articles of diet and might have begun to make use of them for his own purposes e.g. to get rid of his enemies, to catch fish which stupefy or kill them, preparation of poisonous arrows for hunting and for poisoning the live stock or even to increase libido etc. (Chopra *et al.*, 1965).

Today, different plants are used for different kinds of criminal activity e.g. homicide and suicide. Some of the plants are used as stupefying poisons prior to robbery, kidnapping and rape and various methods practiced by the poisoner. Some of these plants are used as abortifacients. Various plants and herbs are also used as love-philtres and as aphrodisiac. The knowledge of poisonous and narcotic plants perhaps is as old as the human race.

The importance of the study of these plants cannot be overrated. On the one hand many plants in regulated doses constitute potent and effective remedies for amelioration of disease yet, on the other, some of them are a serious menace to life and bodily functions of man and animals In criminal investigations forensic scientist has to play a significant role in cases related to plant poisoning It is therefore of fundamental importance to forensic scientists to gain a complete knowledge of such plants, their chemical constituents and physiological action on the human body (Goutam and Goutam 2006). Plants for survival, have evolved to produce an astonishing variety of chemical compounds well-known as secondary metabolites and often serve to deter herbivores, protect against pathogens & mitigate the consequences of radiation, among numerous other uses. Infact, some of these chemicals react with human bodies in specific ways, ranging from organ failure and death to reactions that inspire lifesaving pharmaceuticals.

There are some plants these amazingly, affect the brains and mental states of the humans who ingest them (Melissa Petruzzello) and commonly called as narcotic plants. These plant-originated weapons may be designated as botanical *weapons*. This plant contains substances that cause unusual excitation and subsequent depression of the central nervous system. Many narcotic plants contain phyto-constituents have medicinal properties and used basically as pain relievers. Alkaloids are the principle active constituents of narcotic plants. Among these many of these plants are extremely toxic and when frequently used cause narcomania. Most narcotic plants are of higher plant orders, the only exception being certain fungi. The narcotic plants include:

- Indian hemp: Cannabis *indica*
- Coca plant: Erythroxylum *coca*,
- Opium poppy: Papaver *somniferum*
- Mescal Buttons: Peyote: Lophophora williamsii
- Dhatura plants: D. metel Linn var.fastuosa
- Psilocybe: Magic mushrooms.

Humanity has an enduring and intimate relationship with medicinal plants. From prehistoric times through to the modern era, the use of plant specialized metabolites has helped treat diseases, steer religious ceremonies, and cosmetically augment the body. While modern synthetic chemical methods often provide quicker, safer and more cost-effective production of economically important compounds, many plants remain the sole source of such molecules. On the other hand, several plants containing mind altering hallucinogenic or narcotic chemicals have become infamous for the detrimental societal impacts of illicit drugs derived from them (Restrepo *et al.*, 2019). Therefore, it is imperative to obtain knowledge of these plants. Present review highlights the Chemical, Toxicological and Medico legal aspects of such mind-altering plants.

Cannabis Sativa Plant

Plant Leaves

Cannabis Seeds

Kashmiri Ganja

Bambaiya Ganja

Charas Balls

Crude Charas

Common Name: Hemp, Indian Hemp, Ganja plant, Merihuana, Merijuana, Grass, Pot.

Vernacular Name: Arabic—Hinab, Kanab, Kinnab; Bengali—Bhang, Ganja, Sidhi, Gujarati—Bhang, Ganja; Hindi—Bhang, Ganja, Charas, Ganje ka per; Kashmiri—Bangi, Marathi—Bhang, Bhangacha-Jhada; Punjabi—Bengi, Sabzi; Sanskrit—Chapola, Ganji; Tamil—Bangi-ilai, Ganja-chedi, Kalpam; Telgu—Bangi-aku Ganjari-chettu.

Cannabis sativa is an annual herbaceous plant belongs to the family Cannabaceae. Historically this plant has been used for several purposes like recreational, medicinal, industrial fiber, and seed oil etc. Psychoactive and physiologically active constituents of this plant known as cannabinoids. These are found in the flowers and to a small extent the leaves, and traces in the stems, and seeds.. The cannabinoid, Δ^9-THC is the most active component and is responsible for the plant's behavioural and psychotropic effects. It also has other non-psychoactive cannabinoids such as CBD cannabidiol and CBG cannabigerol and CBC cannabichromene. There are 545 constituents reported in cannabis. The cannabinoids have prospective medical implementation in the treatment of various types of diseases (ElSohly and Gul, 2014).

Structural formula of Cannabinoids

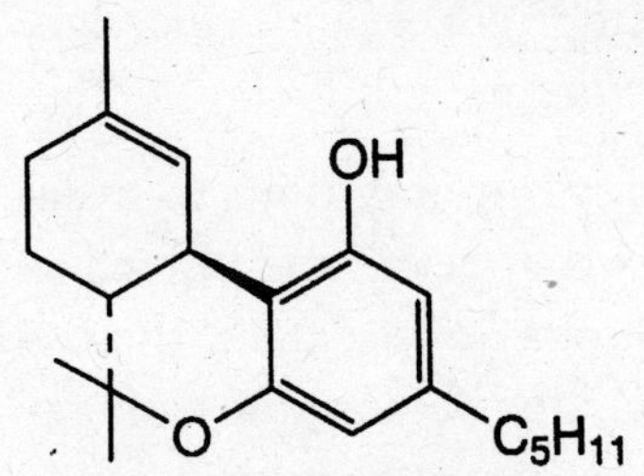

Δ^9-Tetrahydrocannabinol

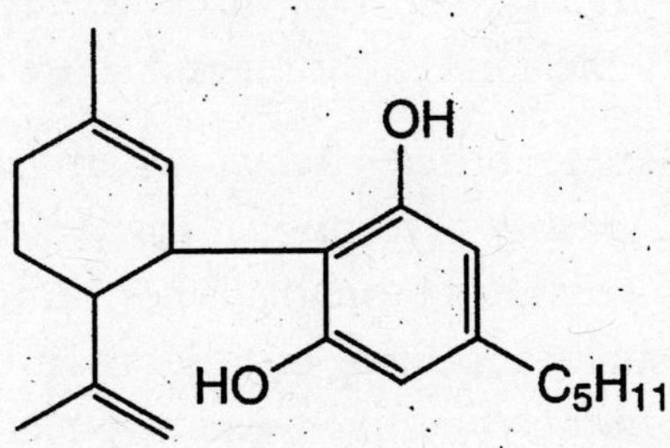

Cannabidiol

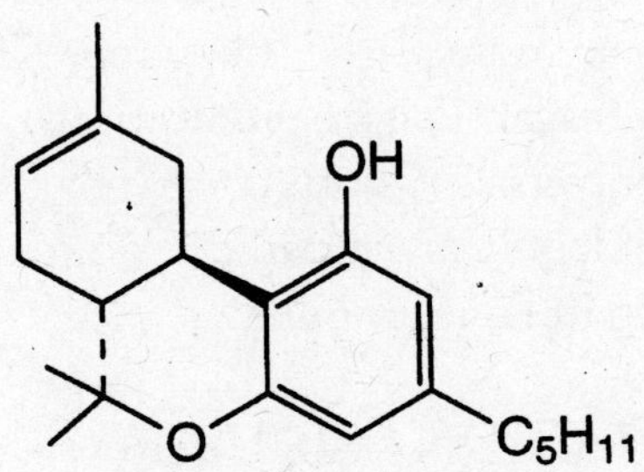

Δ^8-Tetrahydrocannabinol

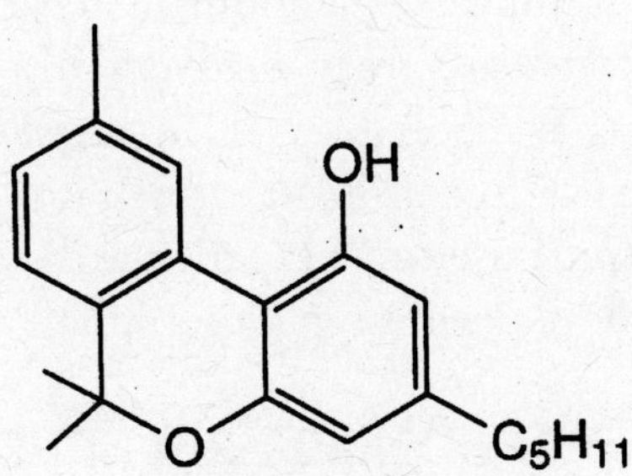

Cannabinol

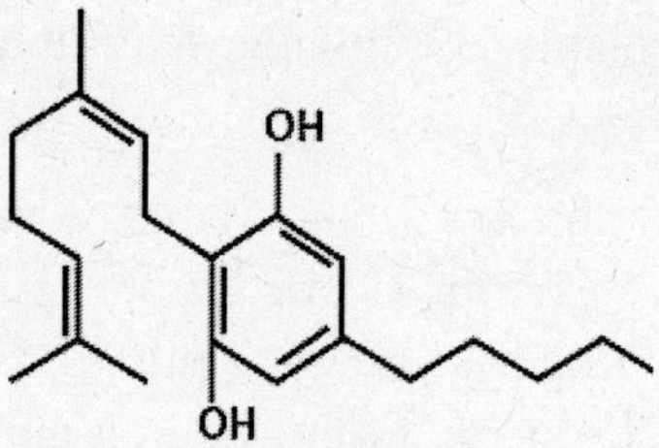

Cannabigerol

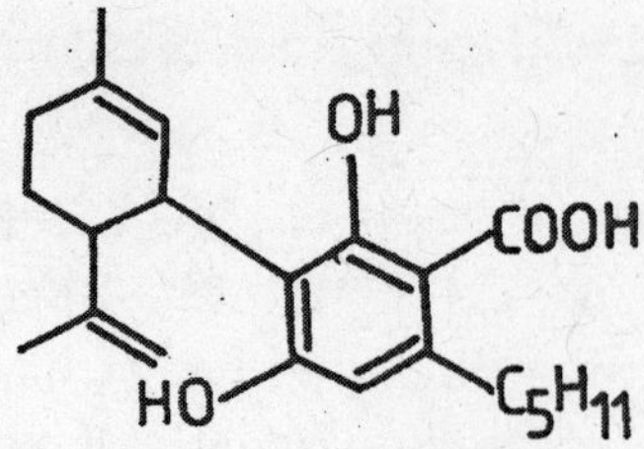

Cannabidiolic Acid

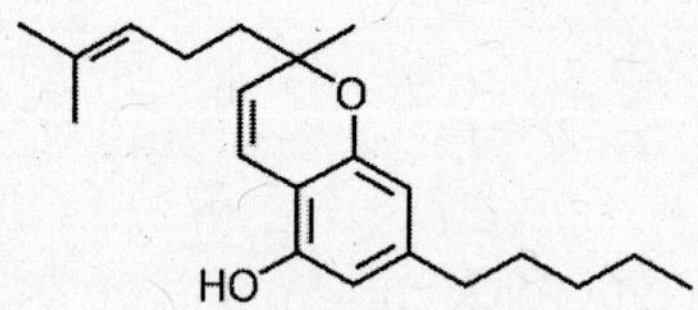

Carmabichromene

EFFECTS OF CANNABIS (MARIJUANA)

Cannabis (Marijuana) is also Known as Mary Jane, weed, grass, bud, herb, pot, ganja, and with different slang terms. It is gray-green dried flowering & fruiting tops of *Cannabis sativa.* When is smoked, active components tetra hydro cannabinol (THC) and other phyto-constituents pass from the lungs into the bloodstream and reaches to the brain. The user is experiencing effect immediately. Some user experiences a pleasant euphoria and sense of relaxation.

There are some other effects, which may vary among user to user: examples- Heightened sensory perception, laughter, Increased appetite and altered perception of time. In a case where cannabis is consumed in foods or beverages, these effects rather delayed—usually appearing after 30 minutes to 1 hour because the cannabis has to first pass through the digestive system. In case of eating or drinking cannabis delivers significantly less Tetra hydro cannabinol into the bloodstream comparatively to smoking an equivalent amount of the cannabis. There may be a reason due to the delayed effects, user may inadvertently consume more THC than they intend to. According to a report by NIDA (https://www.drugabuse.gov/publications). pleasant experiences with marijuana are in no way universal. Contrary to relaxation and euphoria, some user may experience distrust, anxiety, fear, or panic. Commonly these effects are developed when a user inhale the drug in large amount.

SHORT AND LONG TERM EFFECT OF CANNABIS USE

Short-term memory problems: severe anxiety, paranoia, very strange behaviour, psychosis, panic, hallucinations, loss of sense of personal identity, increased heart rate and problems with coordination (impairing safe driving or playing sports). Long term effects: sexual problems (for males), impaired thinking and ability to learn and perform complex tasks, lower life satisfaction, anti-social behaviour including stealing money or lying, financial difficulties, greater chances of being unemployed or not getting good jobs

Medico Legal Aspects

Most cases of poisoning are accidental or due to over indulgence. Its use in chocolates causes intense craving among children for its euphoric effects. The different brands of Munukka tablets are sold in the Indian markets. These contain Cannabis especially Bhang. Majun and charas are sometimes used as stupefying poisons prior to robbery, kidnapping, and rape. Impaired judgment from marihuana use may lead to accidents, sexual excesses, violence, and crime. Rarely, the victims run amok. This is a condition resulting from the continued use of cannabis or even its use for the first time. It is characterized by a frenzied desire on the part of the person to commit murders. The person may then commit suicide or surrender himself to the police. Ganja is taken to steady the nerves before performing some bold act, e.g. homicide. Charas and ganja are sometimes used to dope cigarettes. Smoking such cigarettes is stated to improve memory recall. Sadhus and temple Poojaris (priests) use them to get into a religious mood (Goutam and Goutam, 2006).

Erythroxylum Coca Plant

Leaves

Coca Seeds

Erythroxylum coca leaves are used as a stimulant. Chewing the leaves releases the alkaloid cocaine and when it comes in contact with the saliva. This chewing habit is named as "coqueio" induces a mild stimulation, enabling the user to withstand strenuous work, walking, hunger, or thirst. It produces local anaesthesia when contact with the mucous membranes of mouth and stomach. The psychological and physiological effects are lighter in comparison to the administration of pure extracted alkaloid cocaine. The chewing of coca leaves with alkaline substances such as lime powder is an ancient practice of pre-Incan peoples. The improvement in fatigue, augmentation of cognition, reduction of hunger and enhancement of mood were compelling assets of the plant for indigenous people (https://www.sciencedirect.com/topics/neuroscience).

CHRONIC POISONING

Accidental cases occur from addiction, hypodermic injection and from urethral, vesical and rectal injection. Cocaine is rarely used far homicide or suicide. The sense of well being experienced on administration of cocaine causes a number of persons to drift into addiction, also known as cocainism, cocainophagia or cocainomania. The tongue and teeth of habitual cocaine eater turns black. There is generally ulceration of the nasal septum. When cocaine is used as a snuff the symptoms of chronic cocaine poisoning are characterised by anorexia, weakness, tremors, impotence, loss of weight, moral deterioration and even insanity. The effects of cocaine lead to increased erotic tension in women and nymphomania on the other hand in men, the condition leads to many sexual perversions, mainly homosexuality, and libidinous outrages. Insanity is characterised by many delusions of persecution and hallucinations, chiefly tactile, and visual. It is also believed to be an aphrodisiac and to increase the duration of sexual act by desensitising sensory nerves of glands penis, when used locally. Prostitutes sometimes -inject cocaine solution into vagina to produce local constriction. It causes

Structural formula

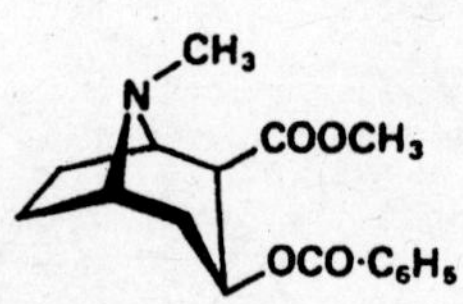

Cocaine

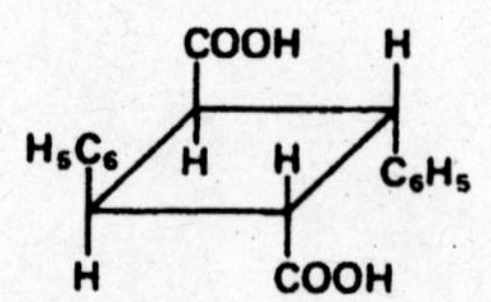

α-Truxillic acid

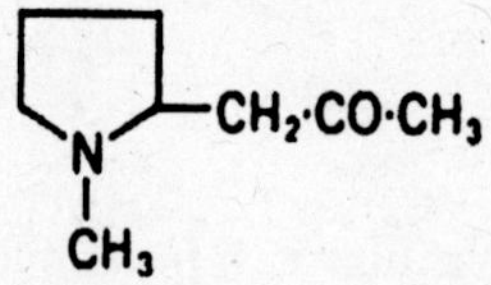

Hygrine

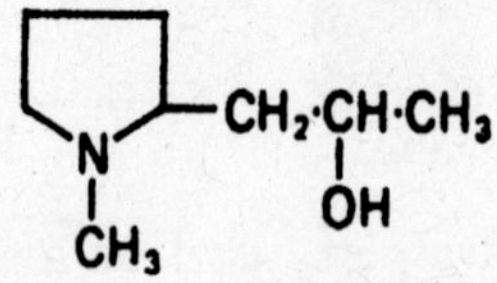

Hygroline

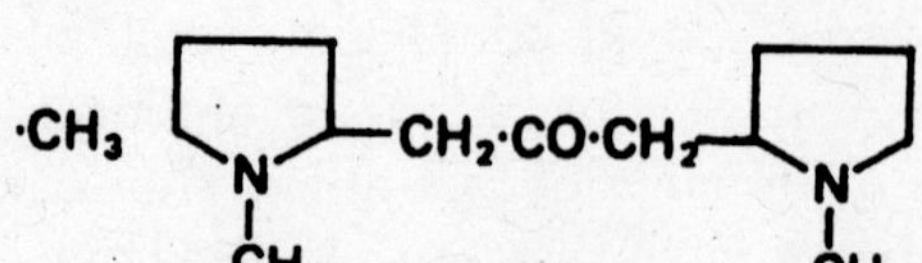

Cuscohygrine

mental derangement in chronic users who may get involved in crimes. Magnan's sign is a clinical sign in which people with addiction of cocaine experience paraesthesia ie feeling like a constantly movement of any foreign body, such as fine sand or powder, under the skin (https://en.wikipedia.org/wiki/Magnan).

In case of acute poisoning when cocaine is used in small doses by cocaine users. They experience restlessness, euphoria and excitability. There is a reduced sense of fatigue, and enlarged capacity for muscular work. Later, hallucinations, dilated pupils, tachycardia, arterial hypertension and abdominal pain is developed. The stimulation is accompanied by depression of the nervous system. Irregular respiration, convulsions, coma, and circulatory failure are observed in acute poisoning. Symptoms of chronic poisoning develop like impaired sensibility of mucous membranes of mouth; may cause ulceration of the mucous membranes; loss in weight; mental deterioration and hallucinations (http://www.inchem.org/documents).

Papaver Sominiferum (Opium Poppy plant)

Opium is the air-dried, milky exude obtained by incising the unripe capsules of Papaver sominiferum (N.O. Papaveraceae). Poppy capsules (Post Ka Doda) when they are ripe and dry contain traces of opium and are used for their sedative and narcotic action. Poppy seeds (Khas-Khas) are innocuous and are used as food. They are sprinkled over some Indian sweets. They yield bland oil known as poppy seed oil (Khas Khas Ka Tel).

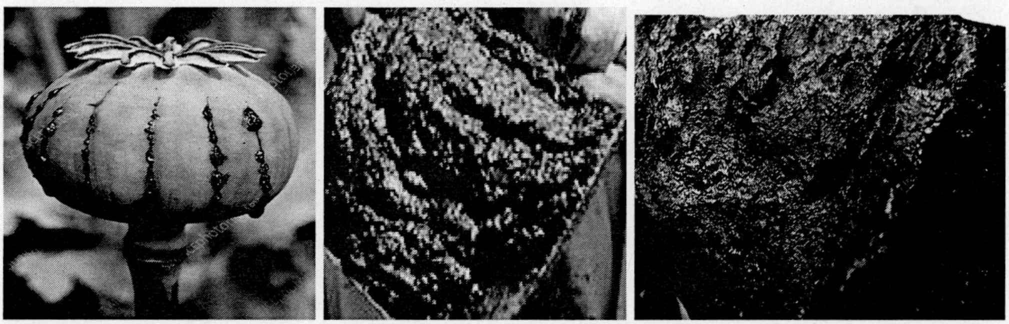

Common Names: Poppy, Opium Poppy, and White Poppy, Carnation Poppy

Vernacular names: Bengali—Pasto, Posto; Gujarati—Afhina, Lhuskhus, Posta; Hindi—Afim, Afyun, Khashkhash, Pest, Post; Marathi—Aphu, Khuskhus, Posta, Afim, Appo, Khashkhash, Posto; Malayalam—Aphim, Khashkhash; Punjabi—Afim, Doda, Khashkhash, Khishkhash, Post; Sanskrit—Ahifen, Ghosa, Khasa, khakasa, Ullasata; Tamil—Abini Gashagasha, Kasakasa, Postaka; Telugu—Abhini Gashagasha, Kasakas and Urdu—Khashkhash sufaid.

Crude opium is sometimes used on special festive occasions, kasoomba, its decoction, is offered to the guests. Opium is also smoked in the form of madak, chandu or opium dross. An infusion of poppy capsules is often drunk by some people in certain districts in Punjab and parts of Rajasthan. A sweet, called halwa, prepared from the juice extracted from green poppy capsules, is also used. Opium is believed to increase the duration of the sexual act. Hence, young men, who get accustomed to the drug by its constant use, often take it. It is also used to steady the nerves for doing some bold act. For instance, in the ancient times, the Rajputs used to take the drug before they took part in battles.

Post Ka Doda

Doda Choora

Active Constituents

The major alkaloids found in opium are morphine, narcotine, papaverine, thebaine, codeine, and narceine. It also contains meconic acid.

Structural Formula of Opium Alkaloids

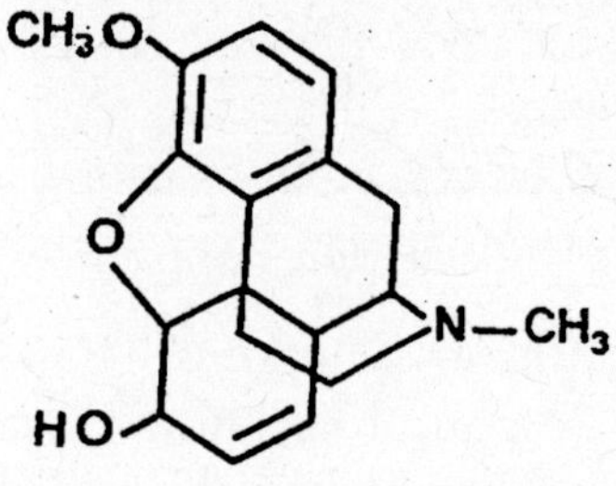

Morphine

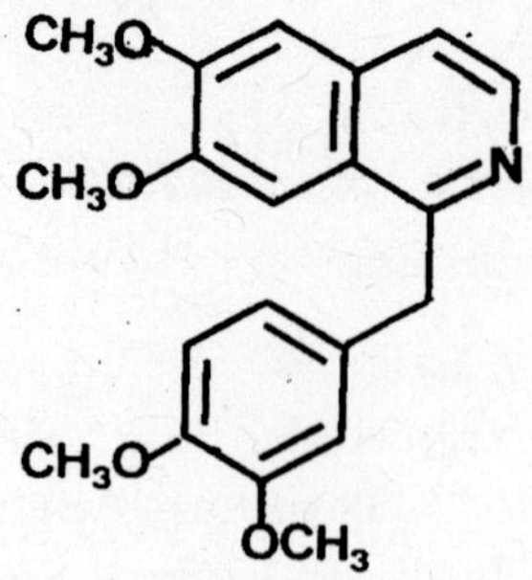

Papaverine

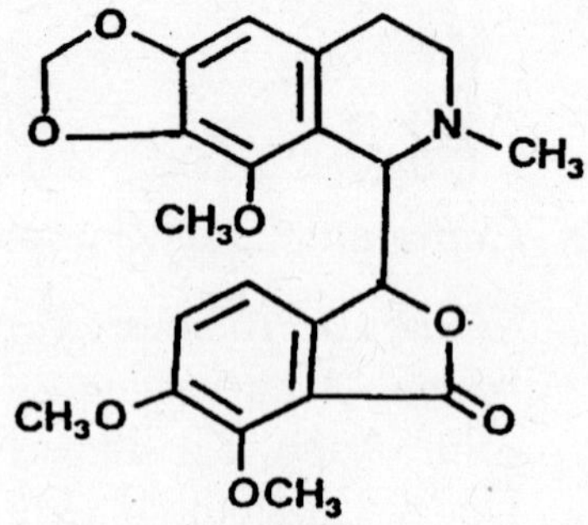

Narcotine

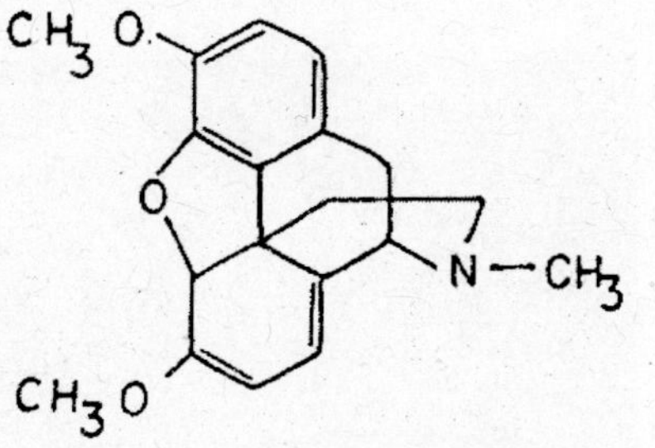

Thebain

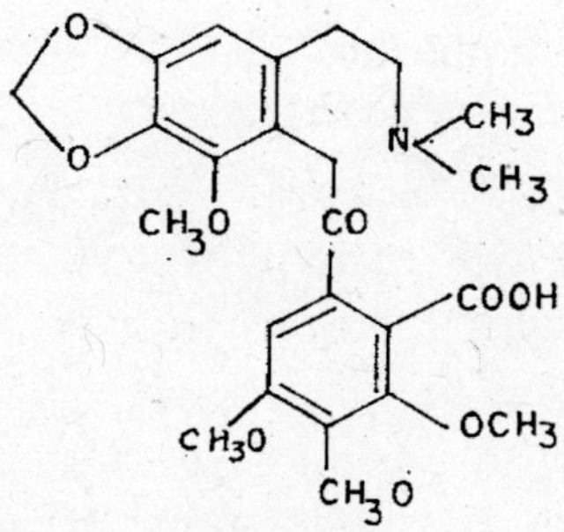

Narceine

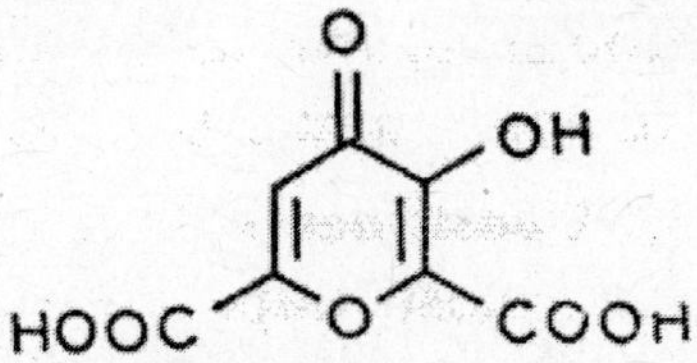

Meconic Acid

Short-Term, Long-Term Effects and Results of Overdose of Opium

Short-term effects include: euphoria, relaxation, analgesia, slower, shallower breathing, lower heart rate, impaired reflexes, temporary constipation and loss of appetite. *Long-term effects:* Regular use of opium may cause: tolerance - needing to use more to get the same effect, irregular periods and difficulty having children, loss of sex drive, constipation, dependence on opium. Symptoms of opium overdose: very slow breathing; loss of consciousness, tiny pupils, and untreated overdose can lead to brain damage and death (https://adf.org.au/drug-facts/opium).

Medico Legal Aspects

Opium is easily obtained everywhere in India and death from its use is so painless that it is the poison of choice for suicidal purposes. On account of its black colour, characteristic odour and bitter taste, it is rarely used for homicidal purposes. It is sometimes used for infanticide. Death has resulted from the breast-feeding of an infant by a woman who had smeared her nipple with tincture of opium with evil intention. Accidental poisoning may occur from drugging of infants and children to keep them quiet or from overdose of a medicinal preparation. Sometimes, opium is used to steady the nerves before doing some bold act, e.g. homicide. It is rarely used for doping racehorses and as a cattle poison. Opium and its preparations cause addiction, of which, heroin (diacetyl morphine), an artificial alkaloid derived from morphine, is the most dangerous. Brown sugar is crude heroin.

Dhatura plants

Dhatura Metel Fruit

Dhatura Stramonium Fruit

Dhatura plants in India are abundant and grow wild all over the country. Dhatura Fastuosa grows in plain and Dhatura Stramonium grows in the range of Himalayan altitudes. In the plains, two varieties of Dhatura fastuosa are available: dhatura alba, a white flowered plant (safed dhatura), and Dhatura niger, a black or rather deep-purple flowered plant (kala dhatura). The flowers are bell shaped. The fruits are spherical and have sharp spines, giving the name thorn apple to the plant. They contain brown seeds resembling chilli seeds. An average sized fruit contains 450 to 500 seeds. Seeds yield what is called 'Dhatura'. All parts of the plant are poisonous but the seeds and fruits are considered to be the most noxious. Dhatura stramonium (Jimsonweed/ apple of Peru/devil's' trumpet/Jamestown weed/ mad apple/ stinkweed/ thorn apple) is an extremely deadly plant. There are about 15 species of Dhatura and while all are poisonous, their fragrance can be sweet or unpleasant depending upon the season.

Vernacular names: D. metel Linn var.fastuosa (Linn)

Bengali: Dhatura, Kala-dhatura

Gujrati: Kala-dhatura, Kalo-dhatura,

Hindi: Kala-dhatura, Kashmiri: Dhather, Malayalam: Kariyummatta

Marathi: Kala-dhotra, Pandra.: dhotara, Punjabi: Dhatura

Sanskrit: Dhattura, phustura, Ummatta, Tamil: Ayigam, Karu-vumattai,

Telugu: Matulaputrakamll, Dutturamu

Uriya: Ambunodo, Khorodushono.

D. Stramonium

Common names: Devil's-apple, Devil's-trumpet, Jamestown Weed, Jimson Weed, Thorn Apple var. tatula, Purple Thorn Apple, Purple Stramonium.

Vernacular names: Bengali: Sada-dhutura, Kashmiri: Dhatura, Malayalum-Matulam Ummam

Punjabi—Dattura, Dhatura, Tattur; Sanskrit—Dhattura, Dhustura, Ummatta

Tamil—Emanaman; Simaiyu—mattai Turutturam, Umatai

Telugu—Dutturamu; Urdu—Dhatura

Uriya—Dhutura, Sukla-dhutura.

Physical and Mental Effects of Dhatura

According to a report, datura has different types of physical effects on the human body: Dilated pupils, Dehydration, High blood pressure, Muscle cramps, Hallucinations and Restless leg syndrome. Mentally Datura can cause amnesia, confusion, psychosis, and hallucinations, in addition to altering mood and emotional expression. If a person takes too much Datura but not enough to overdose, the consumer may still experience something similar to a hangover as the drug metabolizes. The individual may feel some anxiety, dehydration, sleepiness, and light sensitivity, as well as other symptoms (https://www.mhs-dbt.com/blog/datura).

Criminal Activities

Dhatura is employed in India as a stupefying poison prior to robbery, kidnapping and rape It is some time known as Road poison .It is commonly encountered during a journey .The powered seeds are mixed with food, tea drink or in Pann (betel leaf).and given to an unwary travelers by an apparently obliging person. On the ingestion of such material the traveler becomes very drowsy. When he wakes up he finds that his pockets are picked, removable belongings lost and the apparently obliging person vanished. Generally, in the railways and pilgrim places such incidences occur (Parikh, 2011).

Accidental Cases Occur

- When children and adults eat the raw fruit or seeds mistaking them for edible fruits or capsicum seeds respectively.
- From the use of dhatura as an aphrodisiac.
- When the decoction of seeds is added to country liquor or toddy for a greater kick.

Chemical Constituents

The active principle contains the alkaloids, hyoscyamine, hyoscine or scopolamine and traces of atropine. An alkaloid is a complex substance found in various plants. It is so called because it behaves like an alkali and combines with acids to form salts. The distribution of alkaloids in the plant is not uniform: some are concentrated in the roots, others in the seeds, still others in the bark, and so on. They act mainly on some portions of the central nervous system, each having its own individual action.

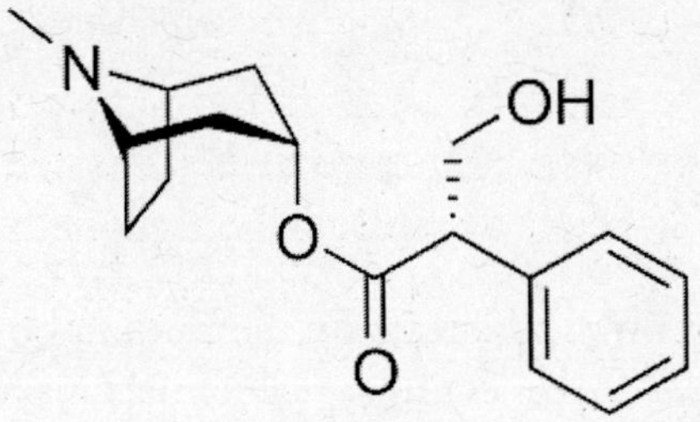

Hyoscyamine

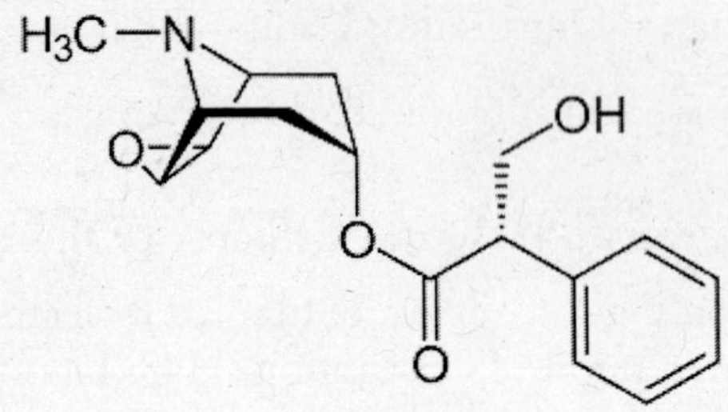

Hyoscine

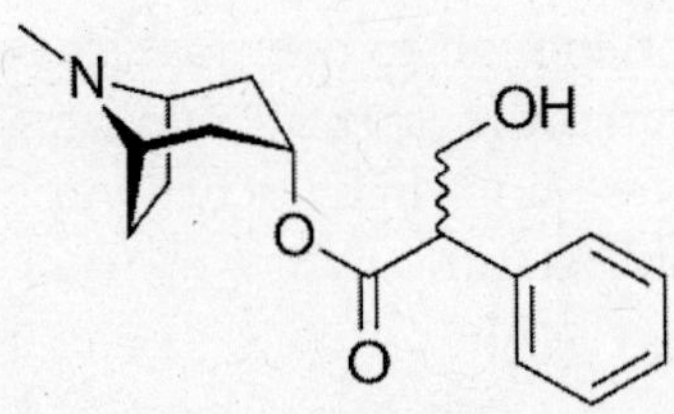

Atropine

Symptoms and Signs

The important signs and symptoms can be summarized under the Os viz: (I) dryness of the mouth and throat (II) difficulty in talking (III) dysphagia (IV) dilatation of cutaneous blood vessels (V) dilatation of pupils, (VI) dry hot skin, (VII) dysuria, (VIII) drunken gait, (IX) delirium and (X) drowsiness leading to coma.

Lophophora Williamsii (Mescal Buttons)

Lophophora williamsii; mescal; peyote a small spineless globe-shaped cactus; source of mescal buttons.

Synonyms: Mescal buttons, mescaline, mescal

Peyote is a small, spineless cactus. The plant has been used tribes for religious and healing purposes since long back. It is a small spineless cactus with particularly mescaline. Peyote has a squat gray-green body with tufted hairs, and pink or white flowers. Centuries before the Spanish explorer Hernando Cortez arrived in Mexico, the Aztec Indians were using peyote—a short, squat, button-shaped cactus that grows in the wild desert countryside. The Aztecs had discovered that peyote had certain mystical powers. During religious rites, they consumed bits of the succulent stem in order to hear and see strange sounds and images, which enhanced their spiritual experience. The practice of chewing often called mescal buttons and still continued among many North American tribes. However the consumption of peyote is illegal in the United States, the law allows it to be used as part of the religious ceremony of the Native American Church, whose membership is largely American Indian.

Chemical Constituents

About 56 individual alkaloid substances in peyote have been identified. The most active and best known of these alkaloids is mescaline, It is a psychotomimetic agent that can alter the mind and produce behaviour similar to that exhibited by psychotic individuals. Some other minor Peyote alkaloids are the phenylethylamines N-methyl mescaline. 3-0-demethylmescaline and hordenine. Certain cacti are of pharmaceutical and pharmacological interest, as they contain protoalkaloids, some of which have hallucinogenic properties. One of these is the cactus *Lophophora williamsii* that has long been used by Mexican Indians. It is known as peyotl. Anhalonium or mescal buttons.

Peyote is a hallucinogen it can cause intense in a person' contortion perceptions of reality, including hearing, seeing and feeling things that appear real but in real sense are not. Hallucinogens can affect neural circuits in the brain involving the neuro-transmitter serotonin responsible for playing a role in mood, sensory perception, hunger, sleep, body temperature and muscle control and sexual behaviour. The effects of peyote depend on the potency and quantity that is ingested, as well as the user's mood, surroundings, expectations, and mental health. Some of the users describe the high as dream-like. The effects are often escalating when the drug is taken combined with alcohol or any stimulant that can definitely harm a person's mental health (https://www.verywellmind.com/how-long-does-peyote).

The Physical and Mental Effects of Peyote

Peyote have similar physical effects include Appetite loss, Increased blood pressure, Increased body temperature, Increased heart rate, Difficulty sleeping, Flushing, Numbness, Severe, Profound sweating nausea and vomiting. Weakness, and Uncoordinated movements. Mental effects include Altered awareness, sense of time and perceptions, Hallucinations, Anxiety Euphoria, Inability in concentration, Panic and Paranoia. Sense of relaxation is also affected (https://www.verywellmind.com/how-long-does-peyote).

Repeated or long-term use of peyote, hallucinogens can cause the following effects

1. Hallucinogen persisting perception disorder (HPPD). The condition causes flashbacks of hallucinations and visual disturbances that do not go away and can interfere with a user's daily life. Symptoms can be mistaken for neurological disorders such as a stroke or a brain tumour.
2. Prolonged psychosis. Include visual disturbances and scattered thinking, as well as periods of paranoia or mood disturbances.

Peyote Alkaloids

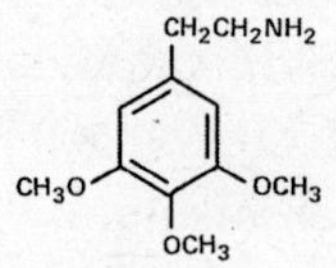

Mescaline

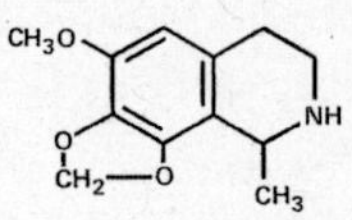

Anhalonine

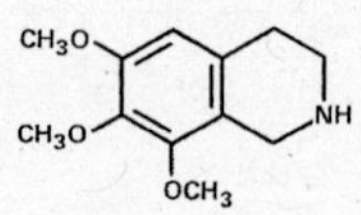

Anhalinine

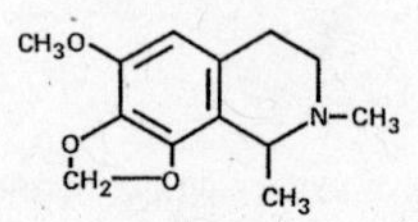

Lophophorine

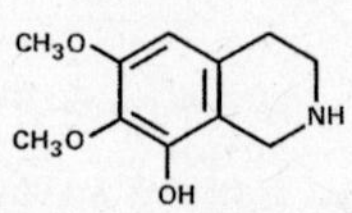

Anhalamine

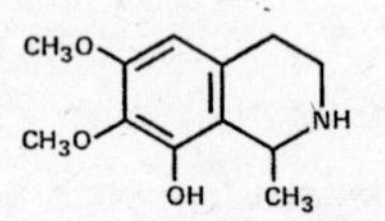

Anhalonidine

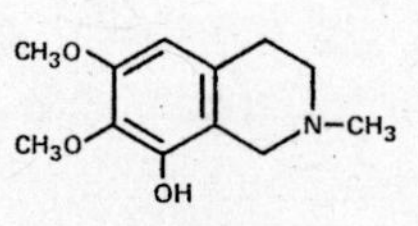

Anhalidine

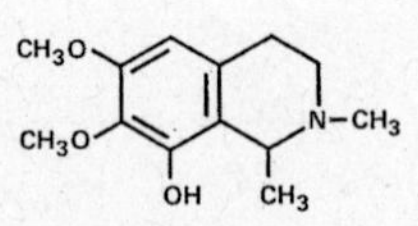

Pellotine

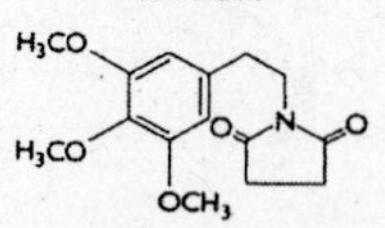

Mescaline succinimide

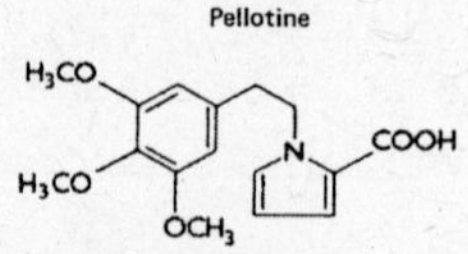

Peyonine

Psilocybe Mushrooms

Psilocybe Semilanceata

Psilocybe Mexicana

Psilocybe Cubensis

Magic Mushrooms

Psilocybin mushrooms, commonly known as magic mushrooms or shrooms, these are a polyphletic informal group of fungi that contain psilocybin and psilocin. Biological genera containing psilocybin mushrooms include Copelandia. Gymnopilus, Incocybe, Panaeolus, Pholiotina, Pluteus and Psilocybe. Psilocybin mushrooms have been and continue to be used in indigenous New World cultures in religious, divinatory, or spiritual contexts. They may be depicted in Stone Age rock art in Africa and Europe, but are most famously represented in the Pre-Columbian sculptures and glyphs seen throughout North, Central and South America.

Various Mushroom Stones (Approx 1 ft tall –1000 BC to 500 AD)

The genus Psilocybe belonging to the family of Strophariaceae, is undoubtedly the most important, being an almost cosmopolitan genus of the hallucinogenic mushrooms. More than 140 different species are known, 80 of them are known to contain psychotropic substances. Other psilocybin containing mushrooms belong to the genera of Panaeolus (Coprinaceae). Conocybe (Bolbitiaceae). Inocybe

(Cortinariaceae), and Pluteus (Pluteaceae). Psilocybe semilanceata and Psilocybe cubensis are the most important two species in view of drug abuse.

Chemical Constituents

The main constituents are Psilocybin, Psilocin, Baeocystin and Serotonin

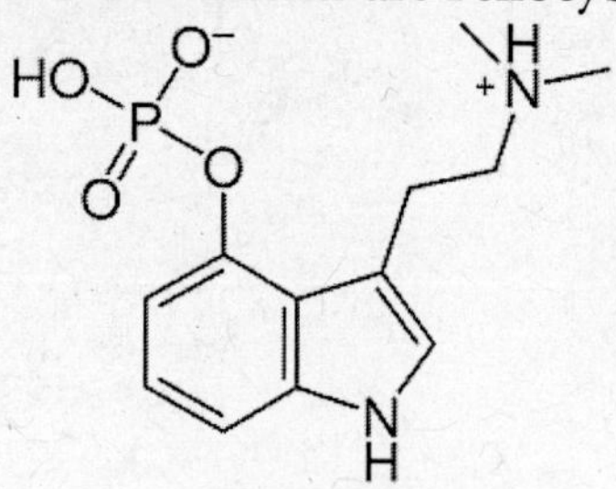

Psilocybin

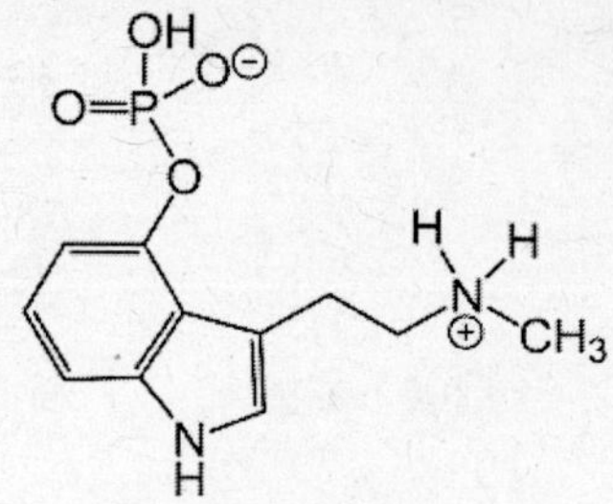

Baeocystin

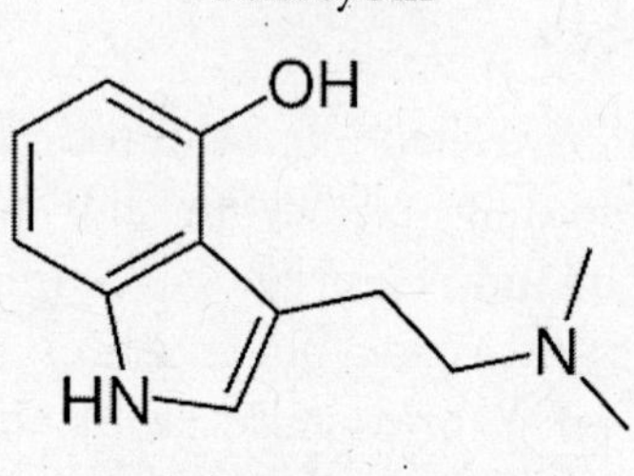

Psilocin

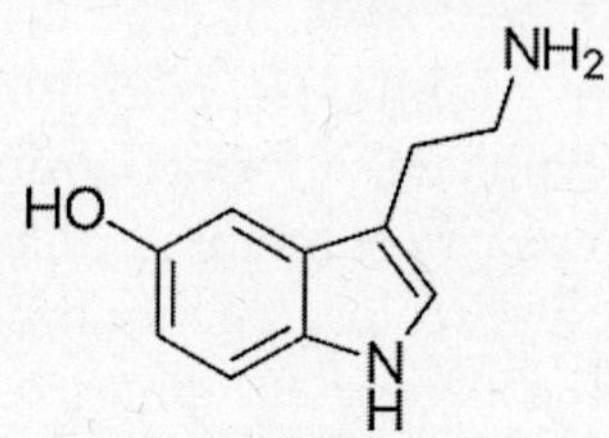

Serotonin

Myths about Magic Mushrooms

Magic mushrooms are hallucinogenic drugs, meaning they can cause you to see, hear, and feel sensations that seem real but are not. The effects of magic mushrooms, however, are highly variable and believed to be influenced by environmental factors (de Mattos-Shipley *et al.*, 2016). For spiritual experiences and self-discovery many myths are associated with Psilocybin mushrooms. Some believe that naturally occurring magic mushrooms, weed, and mescaline are holy herbs. These enable people to godly superior spiritual states. On the other hand, consider magic mushrooms to experience a sense of euphoria and a distorted sense of time. In fact, the active component psilocybin present in shrooms is converted7to psilocin in the body and it is believed to influence serotonin levels in the brain, leading to alter and unusual perceptions. (Daniel and Hagerman 2018).

Side effects of magic mushrooms can include both physical and mental effects

Physical Effects: Dilated pupils, Drowsiness, Headaches, Increased heart rate, blood pressure, and temperature. Lack of coordination, Muscle weakness, Nausea and

Yawning. *Mental effects*: Distorted sense of time, place, and reality, Euphoria, Hallucinations (visual or auditory), Having introspective (spiritual) experiences, Panic reactions, Paranoia, Psychosis and Nervousness.

CONCLUSION

Man (Homo sapiens) since his emergence on the sylvan Blue Planet initiated his search for health and beauty care in addition to food and shelter. People eventually also became aware about his mind and acted at 'mind care'. He utilised leaves, flowers, fruits, and other plant parts for altering his mind to remain unconcerned from his heavy social problems, stress and with incurable diseases. They also endeavoured to use plants for his entertainment. In other words, over the millennia, people discovered, used, and shared ever-increasing knowledge of psychoactive plants and their effects on the physical body, mind, and spirit and they used native plants in religious ceremonies and to heal illness. But in this quest and trial some of them have misused these plants.

Generally, people start taking psychoactive plant drugs because of curiosity, encouragement by friend's or/and a desire to find relief from boredom and worries, pain, anxiety, or depression. But their addiction is harmful not only to the health of the individuals, but also to their families and to the society, which belong. The greatest danger of these drugs is not to the physical health of addicts but to their mental state also. Addiction results in unforeseeable or irresistible behaviour that can cause enormous suffering to an addict's family and society which he belongs. Drugs of abuse change thoughts and behaviour of the abuser and he loses health, wealth and respect in the society. In general, people take these mind-altering drugs for a few reasons to feel good, to feel better and to do better but in the end abuse of these is the end of all kinds of goodness therefore one should be aware of mind-altering plants. Examination of plant materials or remains collected at a crime scene and using them to solve crimes or other legal & medico legal problems comes under Forensic Botany. Forensic botany is playing a valuable role in criminal investigations.

REFERENCES

[1] Chopra, R.N., Badhwar, R.L. and Ghos, S. (1965). Poisonous Plants of India Volume 1, Indian Council of Agriculture Research: New Delhi.

[2] Datura: A Deadly High, (mhs) Mental and Health services, January, 2020https://www.mhs-dbt.com/blog/datura-a-deadly-high.

[3] Daniel, J. and Haberman, M. (2017). Clinical potential of psilocybin as a treatment for mental health conditions. *Mental Health Clinician*, *7*(1), 24–28.

[4] de Mattos-Shipley, K.M.J., Ford, K.L., Alberti, F., Banks, A.M., Bailey, A.M. and Foster, G.D. (2016). The good, the bad and the tasty: the many roles of mushrooms. *Studies in Mycology, 85*, 125–157.

[5] De Sa, I.M. and Elisabetsky, E. (2012). Medical knowledge exchanges between Brazil and Portugal: An ethnopharmacological perspective. *Journal of Ethnopharmacology, 142*(3), 762–768.

[6] Goutam, M.P. and Goutam, S. (2006). Analysis of Poisonous Plants. Selective & Scientific Books, VIII: New Delhi.

[7] Goutam, M.P. and Goutam, S. (2006). Analysis of Poisonous Plants, Selective & Scientific Books, 162: New Delhi.

[8] Mahmoud, A.E., Waseem, G. (2014). Constituents of Cannabis Sativa in Hand book of Cannabis edited by Roger Pertwee, Print Publication.

[9] Melissa Petruzzello Mind-Altering Plants https://www.britannica.com/list/9-mind-altering-plants12.11.2020.

[10] Parikh, C.K. (2011). Text book of Medical Jurisprudence Forensic Medicine and Toxicology, 10:45, CBS Publishers and Distributors Pvt. Ltd: New Delhi.

[11] Restrepo, D.A., Saenz, E., Jara-Muñoz, O.A., Calixto-Botía, I.F., Rodríguez-Suárez, S., Zuleta, P. and D'Auria, J.C. (2019). Erythroxylum in Focus: An Interdisciplinary Review of an Overlooked Genus. *Molecules, 24*(20), 3788.

Sustainable Adaptation of Mishing Traditional House: A Case of North Lakhimpur, Assam

Rupa Jawal

GITAM School of Architecture, GITAM (Deemed to be University), Gandhi Nagar, Rushikonda, Visakhapatnam, Andhra Pradesh

E-mail: rjawal@gitam.edu

ABSTRACT: The Mishing tribes of North Lakhimpur in Assam are constantly prone to floods as they occupy the alluvial strip along the banks of Brahmaputra and its tributaries. Traditional Mishing house is built on stilts to withstand the threats of flood. As bamboo is abundantly available in the entire North Eastern region of India, therefore it is used as a local construction material. Due to flooding and excessive exposure to water, these supporting structures of bamboo tend to decay fast. In such eventuality, the lifespan of these traditional houses is reduced to two years. For the rural poor, owning a house eliminates the threat of being shelter less, thus securing their identity and dignity. These traditional Mishing houses, made of natural materials are on a decline due to its shortened life span, acute shortage of labor, and other resources at hand. More number of people are preferring to live in permanent (pucca) houses. The objective of this paper is to focus on sustainable alternatives for a low cost durable permanent (pucca) house, using bamboo. The methodology for the paper is to study the geographical and climatic conditions of North Lakhimpur, Assam and the impact of flash floods in this area. The study of the culture context and lifestyle of the Mishing community, which would help in integrating the requirements of the community in developing a prototype model house. This prototype model house is a perfect blend of the indigenous architecture and technology, which is resistant to weather conditions, long-lasting, adapted to the cultural context, cost-effective, with low embodied energy and reduced carbon footprint.

Keywords: Bamboo, Carbon Footprint, Embodied Energy, Energy Conservation Building Codes (ECBC), Sustainable.

INTRODUCTION

The Mishing tribes also called Miri are an ethnic group inhabiting the districts of Dhemaji, North Lakhimpur, Sonitpur, Tinsukia, Dibrugarh, Sibsagar, Jorhat and Golaghat of Assam. These Mishing tribe settlements are usually found along the banks of the river Brahmaputra. Although the Mishing people maintain many of their traditional socio-cultural traits, yet modernism has been gradually permeating into their culture. "They have been gradually assimilating themselves with other indigenous people of the Plains of Assam and their culture. But they still maintain their own distinctive socio-cultural system and tribal traditional belief and customs" (Kakoti, 2017). Rivers in this region are in their active stage. These rivers bring enormous amount of silt through erosion which raises the level of the riverbed, thereby causing floods. In Assam, the settlements along the banks of Brahmaputra river are extremely vulnerable due to heavy rainfalls and flash floods for three to four months during monsoon.

Bamboo is a traditionally used construction material and is available in abundance in the entire North-Eastern region of India. It is a temporary material with limited durability, often referred as "poor man's material". Mishing traditional houses are designed to be elevated from ground, called "Chang-Ghar"—which means house on stilts. The reason for building their houses on stilts is to protect their homes from getting inundated during floods and the stilt also doubles up for an area to keep their livestock. Stilt houses also helps in good air flow and ventilation. The predominant occupation of Mishing tribes is farming. Stilts of a Mishing traditional house are also made of bamboo. It is observed that these bamboo supports decay very fast due to over exposure of water in monsoon and floods. This in turn, reduces the lifespan of these houses to two years. For the rural poor, affording a house is not easy. Cost effective relevant solutions, which are sustainable and adapted to the local context, can support communities to thrive. Past and ongoing experience has proven that identifying, understanding, recognizing and, where needed, improving, and strengthening local practices related to habitat and resilience is an extremely valuable approach for preparing efficient and relevant prevention and re-construction strategies (Moles *et al.*, 2017). The main objective of this paper is to focus on sustainable alternatives for a low cost durable permanent (pucca) house using bamboo by integrating local indigenous architecture and technology to develop prototype model house, which is resistant to weather conditions, and adapted to the cultural context.

STUDY AREA

The study area lies between latitude 27.2253°N, 94.1053°E in the state of Assam, India. North Lakhimpur fall under Lakhimpur district, Assam which is one of the worst flood-affected areas in the state (Figure 1). This area falls under "Warm and Humid climate" as per the climatic zones classification of Energy conservation Building codes (ECBC), India. The Mishing settlements of North Lakhimpur are situated on the banks of Ranganadi, which is a tributary of Brahmaputra river. This river is dynamic and periodically alter the geomorphology of the floodplain, along with flooding. Floods are the major hazard of the region. In some years, the floodwaters cover all the villages routes and reaches the interior of the houses, where the entire population was evacuated and hosted in temporary shelters (Partha *et al.*, 2009).

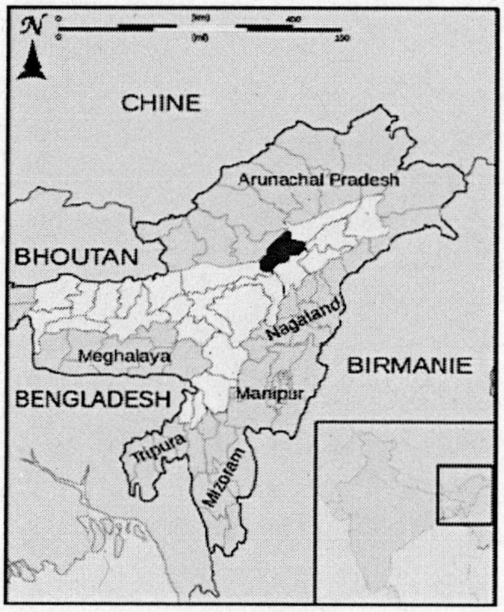

Fig. 1: Location Map of North Lakhimpur

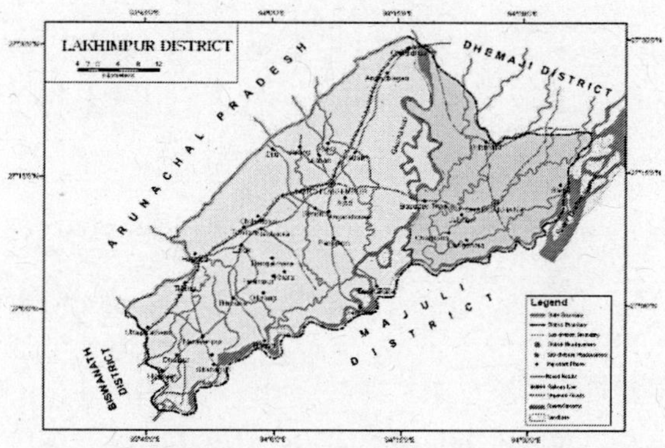

Fig. 2: Ranganadi down Stream of North Lakhimpur

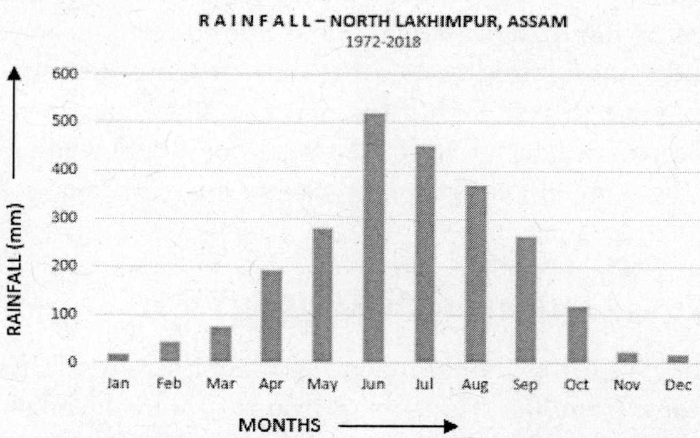

Fig. 3: Average Rainfall Data of North Lakhimpur in Last 45 years

North Lakhimpur receives average annual rainfall over 2500 millimeters (the higher value of the scale). Climate Consultant—energy design tool is used to draw the climatic information for analysis. Climatic data sourced through the software is for Dibrugarh (latitude 27.4728° N, 94.9120° E), which is very close to our study area.

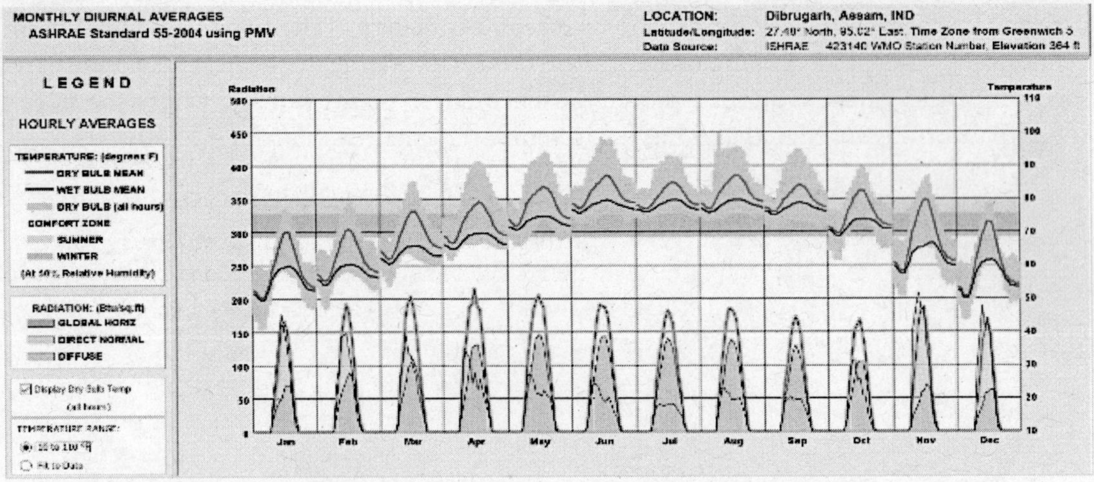

Fig. 4: Monthly Diurnal Average Temperature

The diurnal temperature variations are above 10 degree Celsius for six months in a year while for the month of May to October it ranges between 7 degree Celsius to 9 degree Celsius, this is the time of the year when it really turns sultry and humid. Mean average temperature for the entire year ranges from 17 degree Celsius to 29 degree Celsius. Relative humidity during the rainy month's ranges from 55% to 95% (April-October).

During the rainy months, thermal discomfort is high due to higher relative humidity levels. Nights are pleasant. Due to the hygrothermal properties of bamboo, it is found to be a good construction material in warm and humid climatic conditions. The state of Assam falls under the seismic zone-V of India, making the entire State prone to earthquake of moderate to very high intensity. The State has experienced two major earthquakes in the year 1897 and 1950. Bamboo houses are a suitable alternative for this region being light weight structure to counter any earthquake disaster (Cremin, 2012).

CULTURE OF THE MISHING COMMUNITY

The Mishing tribe or Miri are an ethnic group inhabiting the district of Lakhimpur, Assam. They belong from the Mongoloid group. Originally inhabitants of hills of Arunachal Pradesh, later migrated to plains of Assam. They have their own language, cultures, social customs and traditions, religious faith, and practices (Chungkrang *et al.*, 2016). Mishing tribes were previously dwelling on the hills of Arunachal Pradesh, later migrated to the planes of Assam. The Mishing tribes are the second largest tribe in Assam with a population of over 7 lakhs (2011 census). Farming is their basic occupation. They cultivate paddy on the alluvial banks or islands of Brahmaputra river. Their settlements are along the floodplains of the river. Every year, for almost four to five months, the settlement is prone to rains floods and major destruction to their houses and property (Saikia, 2013).

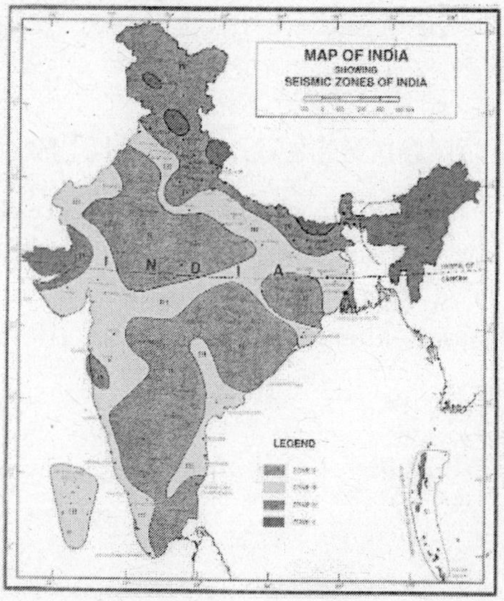

Fig. 6: Map Showing Seismiczones of India

FLOODS: A CONSTANT THREAT

All the rivers in Assam are liable to floods, mainly because they receive heavy rainfall within a short spell of time. The Mishing tribe, with over centuries of co-existence with floods have developed innovative adaptive methods to deal with floods.

Fig. 7: The Mishings Live in Elevated Houses Called Kare Okum (Chang Ghar in Assamese) Built On Bamboo Stilts or Wooden Poles

https://www.eastmojo.com/opinion/2020/06/08/living-with-the-perennial-floods-how-assams-mising-tribe-does-it

An understanding of how 'nature' is placed in the tribe's 'belief system' is important. Floods are accepted in their belief system and they do not fight back with the fury of nature, instead, the community focus on the preparedness, which gets manifested in the living style of the Mishing community starting from their housing design to paddy cultivation to how the village is organised. Their houses are an outcome of adapting to floods.

INTEGRATE LOCAL INDIGENOUS ARCHITECTURE

India is the second largest bamboo-growing nation after China. Bamboo is an indispensable resource of the Northeast culture and its rural population livelihood. The local bamboo ecosystem has a huge potential to play in the sustainable development of the rural communities of Assam and rest of North East India (Loushambam, 2017).

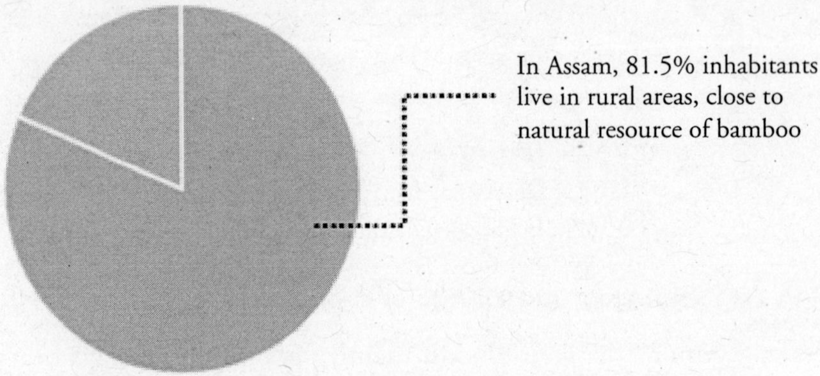

Fig. 8: Rural Communities Inhabiting Close to Natural Resources
(*Source:* As per 2011 census)

Bamboo is considered as poor man's timber. Untreated bamboo is a temporary material and requires periodic replacement and repairs. Due to shortage of labor, and other resources at hand more and more people in the region are making a transition from their traditional bamboo houses to a more durable brick and mortar pucca house. There is a lack of awareness, among the local communities about enhanced durability and longevity of bamboo, once it is treated. State government is arranging much awareness programmes for local communities on treated bamboo and promoting it as a sustainable construction material.

MODEL HOUSE

Mishing communities have been living in harmony in their bamboo houses, referred as "Chang-Ghar" since decades which is well adapted to their cultural context. A traditional Mishing house is stilted. It is built usually with wooden posts, beams, truss and supporting forks, but bamboo is used extensively for flooring and roofing. The granary is built a little close to the house and a cowshed too would not be far away. Mising villages are generally large, consisting of around fifty-to-sixty households on an average. Earlier all villages collectively contributed to community buildings using self-help techniques of construction. Over time, there has been a decline in the community's involvement in self-help construction. This has led to more and more people shifting to pucca house construction over bamboo traditional houses. But rural poor do not have the funds to build RCC houses. The prototype model house is an attempt to enhance the longevity of a traditional Mishing house by addressing the problem area. A Mishing traditional house has two very integral parts of their daily routine- life around the fireplace and co-existing with rains and floods.

Recommended Approach 1

Mising traditional houses are a one room house, with no partitions, and with the kitchen stove (a layered fire stove) at the center of the room. Around the stove they perform all their daily routines - cook, eat, socialize, and sleep.

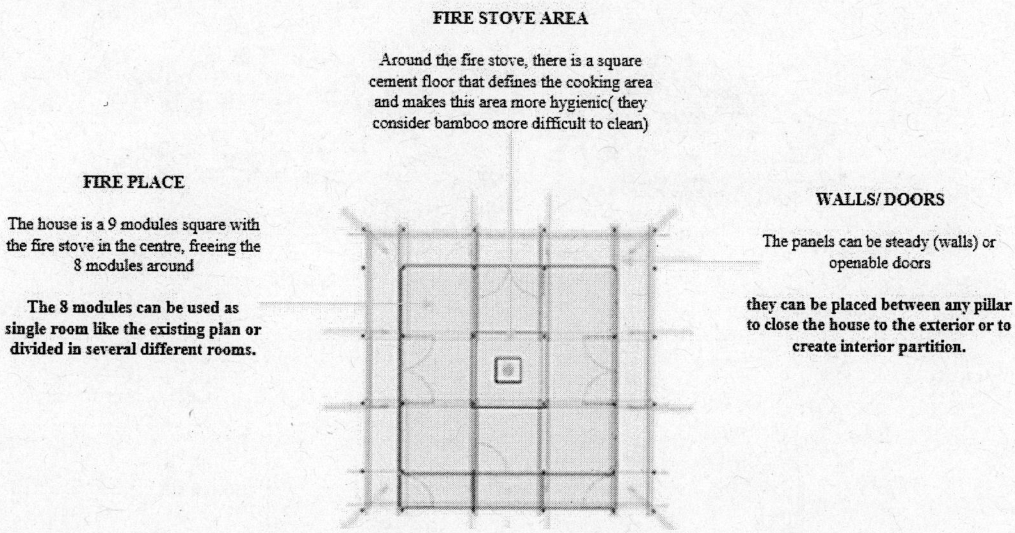

Fig. 9: Plan of a Typical One-Room Mishing Traditional House

Recommended Approach 2

Replacing the bamboo stilts of their traditional house with more durable brick columns. This eliminates the threat of repeated repairs due to bamboo supports decaying with exposure to water.

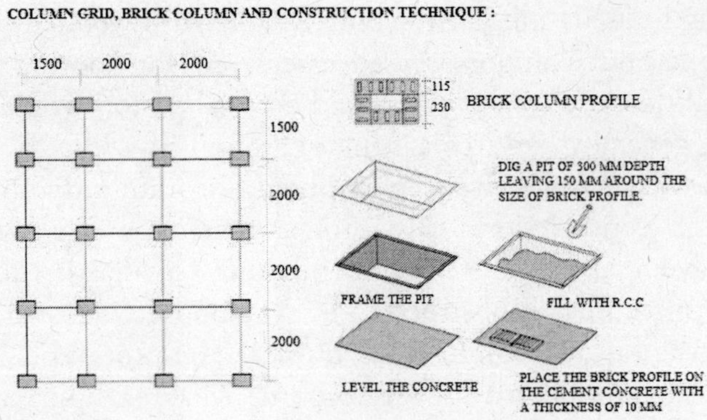

Fig. 10: Proposed RCC and Brick Support Replacing Bamboo Stilts

Recommended Approach 3

Creating more room within the same space by increasing the height of the structure and inducing lofts to accommodate private areas. In the new evolved design, space optimization is achieved by creating a loft in the house where people can sleep or just store things by increasing the height of the structure.

Fig. 11: Evolution of Durable Mishing House

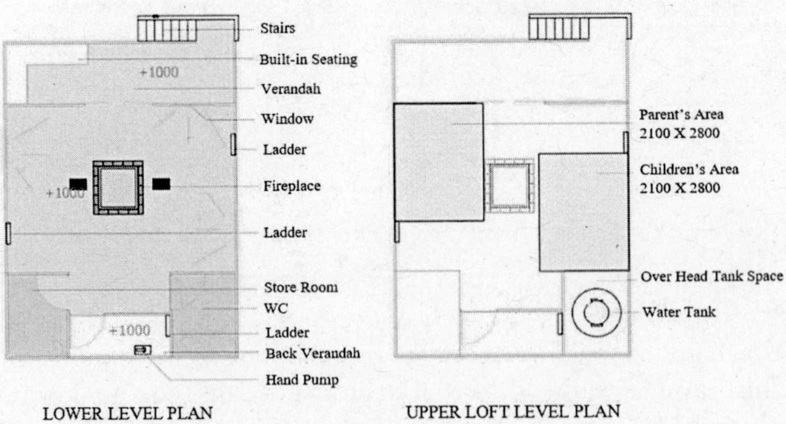

Fig. 12: Floor Plan-Lower Level and Private Upper Loft Level

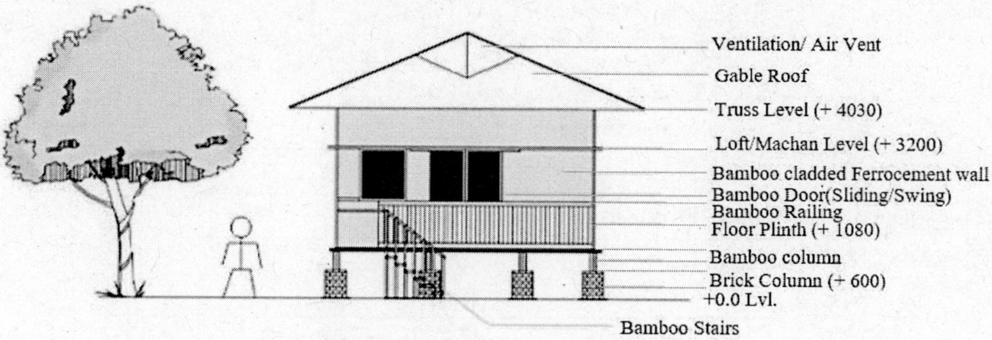

Fig. 13: Elevation of Model House

PROMOTING SUSTAINABILITY

Insensitivity towards the choice of material selection and drifting away from traditional local materials in buildings has led to increased energy consumption, higher manufacturing costs, higher transportation costs and increased waste production (IPE Global Private Limited, Nov 2015). Treated bamboo has various applications in a building as it contributes towards the design of almost all the parts starting from the foundation to roof. CPWD has developed-Sustainability Index, for different building materials. It clearly indicates the environmental impacts of different conventional construction material with respect to natural material. It may not be possible to change the entire scenario of building industry overnight, but small steps can lead to a significant change in the choice of building materials. Promoting bamboo, can contribute to reduced carbon footprint. Bamboo being a rapidly renewable material, has no environmental impact on our natural resource (Nayak, 2006).

Table 1: Proposed Parameters and Their Weightage for CPWD Sustainability Index of Materials

S. No	*Proposed Parameter*	*Weightage*
1.	Recycled Content	10
2.	Embodied Energy	10
3.	Rapidly Renewable	5
4.	Locally available Material	10
5.	Functional Life period	10
6.	Capital Cost	10
7.	Maintenance Cost	10

S. No	*Proposed Parameter*	*Weightage*
8.	Construction waste Management	5
9.	Fly ash Content	10
10.	Reduced Weight	5
11.	Reduced time of Construction	5
12.	Toxicity/Indoor air Quality	10
	Total Points	**100**

(CPWD Sustainability Index and Guidelines for Materials)

Table 2: Embodied Energy and Embodied Carbon Values of Few Conventional Building Materials ("Inventory of Carbon and Energy" prepared by the University of Bath)

Material	*Energy [MJ/Kg]*	*Carbon [CO_2/Kg]*	*Density [Kg/m^3]*
Aluminium	155	8.24	2700
Stainless Steel	56.7	6.15	7850
Copper	42	2.6	8600
Iron	25	1.91	7870
Steel	20.1	1.37	7800
Plywood	15	1.07	540–700
Timber	10	0.72	480–720
Fiber Board	11	0.72	680–760
Bricks	3	0.24	1700
Cement Mortar (1:3)	11.33	0.208	–
Concrete (1:1.5:3)	11.11	0.159	2400
Concrete Block	10.67	0.073	1450
Aggregate	0.083	0.0048	2240
Bamboo	1.5	0.138	500–1100

CONCLUSION

The Mishing community of North Lakhimpur, Assam is extremely affected every year due to floods during monsoon. The rural poor cannot afford to re-construct their bamboo house every two years, which deteriorates due to exposure to floods. The older concept of community building through self-help initiatives have slowly dwindled. Due to the shortage of labour and resource, long-lasting cost-effective solutions will prove rewarding for social and economic sustainability. By adopting the recommended approaches discussed in this paper, the longevity of Traditional Mishing houses can be increased up to 30 years. Bamboo being a locally available material in Assam, can contribute to local economy through local employment and procurement. Bamboo is also a rapidly renewable material with no carbon footprint, use of bamboo also safeguards the climate and reduce the degrading impact of greenhouse gases (GHG) associated with high embodied energy construction materials.

REFERENCES

[1] Chungkrang, L., Phukan, A. and Gogoi, N. (2016). A Study on Mishing Tribes and Their Traditional Costumes of Assam. *International Journal of Textile and Fashion Technology (IJTFT) ISSN (P)*, 2250–2378.

[2] Coelho, S. (2013). *Assam and the Brahmaputra: Recurrent.* IDDRI, 63–73.

[3] Crémin, É. (2012). Wild life conservation and tribal livelihood in the Brahmaputra flood plain-the Case of the Mising tribe in the fringe villages of the Kaziranga National Park (Assam, North-East India). *Nature.*

[4] IPE Global Private Limited, D.A. (Nov. 2015). *Assam Urban Affordable Housing and Habitat Policy. Ministry of Housing and Urban Poverty Alleviation* (MoHUPA).

[5] Kakoti, N. (2017). *The Mising Tribes of North East India—A Glimpse.* Dibrugarh: International.

[6] Loushambam, R.S. (2017). *Bamboo in North East India. Indian Journal of Hill Farming,* pp. 181–185.

[7] Moles, O., Crété, E., Caimi, A., Gutierrez, E.S., Ashmore, J., Nko'o, C.B. and Le Gall, O. (2017). Local building cultures for sustainable and resilient habitats-Examples of local good practices and technical solutions.

[8] Nayak, J. and Prajapati, J.A. (2006). Handbook on energy conscious buildings. *Prepared under the interactive R&D project, 3*(4), 03.

[9] Partha, D., Dadul, C. and Nirupam, H. (2009). Adjusting to floods on the Brahmaputra Plains, Assam, India. *Adjusting to floods on the Brahmaputra Plains, Assam, India.*

[10] Saikia, D.H. (2013). *Missing tribes in Assam.*

The Study of Effect of UV Radiation on Colorant of Black Toner in Printouts of Laser Printer

Anurag Sahu[1] and Priya Tagre[2]
Government Institute of Forensic Science, Aurangabad, Maharashtra
E-mail: [1]anuraggifs@gmail.com; [2]priyatagre@gmail.com

ABSTRACT: Nowadays documents have become important in every aspect of our daily life for authenticity and reliability. In this digitalized era, now e-documents, printouts etc. are widely used in place of handwritten documents. With the advancement of technology in the printing mechanism laser printer is widely used because of its high efficiency, quality and quick response. The aim of this study is to know the degradation of colorant of black toner of laser printer on exposure of UV radiation. Black color printouts from laser printer of HP laser jet having P1007 model were selected and subjected to UV-B radiation at 312 nm wavelength for different time intervals such as 10 mints, 30 mints and 60 mints in video spectral comparator-6000/HS. Black toner was extracted from printouts and loaded in thin layer chromatography. After thorough analysis of these chromatograms, it has been found that colorant of black toner degrade on 60 minutes exposure of UV-B radiation at wavelength of 312 nm.

Keywords: Dye, Long UV, Pigment, Toner, Thin Layer Chromatography.

INTRODUCTION

In our daily life every work depends upon documents because it provides authenticity, reliability, integrity, longevity. Before 40–45 years most of the official, legal, financial documents were written with ball point pen ink. But with the passing of time new inventions have occurred in writing ink like gel pen ink, fiber tip pen ink, marker ink and so on. With the beginning of digital printing era, handwritten documents have been replaced into printouts. Many inventions in digital printers have taken place like ink jet printer, laser printer, 3D printer. Nowadays, laser printers are widely used in office, workplace etc. because of its high-quality text and graphics, high output speed and cost effectiveness. Laser printer works on xerography technology that includes five steps; charging of selenium drum, formation of latent image, development of latent image, transfer of image into plain paper and fusing of toner. Same principle is also applicable for photocopier and fax machine.

The ink used in laser printer is in the form of powder known as toner. Toner is dry ink that creates the image on paper during the printing process used in most copiers and some large printers (Shara *et al.*, 2003). Toner is the fine polymer-based color powder which contains toner binder, a colorant, a charge control agent, a magnetic oxide and other additives. Now toner has become an important part of document examination for identification of document, determination of age of document and comparison of documents. The wavelength and power of the light with which the dyes are irradiated also affect the rate of fading (Brunelle, 2003).

Saini *et al.*, (2016) studied about colored toner components by TLC and HPTLC for forensic identification of document from ink components. Saini *et al.* (2011) added instrumentation technique and used TLC, UV and FTIR for differentiation of color components of toner. But in both the studies researchers did not include black toner. Saini and Sarora (2008) selected samples of black toner from different toner companies and found out suitable solvent system for separation of colorant for TLC but did not touch the area of UV radiation effect on black toner's colorant. The effect of UV radiation on colorant of black toner has remained unexplored. The current study is aimed to understand the effect of UV radiation on colorant of black toner under controlled conditions.

MATERIALS AND METHODS

Collection of Samples

An unprocessed toner (raw) marked S-1 was collected directly from ink cartridge whereas three printouts were collected from HP laser jet printer having model 1007 and marked these printouts according to Table 1. These printouts contained processed toner in the form of texts on A-4 size white color papers having 70 GSM weight. The paper without toner was also collected as a control sample marked S-5.

Table 1: Description and Marking of Toner Samples

Sr. No.	*Marking of Samples*	*Type Of Toner*
1	S-1	Raw (dry powder)
2	S-2	Processed (in printouts)
3	S-3	Processed (in printouts)
4	S-4	Processed (in printouts)
5	S-5	Paper without toner

Sample Preparation

All three printouts having processed toner were placed inside the video spectral comparator-6000/HS under UV radiation at 312 nm wavelength for 10 minutes, 30 minutes and 60 minutes for marked sample S-2, S-3 & S-4 respectively. All the UV exposed processed toner of printouts extracted separately and marked serially. For extraction of processed toner, an aluminum foil was placed over the selected text and the heat was given from back side of the paper with the support of iron (Bajaj iron) for 2–3 minutes (Saini *et al.*, 2003). Only 2 texts were selected to remove sufficient amount of toner from each sample. All extracts were collected into the test tube and mixed generously with 2 ml of chloroform. 0.1 gm of raw toner from ink cartridge was directly taken into test tube and mixed with 2 ml of chloroform. Extract from Sample S-5 was mixed with chloroform. The extracts of all toner samples i.e., S-1, 2, 3, 4 & 5 have been examined by thin layer chromatography (TLC).

Mobile and Stationary Phase

Only one mobile phase i.e., ethyl acetate: ethanol: chlorobenzene (2:2:10) was poured inside the glass chamber for saturation at normal room temperature and the mouth was covered. Two TLC plates (7 × 20 cm and 2.57 × 7.5 cm) were prepared by using silica gel G, dried in the plate at 120°C for 1 hour inside the oven, then cooled at room temperature and was used as a stationary phase. The solvents used in mobile phase i.e., ethanol was purchased from Changshu Hongsheng Fine Chemical Co., Ltd, China (batch no. 20181120), ethyl acetate & chlorobenzene from Thermo Fisher Scientific India Pvt. Ltd., Mumbai, India having product no. 23455 & 22445 respectively. Solvent used in extraction process i.e., chloroform was purchased from Thermo Fisher Scientific India Pvt. Ltd., Mumbai, India having product no. Q12305 while silica gel G for stationary phase purchased from Loba Chemie Pvt. Ltd. Coloba, Mumbai having batch no. L255691802.

All four extracted toner samples were spotted in TLC plate (77 × 20 cm) and one spot for control sample spotted in TLC plate (2.57 × 7.5 cm) with the support of capillary tube. Individual capillary tube was selected for each sample loading. All samples loaded TLC plates were dried at room temperature for 20–30 minutes. Thereafter, dried spotted TLC plates were placed inside the saturated glass chamber carefully and left it to move solvents up to the mark on the plates.

Visualization Process

All the developed chromatograms were visualized under visible and ultra-violet radiation (short and long wavelength), photographs were taken with the support of video spectral comparator 6000/HS and these photographs are demonstrated in Figure 1(a-c). All the visible and fluorescent spots under above said radiations were observed and their retardation factor (*Rf*) was calculated as following:

$$Rf = \frac{\text{Distance travelled by solute}}{\text{Distance travelled by solvent}}$$

Calculated *Rf* value is shown in Table 2.

Table 2: TLC Result of Samples with Number of Spots and Their Rf Value

S. No.	*Samples*	*Under Visible Light*			*Under Short UV Radiation*			*Under Long UV Radiation*		
		No. of Spot	*Color of Spot*	*Rf Value*	*No. of spot*	*Color of spot*	*Rf Value*	*No. of Spot*	*Color of Spot*	*Rf Value*
1.	S-1	1	Light Pink	0.44	–	–	–	2	Sky blue & orange	0.71
2.	S-2	1	Light Pink	0.42	–	–	–	2	Sky blue & orange	0.69
3.	S-3	1	Light Pink	0.38	–	–	–	2	Sky blue & orange	0.68
4.	S-4	1	Light Pink	0.31	1	Blue	0.78	3	Sky blue (2) & orange (1)	0.59
5.	S-5	–	–	–	–	–	–	–	–	–

S. No.	*Type of Radiation*		
	Under Visible Light	*Under Short UV Light*	*Under Long UV Light*
1	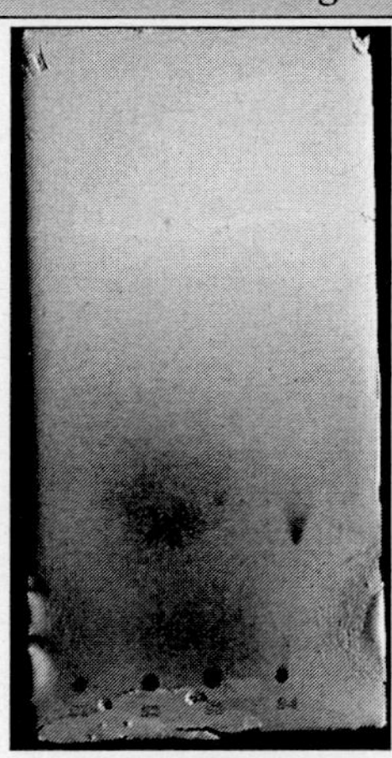	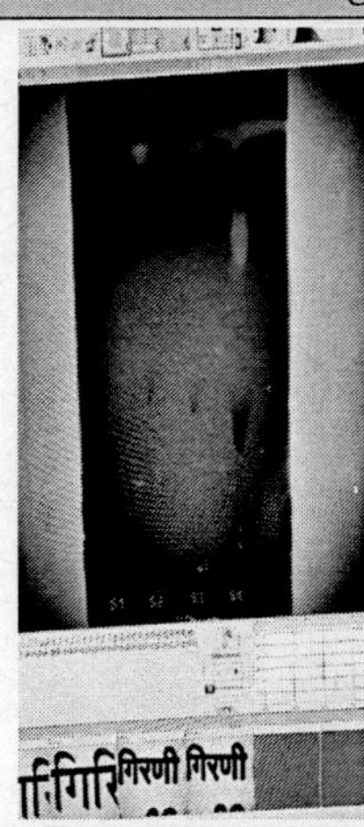	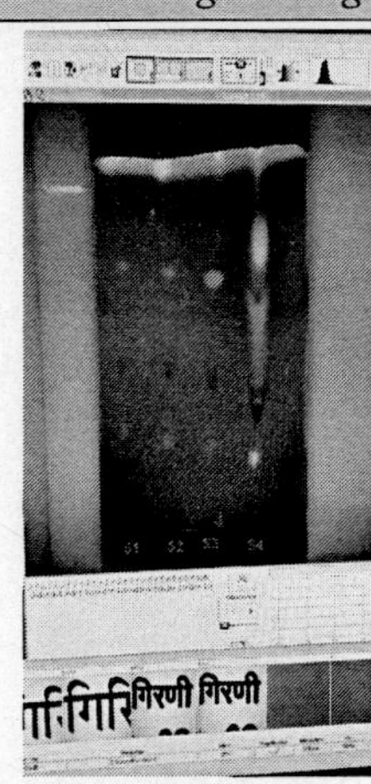

Fig. 1(a-c): Chromatograms under Different Light Sources; a Under Visible Light, b Under Short UV and c Under Long UV

RESULTS

All the samples in the developed TLC plates were observed in visible light and UV light (short and long wavelength). The result has been interpreted on the basis of color, number & *Rf* value of developed spots. Three spots were observed in long UV radiation in sample S-4 whereas only two spots have been observed in sample S-1, S-2 and S-3. In sample S-5 no spot appeared (Figure 2 and Table 2).

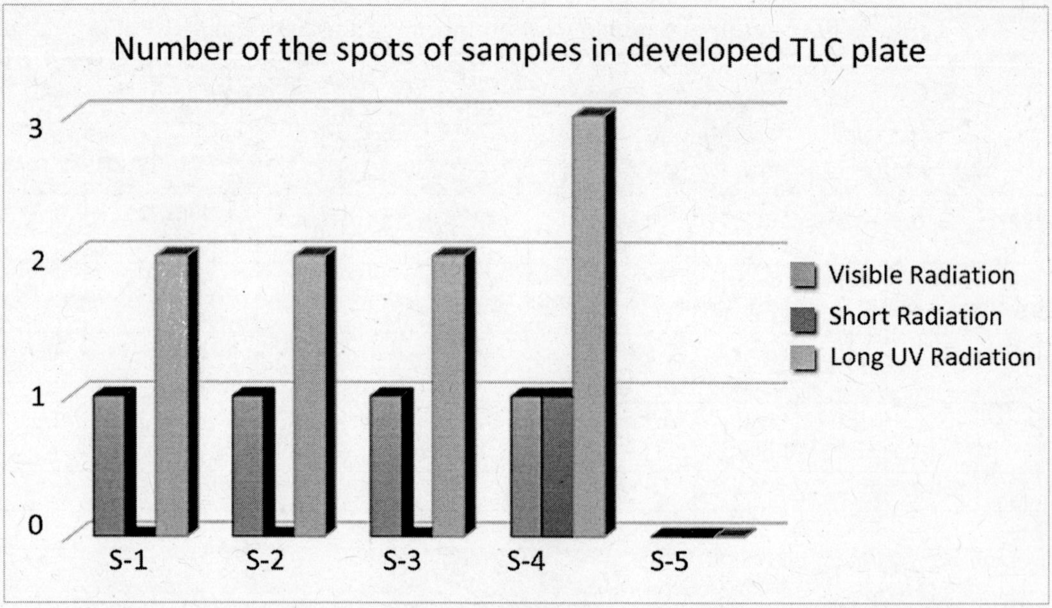

Fig. 2: Number of Developed Spots in Different Toner Samples under Different Radiations

CONCLUSION

After the TLC analysis, in developed TLC plate toner sample S-4 subjected to UV radiation exposure at 312 nm wavelength for 60 minutes degraded and considerable results obtained with distinct separation.

ACKNOWLEDGEMENT

The authors are thankful to Dr. M.P. Goutam, Professor, Shri Vaishnav Vidyapeeth Vishwavidyalaya, Indore, M.P. for his encouragement and motivation. And the authors are also grateful to Director and Head of Department of Forensic Science, Govt. Institute of Forensic Science, Aurangabad, Maharashtra for supporting and guiding to accomplish this project.

REFERENCES

[1] Brunelle, R.L. and Crawford, K.R. (2003). *Advances in the forensic analysis and dating of writing ink*. Charles C Thomas Publisher.

[2] Saini, K. and Sarora, J.S. (2008). Thin layer chromatograpgy for refilled photocopy toner. *Journal of forensic identification, 58*(3), 315.

[3] Saini, K. and Sarora, J.S. (2011). Differentiation of color photocopy toners using TLC, UV and FTIR techniques. *Journal of Forensic Identification, 61*(6), 561–580.

[4] Saini, K., Rathore, R. and Saini A. (2016). Forensic analysis of toners by thin layer chromatography and high performance thin layer chromatography. *Research Journal of Forensic Sciences, 4*(3), 6–20.

[5] Shara, S.I., Aboul El-MAGD, A.A., Moustafa, Y.M., Bakr, A.A. and Aziz, I.A. (2013). Removal of laser printer toner from the paper surface using some chemical methods. *Al-Azhar Bulletin of Science, 24*(2-A), 81–96.

Wireless Sensor Network: Applications and Future Research Directions

Pooja Gulganwa[1] and Saurabh Jain[2]
Shri Vaishnav Institute of Computer Applications,
Shri Vaishnav Vidyapeeth Vishwavidyalaya, Indore, Madhya Pradesh
E-mail: [1]poojagulganwa410@gmail.com; [2]iamsaurabh_4@yahoo.co.in

ABSTRACT: Several applications recently have accepted wireless Sensor Network (WSN) in real-world for varying prospects. It is employed to collect, share and process information. The processed information is promoting sustainable and improved lives using various applications in agriculture, army, health care and traffic management. In all the applications, the sensors are placed with different motive and different kinds of data collection. But during deployment, different types of additional requirements are needed to be fulfilled. Therefore, the category-based deployment and enhancement issues and efforts are highlighted. Then, the application requirements are classified as application-centric and the technological WSN issues in different areas of implementation. At the end of this paper, the future research directions are reported to make it more acceptable for small as well as large scale applications.

Keywords: Application Areas, Information Technology, Internet, Real World, Wireless Sensor Network.

INTRODUCTION

Wireless Sensor Network (WSN) is one of the rapidly evolving technologies. They have grown in a variety of applications from the day of its emerging (Kandris *et al.*, 2020). In many of the real-life applications, an important role is played by WSN, i.e., healthcare monitoring, military surveillance, vehicular tracking, and, so on. It is essential in these applications to secure and real-time data accessing from sensor nodes (Adavoudi-Jolfaei *et al.*, 2019). WSN is made up of many nodes that can measure physical phenomena and send the measurements to the sink using a multiple-hop protocol with the short-range transmission (Barnawi *et al.*, 2019). In smart cities and ecological fields where sensor nodes can be deployed in a thousand numbers, using WSN is an imperative necessity (Sambo *et al.*, 2019).

Significant number of sensor nodes are deployed in many different real-time applications, due to which a number of network issues, i.e., network overload, security, authentication, congestion, power consumption, and other issues are rising.

Additionally, in some of the applications, the application-centric issues and enhancements are required. Therefore, the present paper attempts to provide a presentation of both traditional and most recent applications of WSN. Further, the different categories of applications are identified. Additionally, during the design and deployment of these applications, the key issues and application-centric challenges are explored. In the last obtained application, dependent issues are transformed into the WSN design and implementation requirements are identified according to different application needs. This section offers a key overview of the proposed work involved in this paper. The next sections are providing the applications of WSN in different areas of the real world.

APPLICATION IN AGRICULTURE

Agriculture has an essential role in the survival of the people. The primary economic industry of the country is agriculture. The technological growth in wireless communication and depletion in the size of the sensor is an evolution for several fields. Wireless sensor network also helps in agriculture like prevention from insects, diseases and controlling in irrigation. By using WSNs, data is collected in the farm field and sent the acquired data to the server. Rajasekaran and Anandamurugan (2019) studied the requirements and challenges of wireless sensor networks in agriculture during the implementation of smart farming. Smart farming plays an important role to magnify production in the agriculture. Here some essential issues are discussed to deal with WSN design during agricultural applications.

Large and complex network pose additional difficulty in maintaining and adjusting manually: For automatic delivery and recovery of wireless sensor network nodes a UAV-based scheme proposed which is a combination of special UAV and GNSS-RTK system (Ouyang *et al.*, 2019). Now in agriculture, lot of attention is paid to different natural parameters like temperature, humidity, soil moisture, soil's PH value, and many more which improves the quality and quantity of crops. Using this method natural resource consumption is minimized. Moreover, it can be operational in the unlicensed spectrum. This is a reason for increasing the sensor amount in agriculture.

Accommodation of more sensors extend the lifetime of the WSNs: (NOMA) Relay-aided non-orthogonal multiple access has been introduced (Hu *et al.*, 2019) to transmit several symbols on the same RE by breaking them in the power domain and differentiate them according to power levels. The simulation result shows that WSNs with relay-aided NOMA outperforms in uplink transmission. Lifetime of WSN depends on duty cycle, type of application, and battery state of charge (SoC) level. There are many hurdles in solar energy related to the environment like thermal issues, harvesting, solar energy prediction, solar panel conversion efficiency. To overcome such types of issues, the present study offers a solution of utilizing solar energy for the battery charging of WSN nodes. Using solar energy, WSN lifetime can be maximized (Sharma *et al.*, 2019).

SELECTION OF APPROPRIATE SENSOR AND TECHNOLOGY

Agriculture has been improved upon through various WSN techniques (Thakur *et al.*, 2019). All-natural parameters like soil quality, irrigation schedule, temperature have been monitored to achieve precision in agriculture. They also highlight different technologies and sensors to analyze the impact of WSNs in agriculture.

MILITARY APPLICATIONS

WSNs have received attention in recent years due to its applicability in various fields. The multiplicity of nodes and the cheap cost of nodes has led to massive usage in several applications in military like disaster sensing, battle zone perception and harm occurrence. Due to the advent of smart systems for sensors' data manipulation and connectivity, WSN offers better flexibility and a key technology for military application design. The deployment of military-centric applications has faced the following key challenges:

Better Deployment of Sensors: Ahmed *et al.*, (2016) analysed various applications related to military and found that through the better deployment of sensors, damage in case of militant's attack or enemy's outbreak can be minimized.

Need of Computational Intelligence: Computational intelligence has been used to design various types of sensor networks such as WSN, fixed sensor networks, Mobile Ad hoc Networks (MANET) and cellular networks (Ball *et al.*, 2016). Computational intelligence for sensor network design was described to identify current research challenges.

Military Security Sensing Needs and Sophisticated Protocols: In most of the military applications WSN is deployed for military security sensing needs using more sophisticated protocols. The researchers modified system architecture to perform the military security sense (Jamal *et al.*, 2019).

Detecting and Monitoring the Motion of Mobile Targets: The moving target tracking is essential for detecting and monitoring in many army applications. Different target tracking approaches have been analyzed in line with the several metrics (Zaidi *et al.*, 2015).

CONCLUSION

Wireless sensor network is one of the essential needs of human as in number of real and complex nature of applications services of WSN are utilized. Additionally, it is also helpful in futuristic and sustainable application development. The fundamental and critical issues in deployment have been identified. Based on the applicability of WSN, we can subdivide the issues into two main streams first the issues which are application-centric and second the global issues for the entire WSN systems. The below given Table 1 demonstrate the applications and the relevant application-centric issues and requirements, as well as the global issues. It can be said that by enhancing the network higher degree of security, accuracy, scalability and other prospects of the WSN can be achieved. Based on these observations, the proposed work suggests the following improvements or future research directions in the WSN improvements.

Table 1

Application	*Application Centric Issues*	*WSN issues*
Agriculture	1. Large and complex network, additional difficulty in maintaining and adjusting manually 2. Accommodation of more sensors and prolong the lifetime of the WSNs 3. Selection of appropriate sensor and technology	1. Energy consumption of sensor nodes 2. Handling and maintaining network work load
Military	1. Better deployment of sensors 2. Need of computational intelligence 3. Military security sensing needs and sophisticated protocols 4. Detecting and monitoring the motion of mobile targets	1. Sensor node positioning Accurate sensing Accurate motion detection
Health care	1. Need to track and monitor patient's remotely 2. Sensor faults and false measurements 3. Economically unacceptable due to the high operational and development costs 4. Power issue in sensor nodes inside the human body 5. Information congestion in network	1. Sensor not battery life and wireless charging 2. Accurate data collection and reporting 3. High cost 4. Congestion and fault

FUTURE DIRECTIONS

The new generation technology is based on sensors because in various critical conditions, sensors can collect, share and process the information. Thus, it is required to improve the quality and capability of devices, i.e., sensors and others. In this context, here some significant contributions are collected which provides the baselines and new research directions in the WSN/IoT technology.

1. Scaling the ability of WSN devices using IC-based modifications.

2. Scaling network device capability using software modifications.
3. Development of energy-efficient (EE) routing protocols.
4. Authentication and Access Control.

REFERENCES

[1] Adavoudi-Jolfaei, A., Ashouri-Talouki, M. and Aghili, S.F. (2019). Lightweight and anonymous three-factor authentication and access control scheme for real-time applications in wireless sensor networks. *Peer-to-Peer Networking and Applications, 12*(1), 43–59.

[2] Ahmad, I., Shah, K. and Ullah, S. (2016). Military applications using wireless sensor networks: A survey. *International Journal of Engineering Science and Computing, 6*(6), 7039.

[3] Ball, M.G., Qela, B. and Wesolkowski, S. (2016). A Review of the Use of Computational Intelligence in the Design of Military Surveillance Networks. *Recent Advances in Computational Intelligence in Defense and Security*, 621, 663-693.

[4] Barnawi, A.Y., Mohsen, G.A. and Shahra, E.Q. (2019). Performance analysis of rpl protocol for data gathering applications in wireless sensor networks. *Procedia Computer Science, 151*, 185-193.

[5] Ez-Zaidi, A. and Rakrak, S. (2016). A comparative study of target tracking approaches in wireless sensor networks. *Journal of Sensors, 2016.*

[6] Hu, Z., Xu, L., Cao, L., Liu, S., Lou, Z., Wang, J., Li, X. and Wang, L. (2019). Application of Non-Orthogonal Multiple Access in Wireless Sensor Networks for Smart Agriculture. *IEEE Access*, 7, 87582–87592.

[7] Jamal, T. and Butt, S. A. (2017). Low-energy adaptive clustering hierarchy (LEACH) enhancement for military security operations. *Proc. of Journal of Basic and Applied Scientific Research, ISSN*, 2090–4304.

[8] Kandris, D., Nakas, C., Vomvas, D. and Koulouras, G. (2020). Applications of wireless sensor networks: an up-to-date survey. *Applied System Innovation, 3*(1), 14.

[9] Ouyang, F., Cheng, H., Lan, Y.,Zhang, Y., Yin, X., Hu, J., Peng, X., Wang, G. and Chen, S. (2019). Automatic delivery and recovery system of Wireless Sensor Networks (WSN) nodes based on UAV for agricultural applications. *Computers and electronics in Agriculture*, 162, 32–43.

[10] Rajasekaran, T. and Anandamurugan, S. (2019). Challenges and Applications of Wireless Sensor Networks in Smart Farming—A Survey. *Advances in Big Data and Cloud Computing*, 750, 353–361.

[11] Sambo, D.W., Yenke, B.O., Förster A. and Dayang, P. (2019). Optimized Clustering Algorithms for Large Wireless Sensor Networks: A Review. *Sensors*, 19(2).

[12] Sharma, H., Haque, A. and Jaffery, A.Z. (2019). Maximization of wireless sensor network lifetime using solar energy harvesting for smart agriculture monitoring. *Ad hoc Networks*, 94.

[13] Thakur, D., Kumar, Y., Kumar, A. and Singh, P.K. (2019). Applicability of wireless sensor networks in precision agriculture: A review. *Wireless Personal Communications, 107*(1), 471–512.

Epilogue

The purpose of this part of the book is to draw attention of the readers to key indicators given in each of the preceding chapters sequentially. The number coincides with the numbers of chapters in the book.

1. Manual or conventional methods of handwriting examination may prove to be unreliable in circumstances where they fail to identify the minute peculiarities in the handwriting like pressure identification and recognition of characters. Computational methods may prove to be useful in reproducing the results, but cannot help to resolve the legal concerns raised over the admissibility of handwriting as an evidence. In spite of this, each method has its own advantages.
2. Flood Routing is very important subject of research in water engineering and related fields. Swarm intelligence approach—Bat Algorithm has gained more interest in predicting flood routing. It has given very good optimal values and also reduced error when compared to other evolutionary algorithms which were used as a benchmark for comparing the performance of BA in predicting flood routing characteristics.
3. E-waste recycling in organized sector is at its nascent age in many developing countries especially in India. With the result, many of the e-waste recyclers are novice in the organized sector and are unacquainted with the professional expertise expected of them. Lack of awareness regarding disposal of e-waste and expectations of monetary incentives is creating collection issue before recyclers. Educating people regarding the need of proper disposal of e-waste is must. A series of parallel actions need to be taken to address the issues associated with e-waste management.
4. Blooms Taxonomy can be an optimum tool to formulate assessment parameters and help institutions in achieving their goals towards shaping intellectually mature, critical minded, skilled, ecologically sensitive and socially responsible architects for the future. Institutes can reflect critically on the weaknesses observed and formulate future educational enhancement initiatives in those specific areas to overcome realised gaps. Students will equally be able to self-assess their weaknesses in focused areas and work towards overcoming them.
5. Coopetition is portmanteau in nature as it derives its significance from both cooperation and competition simultaneously. It is a phenomenon where at the same time firms are involved in cooperative and competitive relationships. They share their complementary resources and capabilities with each other to create synergies. Although, it is a common business strategy followed by larger firms;

but it has been reported that small and medium firms (SMEs) can gain competitive advantages too, if they pursue coopetition from strategic perspectives.

6. Sustainable construction materials are those that are locally manufactured or purchased. Recycled and industrial waste includes this material. Sustainable materials have an occasional environmental effect and perform physically well. Compared to modern or conventional building materials, the assembly of such building materials requires little energy in manufacturing. The benefits of choosing sustainable building materials are that they not only function economically, but also minimize toxicity and thereby decrease the impact on the environment.
7. Retail sector in India has undergone steep changes in recent years. This has happened mainly because of increase in use of internet and smart phones. Online retailing business is growing with growth in technology. There is an impact of age, gender, and income on sales assistance, purchase involvement, retailer's sales motive, flexible transaction facility, product accessibility and entertainment values factors of off-line retailing.
8. The experience of emerging realities is a key generator of engagement and has significance of social collaboration and peer-to-peer interactions (experience of collective intelligence); the observable rise in engagement and willingness to contribute when real business situations, especially labelled as 'strategic issues' are discussed and the role of image-capturing ('snapshot experience') and creates an engaging learning experience.
9. The new definition of human intelligence by Gardner that goes beyond the realms of psychology includes musical, interpersonal, spatial-visual, and linguistic intelligence, etc. that human beings are gifted with. However, in this article, it is proposed if Communication Intelligence could be an added dimension of human intelligence. Although different facets of Communication intelligence is already a part of Gardner's multiple intelligences for example verbal intelligence; Intra and Interpersonal communication and nonverbal communication but these and many other facets of Communication can be brought together under one umbrella that could be labeled as Communication Intelligence.
10. Store atmosphere act as a pivotal contributor to the customer experience, which is arguably one of the most significant elements of the retail business today. As a result, businesses need to seek strategies that will differentiate their brand from the competitors, and one way to do it is by providing pleasant and engaging shopping ambience. For providing superior store atmospherics and integrated view of the situations should be taken into account while working on multi-pronged strategies.
11. The burning of the documents is the most common phenomenon used by the criminals in order to destroy the evidences. Video Spectral Comparator (VSC)

can be used for the decipherment of writings on partially burned documents using the effect of floodlight and white spot. It was found that these are the most prominent lights for decipherment of writings on the partially burned documents.

12. The role played by religion, tradition and culture is determining in the evolution of folk art and is the assimilating force behind the aesthetic creativeness. The themes get visual expression in a painting by fundamental values of culture and the devotional minds. They wrote verses and poems in which Radha's adventures with Krishna and their romance were described devotedly and aesthetically which gave the artist a wider imagery to illustrate and narrate. Krishna has been one of the most cherished themes of arts, who has been illustrated from ancient times as well narrated in folk and tribal arts of contemporary period.
13. Hempcrete being a vegetal concrete mixture reduces the carbon footprint and has a high absorption capacity of CO_2 as compared to any other conventional walling material but has been disregarded due to paucity in awareness about the material and its energy saving characteristics. Burnt red bricks, a conventional material, have high embodied energy & carbon footprint and can be replaced by energy efficient hempcrete blocks.
14. The novel *The Fifth Child* is presented as a dilemma story initially but closely it portrays the patriarchal forces, social relations and the institution of motherhood. Feminist critics opine that subsequent gender roles have caste women in a second position in societal structure. To blame the mother for mistakes and wrongdoings is a normal phenomenon. She is held responsible for molding the child in such a way so that he grows into a healthy citizen who functions normally within the set norms of the society. Motherhood is a part of parenthood. It is a collaborative responsibility which society narrows down to gender role.
15. Positive ageing suggests that older persons can actively manage resources. In doing so, they initiate at will and start intervention. The concept of positive ageing emphasizes fitness, lifelong activity, good health, and high self-esteem. Older people can make choices that will preserve and enhance their well-being. In particular, taking measures to maintain good physical health, seeking personal or intellectual growth experiences, and developing a reliable network of social relationships can be helpful in maintaining well-being in old age. Positive-ageing framework defies previous notion that ageing is inexorably associated with detachment, inactiveness and waning.
16. There are various parameters inside and outside the school which contribute to the quality education. The key role of the educators is to teach their students effectively so that students are able to demonstrate higher performance in their studies. It is necessary to understand the role of various parameters in the

academic achievement of students. Teachers, teaching approach and school environment are primary parameters of quality education, followed by content, method of assessment, caliber of students, infrastructure and involvement of parents.

17. The use of self-healing biomimetic materials not only help in achieving economic and environmental sustainability, but it also ensures a safe and secure built environment for the future generations to enjoy and live in. Moreover, the requirement of high humidity levels for the bacteria in these materials to carry out the processes of self-repairing shows that they can be the best possible solutions for overcoming the issues related to cracks that appear in the buildings located in the Warm and Humid climatic zones. Such materials also increase the lifespan of the buildings and reduce the maintenance and repair costs as well as the amount of the demolition wastes.
18. Humanity has a perpetual and strong relationship with medicinal plants. On the one hand, many plants in regulated doses constitute potent and effective remedies for amelioration of disease, on the other, some of them are a serious menace to life and physiological activity of man and animals. Nowadays mind altering hallucinogenic or narcotic plants have become prominent for the detrimental societal impacts. There is a need to get the complete knowledge of these plants.
19. Long-lasting cost-effective solutions can prove rewarding for social and economic sustainability. Bamboo being a locally available material in Assam, can contribute to local economy through local employment & procurement. Bamboo is also a rapidly renewable material with no carbon footprint, use of bamboo also safeguards the climate and reduce the degrading impact of greenhouse gases (GHG) associated with high embodied energy construction materials.
20. Nowadays documents have become important in every aspect of our daily life for authenticity and reliability. In this digitalized era, now e-documents, printouts etc. are widely used in place of handwritten documents. With the advancement of technology in the printing mechanism laser printer is widely used because of its high efficiency, quality and quick response. Thorough analysis of chromatograms has revealed that colorant of black toner degrades on 60 minutes exposure of UV-B radiation at wavelength of 312 nm.
21. Wireless sensor network is one of the essential needs of human and is helpful in futuristic and sustainable application development. By enhancing the network, higher degree of security, accuracy, scalability and other prospects of the WSN can be achieved. Based on the applicability of WSN, it can be subdivided into two main streams- first the issues which are application-centric and second the global issues for the entire WSN systems.

Subject Index

Author Index